Language and Poverty

D1555344

PEFC

PEFC/16-33-111

CATG-PEFC-052

www.pefc.org

MULTILINGUAL MATTERS
Series Editor: John Edwards, *St. Francis Xavier University, Canada*

Multilingual Matters series publishes books on bilingualism, bilingual education, immersion education, second language learning, language policy, multiculturalism. The editor is particularly interested in 'macro' level studies of language policies, language maintenance, language shift, language revival and language planning. Books in the series discuss the relationship between language in a broad sense and larger cultural issues, particularly identity related ones.

Full details of all the books in this series and of all our other publications can be found on http://www.multilingual-matters.com, or by writing to Multilingual Matters, St Nicholas House, 31-34 High Street, Bristol BS1 2AW, UK.

MULTILINGUAL MATTERS
Series Editor: John Edwards, *St. Francis Xavier University,*
Canada

Language and Poverty

Edited by
Wayne Harbert with help from Sally
McConnell-Ginet, Amanda Miller and
John Whitman

MULTILINGUAL MATTERS
Bristol • Buffalo • Toronto

'Of what they had before the late conquest of their country, there remain only their language and their poverty'

Samuel Johnson, *A Journey to the Western Isles* (1775: 97)

Library of Congress Cataloging in Publication Data
A catalog record for this book is available from the Library of Congress.
Language and Poverty
Edited by Wayne Harbert with help from Sally McConnell-Ginet, Amanda Miller and John Whitman.
Multilingual Matters: 141
Includes bibliographical references.
1. Sociolinguistics. 2. Poverty. 3. Language and languages–Economic aspects.
4. Language maintenance.
I. Harbert, Wayne. II. McConnell-Ginet, Sally.
P40.L2833 2008
306.44–dc22 2008026643

British Library Cataloguing in Publication Data
A catalogue entry for this book is available from the British Library.

ISBN-13: 978-1-84769-118-7 (hbk)
ISBN-13: 978-1-84769-119-4 (pbk)

Multilingual Matters
UK: St Nicholas House, 31-34 High Street, Bristol BS1 2AW, UK.
USA: UTP, 2250 Military Road, Tonawanda, NY 14150, USA.
Canada: UTP, 5201 Dufferin Street, North York, Ontario M3H 5T8, Canada.

The policy of Multilingual Matters/Channel View Publications is to use papers that are natural, renewable and recyclable products, made from wood grown in sustainable forests. In the manufacturing process of our books, and to further support our policy, preference is given to printers that have FSC and PEFC Chain of Custody certification. The FSC and/or PEFC logos will appear on those books where full certification has been granted to the printer concerned.

Typeset by Datapage International Ltd.
Printed and bound in Great Britain by MPG Books Ltd.

Contents

Acknowledgements

The editors wish to thank Tova Friedman, Bill Price and Sally Kim for their exacting and insightful work in the editing of this volume, and Sheila Haddad for her steadfast support throughout the project. Special thanks go to our anthropology colleague Magnus Fiskesjö for his careful reading of the manuscript, which has benefited enormously from his thoughtful and expert comments. The language and poverty project out of which this volume grew was generously supported by NSF Grant number 0514174 and by Cornell's Poverty, Inequality and Development Initiative.

Contributors

Neville Alexander is Director of the Project for the Study of Alternative Education in South Africa at the University of Cape Town. He has been advisor on language policy to various government departments. In 1995–1996, he chaired the Language Plan Task Group, which drew up the outline for a national language plan for South Africa. Until March 1998, he was Vice-Chairperson of the Pan South African Language Board. He has been special advisor on language policy and planning to the Minister of Arts, Culture, Science and Technology and a member of the Western Cape Language Committee. Alexander is a member of the Governing Board of the African Academy of Languages.

Helen Aristar Dry is a Professor of Linguistics at Eastern Michigan University, where she specializes in text analysis and language technology. She is a comoderator of The LINGUIST List and Principal Investigator on several projects focused on the digital documentation of endangered languages and the creation of Internet infrastructure for linguistics. These include E-MELD (http://emeld.org), LL-MAP (http://llmap.org) and MultiTree (http://linguistlist.org/multitree/). She serves on the Advisory Board of the Open Language Archives Community and is a founding member of DELAMAN (Digital Endangered Languages and Musics Archive Network). She is the editor (with John Lawler) of *Using Computers in Linguistics: A Practical Guide*.

Herman M. Batibo is Professor of African Linguistics at the University of Botswana, Southern Africa. His main interest, in recent years, has been the study of minority languages, especially with regard to marginalization, endangerment and death. He has carried out extensive sociolinguistic research in both Eastern and Southern Africa, particularly Tanzania and Botswana. His major publications include *Language Decline and Death in Africa: Causes, Consequences and Challenges* (2005), *Botswana: The Future of Minority Languages* (edited with B. Smieja, 2000), *The State of Khoesan Languages in Botswana* (edited with J. Tsonope, 2000), *Role of*

Language in the Discovery of Cultural History (1996) and *Le kesukuma, langue bantu de Tanzanie: Phonologie et morphologie* (1985).

John Baugh is the Margaret Bush Wilson Professor in Arts and Sciences, Washington University, where he serves as Director of African and Afro-American Studies. He is professor of Psychology, Anthropology, Education and English. He has previously held academic appointments at Stanford University, The University of Texas at Austin and Swarthmore College. He has conducted extensive research on linguistic profiling and other forms of language-related discrimination. His scholarship evaluates the social stratification of linguistic diversity with special attention to policy implications in medicine, education and the law. He is a past president of The American Dialect Society. He has published extensively regarding African American linguistic behavior and its educational and legal relevance. His books include, *Out of the Mouths of Slaves: African American Language and Educational Malpractice* (1999, University of Texas Press) and *Beyond Ebonics: Linguistic Pride and Racial Prejudice* (2000, Oxford University Press).

Matthias Brenzinger is a tenured researcher at the Institut für Afrikanistik, University of Cologne, Germany. He organized several international conferences focusing on endangered languages and edited two volumes on language endangerment in Africa (1992, 1998) and a worldwide overview on endangered languages (2007). Fieldwork and publications on endangered languages on the African continent were conducted among the Yaaku in Kenya, Ma'a in Tanzania, Bayso in Ethiopia and Khwe in Namibia, Botswana, Angola and Zambia. He supported communities' language maintenance activities, such as the development of a practical orthography for Khwe, and assisted as a consultant in the implementation of mother tongue education in Ethiopia. Since the mid-1990s he is involved in UNESCO activities and projects related to endangered language issues, together with Akira Yamamoto as chairperson of the UNESCO Ad-hoc Expert Group on Endangered Language. He is Secretary General of WOCAL (World Congress of African Linguistics) and organizer of WOCAL6, which will be held at the University of Cologne in 2009.

Ofelia García is Professor of Urban Education at the Graduate Center of the City University of New York, and has been Professor of Bilingual Education at Columbia University's Teachers College and at The City

College of New York, and Dean of the School of Education at Long Island University. Her latest books include *Bilingual Education in the 21st Century: A Global Perspective* (in press), *Imagining Multilingual Schools* (with Skutnabb-Kangas and Torres-Guzmán) and *A Reader in Bilingual Education* (with Colin Baker). She is a Fellow of the Stellenbosch Institute for Advanced Study (STIAS) in South Africa, and has been a Fulbright Scholar and a Spencer Fellow of the US National Academy of Education.

Lenore A. Grenoble is Associate Dean and Professor of Russian and Linguistics at Dartmouth University and specializes in Slavic and Tungusic languages. In 1998 she edited (with Lindsay Whaley) *Endangered Languages: Current Issues and Future Prospects* (Cambridge University Press), and she is the coauthor (with Lindsay Whaley) of the recent *Saving Languages: An Introduction to Language Revitalization* (Cambridge University Press).

Leah Mason is a Doctor of Education Candidate, focusing on the implementation of language education policy in the USA and the European Union in the Department of International and Transcultural Studies at Teachers College, Columbia University. Leah is also a Research Assistant for the National Center for the Restructuring of Education, Schools, and Teaching and a site assistant for the Student Press Initiative at Teachers College. She is a Center for the Advancement and Study of International Education Research Fellow, Campaign for Educational Equity Student Research Grantee, Arthur Zankel Urban Fellow, Teachers College Policy and Research Fellow, Austrian Fulbright and Ministry of Education teaching assistant and a Rotary Ambassadorial Scholar.

Ajit Mohanty was a Fulbright Senior Scholar (University of Wisconsin, Madison), Killam Scholar (University of Alberta), Senior Fellow (Central Institute of Indian Languages), Visiting Scholar (Universities of Geneva and Chicago) and Fulbright Visiting Professor (Columbia University). Currently, Ajit Mohanty is a Professor in Jawaharlal Nehru University, New Delhi. He has published in the areas of psycholinguistics, multi-lingualism and multilingual education, focusing on education, poverty and disadvantage among linguistic minorities. His books include *Bilingualism in a Multilingual Society* (1994), *Psychology of Poverty and Disadvantage* (2000) and *Perspectives on Indigenous Psychology* (2002). He is in the Editorial Boards of the *International Journal of Multilingualism, Language Policy and Psychological Studies*.

Keren Rice is a Professor in the Department of Linguistics at the University of Toronto and is Director of the Centre for Aboriginal Initiatives. She is also editor of the *International Journal of American Linguistics*. She has been involved with work on Aboriginal languages of Canada for some time.

Norvin Richards is a Professor in MIT's Department of Linguistics and Philosophy. He does linguistic fieldwork and language revival work with the Lardil in Northern Queensland, with the Maliseet in New Brunswick and with the Wampanoag in Eastern Massachusetts. He also runs the MITILI program, which offers training in linguistics to members of communities with threatened languages.

Suzanne Romaine has been Merton Professor of English Language at the University of Oxford since 1984. She has received honorary doctorates from the University of Uppsala and the University of Tromsø. She has published numerous books and articles on linguistic diversity, multilingualism, language change and contact. One of her most recent books, *Vanishing Voices. The Extinction of the World's Languages* (Oxford University Press, 2000), coauthored with Daniel Nettle, won the British Association for Applied Linguistics Book of the Year Prize in 2001 and has been translated into Italian, French, Turkish, Japanese, Dutch and Catalan.

François Vaillancourt is a professor in the Département de sciences économiques, Université de Montréal. His specialization is public policy (fiscal federalism, taxation, language policy). He has been a visitor at the University of Toronto, the Australian National University, the Université Libre de Bruxelles, the École Normale Supérieure –Cachan, FUCaM, Kennesaw State University-Fulbright Canadian Research Scholar (2007) and the Andrew Young School of Policy Studies (2007). He has been a consultant for various bodies, including the Conseil de la langue française, the OECD, Statistics Canada, the UNDP and the World Bank.

Peter Whiteley is Curator of North American Ethnology at the American Museum of Natural History, New York. He holds degrees in Anthropology from the University of New Mexico (PhD) and Cambridge University (MA). Since 1980, he has conducted extensive ethnographic research with the Hopi, and briefer periods with Hupa, Cayuga, several Rio Grande Pueblos and Akwesasne Mohawk. Principal publications include *Rethinking Hopi Ethnography* (1998) and *The Orayvi Split* (Anthropological Papers of the American Museum of Natural History, 2008). His paper 'Do "Language Rights" Serve Indigenous Interests? Some Hopi and Other Queries' (*American Anthropologist*, 2003) questions global language-rights discourse vis-à-vis local sociolinguistic ideologies.

Chapter 1

Introduction

WAYNE HARBERT, SALLY MCCONNELL-GINET, AMANDA MILLER and
JOHN WHITMAN

This volume explores aspects of the relationships between language and
poverty, singling out two central questions from the complex intercon-
nections in that domain and examining them from the perspectives of
linguistics, economics, anthropology, sociology, and language policy and
planning.

On the one hand, it addresses the question of how poverty affects
language survival. In contexts of competition between languages, shift to
the dominant language and abandonment of the minority language are
most often determined by factors that are broadly economic. These may
include perceived economic advantages for oneself or one's children in
switching to the dominant language or changes in local economies which
result in the destabilization or dissolution of minority language communities. Language maintenance efforts, too, depend on financial resources
for such things as teacher training and employment, materials development and technological support. Government and other funding agencies, even when favorably disposed toward minority languages, are often
confronted with difficult questions of priority. How are efforts to
maintain indigenous languages to be valued relative to other societal
needs such as public education, health, sustainable utilization of
resources and economy building? Are these either/or choices or is it
possible to promote minority languages indirectly by steering resources
toward the economic needs of the communities in which those languages
are used? To what extent do indigenous languages count as a part of the
wealth of the communities in which they are spoken? Is it possible to
assign a value to cultural assets such as indigenous languages and to the
cultural impoverishment attendant on their loss? How do – or can – such
languages factor into the material economies of the language community?

On the other hand, it examines the role of language in determining the
economic status of speakers. Speaking certain languages, or not speaking

certain others, often leads to poverty by affecting individuals' access to jobs and education, as well as their ability to participate on an equal footing in the functions of the society. Issues involved here include discrimination in employment based on language, accommodation or nonaccommodation of minority languages in education and public services (such as, e.g. ballots, licensing examinations and the dissemination of information), the question of official languages, and the subsidizing of efforts by minority language speakers to acquire the dominant language.

Questions involving the relationships between language and economics are of practical concern to people in a wide range of disciplines and professions, including politicians, educators, social workers, language planners and others in all situations in which more than a single language is used. The issues encompassed by both of our themes have grown in significance in an era of increasing globalization and accelerating change in economies, technologies, and social, cultural and political traditions. These developments in turn impose a growing obligation on the academic disciplines at whose intersections these questions lie and which should be prepared to offer advice, guidance and advocacy to those responsible for planning and policy. These questions are also increasingly of direct concern to linguists and other field researchers who work with minority languages and minority language communities. Fieldworkers in communities whose languages are highly endangered are often the only individuals, aside from community members themselves, who are aware of the existence, the richness and the imperilment of those languages. Their experience and training, as well as their presence in the community, position them to serve not only as advisors and advocates for the community and its language to the outside world, but as resources within the community who can help shape its response to language endangerment. Beyond this, however, by the nature of their professional activity, fieldworkers become a part of the economies of the languages they study. Increased awareness of the significance of this role has led to ongoing reassessment of the implications, obligations and practical questions it raises.

This volume attempts to explore some aspects of the relationships between language and poverty, in both their scholarly and practical aspects, from a cross-disciplinary perspective appropriate to their scope. It is organized into four sections. The first contains chapters by Herman Batibo (Chapter 2) and Matthias Brenzinger (Chapter 3), addressing the role of poverty as a factor in language maintenance and language death. These chapters make specific reference to the situation in Africa, where linguistic density is particularly high (with approximately one third of the world's languages) and where poverty, with its attendant threats to continued linguistic diversity, is particularly acute (though, as Brenzinger notes, poverty and linguistic diversity do not necessarily co-occur in individual countries). The second section addresses the ways in which access by individuals to resources in multilingual contexts is affected by the languages they do or do not speak. Such effects manifest themselves in a variety of different ways. In nations with a colonial history, for example, the language of former colonizers often continues to exist in a complex relationship with indigenous languages, and the opportunities for advancement in such contexts often depend on the mastery of languages that are native to a very small percentage of the population. Two of the chapters in this section address the problem of linguistic restrictions on opportunity in such situations. Neville Alexander (Chapter 4) discusses the effects of former colonial languages on access to education in Africa, with specific reference to English in South Africa. Ajit Mohanty (Chapter 7) discusses the problem of language policy in education in India and its role in the perpetuation of poverty and inequality. However, the role that language plays in determining prosperity is not limited to postcolonial contexts, nor to developing nations, but is in evidence even in affluent Western democracies – a context on which the remaining chapters in this section focus. John Baugh (Chapter 5) offers an overview of language-based discrimination in the USA, while Ofelia García and Leah Mason (Chapter 6) look specifically at Spanish in the USA, contrasting a traditional ideology that constructs US Spanish as a language of poverty (thus hindering its speakers) with an alternative ideology that considers the linguistic skill of Spanish–English bilinguals in the USA to be an increasingly valuable potential resource in the global marketplace.

These first two sections are primarily linguistic in their orientation, offering the perspectives on the volume's central themes of those for whom language is the main object of interest – field linguists, socio-linguists and language planners. By contrast, the third section situates this discussion in a wider context, bringing to bear the perspectives of other disciplines. Suzanne Romaine (Chapter 8) discusses global linkages between linguistic diversity, wealth and ecological diversity, and envisions an approach to saving threatened languages, meliorating poverty and maintaining biodiversity which views all of these as a common problem, amenable to a unitary solution. François Vaillancourt (Chapter 9) examines the nature of language-poverty relationships from the perspective of economics, pointing out the challenges of taking language into account in economic models. Peter Whiteley (Chapter 10) addresses the subject of language and poverty as an anthropologist, and develops the concept that indigenous languages are themselves a form of wealth, and that their loss and the loss of the aspects of culture to which they are bound are also forms of impoverishment.

The final section advances yet another perspective. Shifting the focus from languages, their speakers and settings, to the roles and responsibilities of those who make a profession of studying them, it raises the question of the standing of linguists and other field researchers in the local economies of minority or endangered language communities, with particular emphasis on their role as producers of resources for community-based language revival and maintenance activities. Lenore Grenoble, Keren Rice and Norvin Richards (Chapter 11) develop the theme that researchers are unavoidably a part of the local economies of the languages and speakers with which they work, and explore the concept that in carrying out their research, field linguists incur an obligation to the languages and the speakers which requires that they return value to the language community. They then touch on practical ways of discharging this debt, by providing documentation, training and materials development in support of language maintenance and revitalization. The concept of returning value to endangered language communities is developed further by Helen Aristar Dry (Chapter 12), who offers specific examples of how technological resources now available to researchers can be deployed in the service of community language maintenance and revival initiatives (or where priorities do not allow for such initiatives, can at least be used to preserve linguistic wealth for the future).

A word should be said at the outset about how *poverty*, a major thematic anchor point of the volume, is understood. As will be evident to the reader, the notion of poverty is extremely complex, not only subject to a variety of different measurements, but in fact construed differently in different disciplines. As a first, very narrow approximation, we can take poverty to be the (relative) inability to provide for the basic needs of life. Even so defined, poverty can be measured in a variety of ways. Vaillancourt, for example, enumerates monetary and nonmonetary measures of poverty, each with its own means of assessment. Nonmonetary measures include education poverty, health poverty and nutrition poverty. His own chapter focuses on monetary measures, as those are the ones with which economists have the greatest expertise. As Brenzinger points out, famine and the AIDS epidemic make the non-monetary measures of nutritional poverty and health poverty especially salient components of the problem in Africa.

Grenoble, Rice and Richards observe further that the standards by which these measures are assessed vary from one economic context to another; the standards for poverty are not the same in postindustrial countries as in developing countries. In the extreme case, the resources of a community are not sufficient to provide the basic necessities for the maintenance of life. This condition is labeled *extreme poverty* by Grenoble, Rice and Richards (following the UN definition) and *absolute poverty* by Brenzinger. According to Grenoble, Rice and Richards, the World Bank estimates that 1.1 billion people live in extreme poverty.

Brenzinger contrasts absolute poverty with *relative poverty*, in which one group experiences 'exclusion from symbolic and material markets and denial of access to tangible or intangible resources' enjoyed by neighboring groups. In its extension to symbolic as well as material markets, and in its characterization of poverty as a constraint on the ability to participate in such markets, rather than as simply a matter of quantities of goods or property possessed, this definition departs significantly from our starting point.

Mohanty takes such exclusion from participation as the core notion of poverty, a reconceptualization which, he claims, is essential to understanding its nature and causes. Citing Amartya Sen, he defines poverty as *capability deprivation* – the denial of opportunities for choice. Related to this, as pointed out by our colleague Magnus Fiskesjö, is the conception of poverty as a manifestation of inequality in power relationships. Numerous instances of such inequalities are treated in the chapters that follow, including, for example, the lack of control by local communities over the language of education, as discussed by Mohanty and others, and the denial to local communities of a voice in decisions about the utilization of the resources on which their livelihood depends, as discussed by Romaine. Thus, poverty is not merely an economic, but also a political concept. Finally, some of the authors in this volume, including Whiteley, as noted, as well as Grenoble, Rice and Richards, put forward the concept that indigenous languages and the cultures whose transmission depends on them are themselves a form of wealth, and that their loss is therefore a form of impoverishment, sometimes leading to material loss when it results in a loss of traditional knowledge of nutritional or medicinal resources, and almost always adversely affecting what Pierre Bourdieu calls 'symbolic capital'. Attendant on such loss is also a loss of the ability to make choices about one's language – hence an instance of capability deprivation, in Mohanty's sense.

We make no attempt here to harmonize these very different views of poverty, but we direct the reader's attention to Romaine's assertion that more is at stake here than mere terminological quibbles or differences in disciplinary perspective. Stating that 'whoever controls the language of poverty controls the agenda on poverty, how it is conceptualized, and how it is to be remedied', she goes on to argue that shortcomings in the efforts of international organizations to address poverty as a global problem have resulted in part from preconceptions built into the discourses in which the problem has been framed.

The points of potential contact between language and poverty are, as Grin (1996b, 1996c) observes, manifold, complex and still largely unexplored. It is thus impossible to address them exhaustively in a single volume. Moreover, these interactions play out in so many different ways in different contexts around the world as to preclude the possibility of comprehensive geographical coverage. The geographic scope of the present volume is, for the most part, limited to the language areas in which the individual contributors have worked, though we are confident that the lessons drawn from the case studies reported here are of relevance in other geographical settings as well. The volume is also selective with respect to the disciplinary lenses through which this complex problem area is viewed and the particular thematic threads it has pulled from that tapestry for particular scrutiny. To a considerable extent, the emphases and the omissions of the book reflect the ways in which questions in this field of inquiry relate to general intellectual concerns of the times. Thus, for example, this volume overlaps very little with another volume published almost 40 years ago under a similar title (*Language and Poverty: Perspectives on a Theme*; Williams, 1970a). That earlier work focused primarily on how poverty affected the linguistic performance of individuals in the American classroom. The central question was framed by its editor as 'the deficit-difference controversy' – the debate about whether differences in linguistic behavior between children of poor and middle-class families were most appropriately regarded as reflecting 'deficits' or 'developmental lags' in the linguistic preparation of the former, or simply as reflecting linguistic differences.[1] One advocate of the former view was Engelmann (1970), who opened his contribution to the volume with the following striking assertion about 'the poverty child':

> The child of poverty has language problems. These are problems far more crippling than mere dialect problems. Too frequently, a four-year-old child of poverty does not understand the meaning of such

words as *long, full, animal, red, under, first, before, or, if, all* and *not*. Too frequently, he cannot repeat a simple statement such as, "The bread is under the oven", even after he has been given four trials... Too frequently, he cannot succeed in a task in which he is presented with a picture of two boys and two girls and is asked to "Find the right ones: He is big... She is not standing on the floor... She is next to a chair" and so on... In brief, the child of poverty has not been taught as much about the meaning of language as a middle-class child of the same age. (Englemann, 1970: 102)

The contributions by the linguists Labov and Shuy to that volume, on the other hand, represent an alternative view (shared by the editor), under which

speech variations among groups of people should not be assumed to be variations in degrees of linguistic complexity, sophistication, or development, nor capricious errors. Rather such variations may reflect distinctions among quite normal and well-developed, but different linguistic or dialect systems. This reasoning reflects the theoretical view of most linguists that no natural language or dialect can really be considered more primitive, rudimentary or under-developed than another. In brief, as applied to the deficit position on the language of the poor, this group of linguists is arguing that what we are observing are often language differences, and if there is a discrepancy between the demands of the school, for example, and the performance of the child, we are seeing the consequences of forcing a child to perform in a linguistic system other than his primary one... They are arguing that the United States is a polycultural society with monocultural schools, and this is the first and perhaps most damaging inequity foisted upon the poverty child. (Williams, 1970b: 5)

Some of these ideas do recur in the present volume. In particular, the chapters by Alexander, Batibo and Mohanty address the global problem of disadvantage imposed on individuals who are required to receive their education in a language not their own, echoing the concern that Williams (1970b: 5) raises in the last sentence of the quotation. The chapter by Baugh addresses the still-widespread tendency to equate difference with deficit, sometimes resulting in linguistic discrimination on the basis of dialect. For the most part, though, the present work is informed by different sets of general ideas and concerns, carving out a different set of themes from the rich set of interactions between language and wealth or poverty. It too takes language and poverty as its theme (and its title), but focuses on one particular bidirectional subset of the relationships between them. On the one hand, it considers the role that poverty plays in determining the fate of minority or endangered languages and, on the other hand, how languages people do or do not speak determine their economic well-being and access to resources.

Again, these particular choices are shaped in part by more general concerns of our times. The question of the role of poverty in language death is made particularly timely by the growing awareness among linguists, and increasingly, the general population, that the linguistic world in which we live is on the threshold of momentous changes. It is widely accepted (see Crystal, 2000; Nettle & Romaine, 2000; and references cited therein) that languages have been disappearing at an unprecedentedly rapid rate in recent decades. Under projections that are generally regarded as conservative and realistic, by the end of the present century as many as half of currently spoken languages will have disappeared as community languages. This 'vanishing languages crisis' has received a great deal of scrutiny by linguists since it was raised to prominence by the essay of Hale *et al.* (1992). Recent treatments of the problem include Abley (2003), Bradley and Bradley (2002), Crystal (2000), Dalby (2003), Fishman (2001), Grenoble and Whaley (1998, 2006), Harrison (2007), Hinton and Hale (2001) and Nettle and Romaine (2000). The questions posed in this growing literature have ranged from historical questions such as 'What forces have brought us to this point?', to philosophical ones such as 'What does humanity lose in terms of intellectual wealth when a language – even a small and marginalized one – is lost?' to practical ones such as 'What, if anything, can linguists and communities do to arrest and reverse language loss?'

Except in rare cases, the proximate cause of language death is language shift, which consists of a switch (gradual or abrupt) of its speakers to another language and a cessation of its transmission to new generations. There is widespread agreement with the assessment of Grenoble and Whaley (1998: 52) that the most significant causes of language shift are, broadly speaking, economic. Economically driven language shift can take a variety of different paths. Very typically, it is an outcome of population movement – the migration of all or part of the population speaking the language to another region in which it is not spoken as a community language (see Batibo (Chapter 2) for a discussion of numerous instances in Africa). Such migrations can result on the one hand in the depopulation of the language community, and on the other in the isolation of displaced speakers of local languages from one another and their submersion in linguistic environments dominated by languages other than their own. Movements of this sort are typical of the global phenomenon of increasing concentration of populations into urban areas (Batibo, Chapter 2 and Brenzinger, Chapter 3). Conversely, linguistic communities can be disrupted by the expansion of neighboring speakers of other languages into their territories (Batibo, Chapter 2), resulting in dilution and in extreme cases submersion of the local language community. In some instances, as in the case of Welsh, the two directions of migration are linked; housing and businesses which have been abandoned by economically motivated emigration of speakers of the minority language draw in immigration of speakers of outside languages, attracted by lower prices and the appeal of life outside large cities. Population movement and the attendant disruption of language communities can be set in motion by a number of factors, including wars and ethnic-cleansing campaigns as in the present case of Sudan (see Brenzinger, Chapter 3), and natural disasters, but they most often arise from circumstances that affect the tenability of traditional modes of livelihood. Those circumstances, in turn, are of a wide variety of types. Some are the results of political and economic decisions, such as settlement programs or dam building, that disrupt local means of livelihood and therefore the economic basis of language communities; examples come from areas as diverse as the American Southwest (Hale & Hinton, 2001: 76) and Thailand (Nettle & Romaine, 2000: 10). Some are the cumulative result of human activity (deforestation and other habitat destruction, overhunting, climate change, overpopulation). Still other cases result from changes in the economic expectations of individuals – the perception that a life of greater prosperity is possible outside the language community.

Language shift also occurs without migration. In these cases, the community of speakers often remains intact while the language of the community shifts from the local language to the surrounding regional language, sometimes across intermediate stages of bilingualism. Again, such shifts do not always have direct economic motivations; they may be motivated by patriotic desires to conform to a national identity, for example (Brenzinger, Chapter 3). In the large majority of cases, though, the causes of the shift are economic, ranging from changes in the local economy which demand increased levels of individual interaction in the regional language, to the simple perception that it is to one's own economic advantage or that of one's children, to learn and use the regional language. Decisions to abandon local languages are typically bolstered by a widely held perception that one must choose between competing languages and also make such a choice for one's children in light of assessment of direct economic value. Again, the shift is sometimes enforced by policies that, for example, deliberately give some languages preference over others in education and in other public functions. In other cases, the shift accompanies more general changes in economies; as Brenzinger observes, it sometimes accompanies the adoption of new modes of living from neighboring cultures.

The rise in interest in the loss of linguistic diversity is also connected to the increasingly salient and urgent general concern about growing ecological impoverishment – degradation and attrition of ecosystems and loss of biological diversity. The connection between the two is more than simply conceptual; as observed by Nettle and Romaine (2000: 43), 'those areas which are rich in languages also tend to be rich in biodiversity value. Biodiversity is concentrated through the tropics and tails off towards the poles, just as linguistic diversity does... Thus, we can really speak of a common area of biolinguistic diversity'. And consequently, it is precisely in these areas that the threat of loss of diversity – linguistic and biological – is greatest. Thus, the rising concern about language loss is often embedded in a larger concern about loss of ecological richness. Moreover, both linguistic and biological diversity are connected, in ways still not fully understood, with poverty; the areas of threatened biological and linguistic wealth, as Batibo, Brenzinger and Romaine point out, are also often areas of economic impoverishment as typically measured. There is at least a rough correlation between areas of the world with the highest language densities and those with the highest incidence of poverty. According to these investigators, poverty is linked with threatened biological and linguistic richness not just areally, but causally, though the causal connections are complex. Vaillancourt (Chapter 9) and Brenzinger (Chapter 3) point out that poor minority language groups are often poor in part because they have been forced into (or allowed to continue to occupy) regions which are economically marginal, and therefore of relatively little economic interest to their more numerous and powerful neighbors. Brenzinger, as well as Grenoble, Rice and Richards (Chapter 11), note the apparent irony that marginalization and poverty – already identified as key factors in language death – have also '"saved" large numbers of African languages' (as Brenzinger puts it), by making the territories in which they are spoken economically undesirable to other groups. The poverty of the language community in such instances is not in itself destructive to the language (nor, as Romaine emphasizes, to the ecosystem from which it makes its livelihood), and in fact may serve to ensure its stability. Thus, it is not poverty itself that puts languages at risk. Rather, language endangerment seems to begin with economic disruption. Such disruption can come about in various ways. First, local resources previously unnoticed by or deemed unworthy of economic exploitation by outside groups sometimes come to be desired by those groups. Deforestation of previously untouched areas can arise because better technology or transportation or increased scarcity of resources elsewhere has increased the value of the trees as commodities. The agricultural potential of the land on which trees are growing may also ensure their removal. Similar factors can lead to the building of hydroelectric dams on previously untouched waterways. Such considerations also extend naturally to biodiversity; some areas of high biological diversity have managed to remain so far only because, for reasons of history or technology, large-scale exploitation of their resources, extensive human occupation and the introduction of industry or monocultural farming practices have not yet been deemed economically worthwhile. This state of affairs, too, is subject to disruption by changes in technologies, perceptions or policies.

In the extreme case, disruption of the local economy can take the form of changes that cause the poverty of an area to become absolute, in the sense defined earlier. This leads to the disappearance of language communities by emigration or starvation. Relative poverty, in the sense defined earlier, does not in itself lead to language death unless a disruptive factor comes into play. The disruptive factor may simply be a change in the perceptions and expectations of that language community – for example, dissatisfaction generated by the realization, due to increased contacts, that neighboring groups are materially better off. However, in his discussion of the striking case of Khwe communities in Namibia, who remain steadfastly loyal to their language in spite of enormous poverty, Brenzinger illustrates that such outcomes are not inevitable.

As the second of its twofold themes, this volume focuses on how language – the languages one speaks or fails to speak – affects the economic status or access to resources of its speakers. The linguistic inequities at issue here are diverse. On the one hand, lack of proficiency in (*de facto*) official languages can deny nonspeakers of those languages access to information crucial to their well-being and advancement. As a particularly widespread and consequential manifestation of this, in many parts of the world, the language of education (even in primary grades) is not the native language of the large majority of students, who are consequently disadvantaged in the classroom (see, in particular, the Chapters 2, 4, 8 and 7 in this volume). As Mohanty notes, linguistic impediments to education are obstacles to economic advancement: '[w]hile education is the enabling factor for economic development, language is the enabling factor for access to quality education'. Alexander and Mohanty point out that it is often the case in countries with colonial histories that former colonial languages continue to be privileged over indigenous languages in such functions – a practice often defended by reference to the purported neutrality of those languages, but one that constructs and legitimizes a 'power hierarchy of languages' that contributes strongly to socioeconomic stratification. As Brenzinger notes, the problem is not wholly addressed by the move toward 'Mother Tongue education' policies. As these policies typically privilege a handful of regionally or nationally dominant languages (only 20% in the case of Africa), most students are still denied access to education in their native languages. Economic problems created by unequal access to the language of public information transfer are not limited to language choice in schools. For example, Brenzinger (Chapter 3) proposes that dissemination of health information in indigenous languages is an indispensable step in countering the AIDS crisis in Africa, which he asserts is fundamental to overcoming poverty on that continent.

The topics of this problem area – linguistically-based discrimination, linguistic impediments to access to services, education and employment and language rights – have also been brought into salience in recent times by a growing general interest in protecting the rights of minorities. This interest has been fostered by the wane of colonialism, worldwide struggles for autonomy and self-determination and even changes in theories of international law. The changes in attitude here are also in part a consequence of globalization. The increasing importance of supranational political and economic organizations, and a corresponding reduction in the importance of nations, has created an environment for reassessment and reassertion of local regional identities (Crystal, 2000: 165; Grenoble & Whaley, 2006: 3). Language rights – the right to speak, be educated and receive public services (including access to information by print broadcast and other media) in one's native language – are increasingly receiving official recognition as one of the categories of basic human rights. Grenoble and Whaley cite, among many other similar documents, UNESCO's Universal Declaration on Cultural Diversity, which states that 'all persons should therefore be able to express themselves and to create and disseminate their work in the language of their choice, and particularly in their mother tongue; all persons should be entitled to quality education and training that fully respect their cultural identity' (Article 5, cited in Grenoble & Whaley, 2006: 2).

The concerns of the two themes of the volume converge in the case of small, indigenous, linguistic minorities; measures that help to remove financial, social and legal encumbrances on the use of minority languages by individuals also help to prevent language death. As Hinton and Hale note, 'Because the loss of indigenous languages is tied closely to the usurpation of indigenous lands, the destruction of indigenous habitats, and the involuntary incorporation of indigenous peoples into the larger society (generally into the lower class margins of that society), language death has become part of a human rights struggle' (Hinton & Hale, 2001: 4).

Pronouncements on language rights by national and international official organizations are one promising sign of a change in the intellectual climate – a change to which the present volume is in part a response. There is cause for optimism here. That being said, it is still the case that the right to use one's native language without economic, political or social penalty is far from universally assured. In the USA, for example, the spirit of such declarations is countered by the widespread and very successful movement to make English the official language of individual states, and the (so far less successful) initiative to make bilingual education illegal, as discussed in Garcia and Mason (Chapter 6) and Romaine (Chapter 8). There are even instances in which official pronouncements are at odds with each other; Grenoble and Whaley (2006: 26) note that 'the Native American Languages Act guarantees the right to education and development of Native American languages, yet the No Child Left Behind Act requires standardized testing in English'. Even where linguistic rights are legally protected, the protections are often not effectively exercised in practice. In a case in Wales that has made the headlines just as this introduction is being written, a Welsh office of a travel agent was the target of protest for having instructed its Welsh-speaking personnel not to use Welsh for work-related purposes. The company replied that it had not forbidden its employees to use Welsh 'privately', but then went on to state unapologetically its policy that 'the company has always requested that its staff, regardless of any geographical location, speak English to other staff members when discussing work-related matters in the work place. This ensures clear communication at all times and is respectful to team members who do not speak other languages' (BBC News, 11 June 2007). And finally, of course, changes in policy and attitudes at the official level will always prove to be insufficient until those new attitudes gain currency in the general population. Failing that, economic and social penalties will continue to be exacted from those who are perceived as speaking the wrong language, or even having the wrong accent. See Baugh (Chapter 5) and Garcia and Mason (Chapter 6) for discussion of these issues.

Once it is established that there are substantive causal relations between languages and poverty, the ideal next step would seem to be the establishment of dialogue among the various individual disciplines with a stake in them, given that the problems involved are inherently cross-disciplinary. On this front, in spite of some promising beginnings, there is still much to do. On the one hand, the field of economy of language, heralded in an important special issue of the *International Journal of Sociolinguistics* (Grin, 1996a) and developed subsequently by Grin and Vaillancourt (1997, 1999) and a few others, has remained a relatively peripheral subfield in economics. This is in part for discipline-internal reasons, and partly because language plays such multifaceted roles in human society, that it has proven highly difficult to reduce it to a variable of a particular type. See Vaillancourt (Chapter 9), who points out that it does not suffice to regard language only as a type of human capital, a means of (or a barrier to) communication or an ethnic attribute or marker. On the other hand, social scientists in other fields have tended to adopt the jargon of economics without real understanding in discussing these issues (Grin, 1996c: 29). Grin summarizes the challenge, and its resolution, as follows:

> In short, combining economics and the sciences of language is not without its perils, among which inadequate analogy looms large; in my opinion, this can best be countered by a firm commitment to interdisciplinary collaboration. (Grin, 1996c: 30)

Economists have studied extensively the second of the two themes of the present volume (how the wealth [earning power] of an individual is affected by his or her linguistic attributes) in some multilingual situations, particularly among Francophone speakers in Quebec and among Hispanic speakers in the USA (see the chapters by Vaillancourt and by Garcia and Mason). Much of this work has dealt with the question of whether and to what degree speakers of minority languages are economically disadvantaged by that status. A few studies, though, have focused on the somewhat different question of whether minority languages can be turned into economic assets for their speakers in some contexts. This prospect is addressed in Sproul (1996), for example, and is taken up by Garcia and Mason in the present volume. The first theme of this book – the role of economic considerations in language shift – has been studied less extensively. Grin (1996c: 23) lists a number of theoretical studies in this area, but only one empirical study, of Irish-to-English language shift. In fact, in typical cases of language shift among the most highly endangered languages, such empirical studies might be difficult to carry out. By the time they have acquired this status, such languages are spoken by no more than a few dozen to a few thousand economically marginalized speakers whose participation in the main-stream monetary economies of the countries in which they live is negligible, though even in those cases the dynamics of the shift may be amenable to economic modeling.

A cross-disciplinary view of language and poverty interactions sufficient to encompass the problem area must also take into account the non-monetary value attached to languages. Languages have intrinsic worth to their speakers; the speakers may therefore remain attached to those languages in spite of the possible economic disadvantages of that allegiance. This is well-illustrated in Brenzinger's example of Khwe and by many other languages around the world. Moreover, as argued by Whiteley (Chapter 10), the knowledge and understanding of the world that are encoded exclusively in those languages are also a part of the wealth of individual speakers and language communities; the loss of those languages is another form of impoverishment. These two concepts of value may sometimes converge; according to a recent line of argument represented in Nettle and Romaine (2000: 166f), Harrison (2007) and Romaine (Chapter 8), local languages may embody systems of knowl-edge that are the key to the repair of local economies. Imported modes of exploiting local resources have often proven to be economically and ecologically ruinous and not sustainable in the long term. The way to re-establish sustainability in such economies is to return to modes of resource utilization based on those established over millennia by the indigenous population. The traditional knowledge required for this is encoded in the conceptual systems that find expression in the local languages, however, and is in danger of being lost along with them. Thus, the preservation of endangered languages is important not only for their own intrinsic cultural worth, but also for their potential value to the local economy (and potentially even to the world economy – see Harrison, 2007: 15).

Once we have arrived at a cross-linguistic, multidisciplinary picture of language-poverty interactions, what is the next step? How do we proceed from scholarly insight to practical policy and planning with respect to these interactions? Are we in fact obliged to do so? There is a growing though not uncontroversial view that scholars are in fact ethically obligated to engage with societal problems. Alexander (Chapter 4) formulates this ethical imperative in the following way: 'the international rhetoric around the *Make Poverty History Campaign* compels all scholars to examine their particular disciplines in terms of the ways in which their practices and their theoretical positions *a priori* either exacerbate or alleviate poverty in the world or in their relevant spaces'. Similarly, Baugh (Chapter 5) expresses a 'hope that linguists and linguistic science may be employed to help advance social justice and equality'. Such calls to engagement raise a variety of questions: what is it that we, as specialists in particular disciplines and as members of a general intellectual community, ought to be doing, what are we in a position to do, and how should we go about doing it? Only a few members of that intellectual community – fieldworkers in impoverished communities, language planners and educators, for example – are well-positioned to take direct action (for good or ill), but the rest are situated to take indirect action through advice or advocacy directed at those responsible for planning or policy. What advice should we offer on questions of balancing the linguistic rights of individuals with societal needs, for example? How does Alexander's call to alleviate poverty rank relative to other worthy objectives such as preventing the extinction of languages or the degradation of the environment? Vaillancourt states that in cases in which a poor language community subsists in an economically marginal area, the options for addressing poverty seem to be limited to encouraging outward mobility or to carrying out regional development policies to reduce poverty. The first of these, he notes, is potentially at odds with the alternative goal of language maintenance. The second, however – policies that effect changes in the local economy with the intention of enhancing it – can also be risky from the point of view of language maintenance. As Batibo points out, such initiatives in the case of African communities have led to an influx of speakers of mainstream languages and the consequent disruption of the indigenous language community – an experience echoed during the implementation of similar schemes in the Irish *Gaeltacht*. Some have even suggested, as Nettle and Romaine (2000: 155) note, that the preservation of multilingualism is an obstacle to economic progress. Must we therefore choose between them? Romaine (Chapter 8) argues that a view of poverty constructed exclusively within the conceptual and terminological framework of standard economics privileges certain kinds of policies that are not necessarily the best ones. She takes issue with the currently prevalent idea that the elimination of poverty in third-world countries is best achieved through job creation and urbanization on Western models, thereby placing that goal at odds with the maintenance of traditional language communities. Rather, she advances the idea that the most workable resolutions of these three crises

– poverty in marginal communities, loss of biological diversity and language death – all converge on the promotion of traditional local economies.

These questions arise with particular immediacy for fieldworkers in impoverished linguistic communities, who experience to some degree the poverty of those communities and who become, virtually unavoidably, a part of their economy. These members of the scholarly community are confronted with a special set of philosophical, ethical and practical questions. Is it proper for the fieldworker to become an activist, engaging with the community on issues like language revitalization? If so, how is this role to be balanced with the professional imperative of scholarly research? How ought the linguist (or other fieldworker) act so as to give proper weight to the now universally accepted understanding that the knowledge the fieldworker takes away from the community is the intellectual property of that community and its individuals, and an object of value in multiple senses? These intellectual property rights extend, ultimately, to the decision to maintain the language or to let it go. If the linguistic fieldworker believes that the community undervalues its linguistic wealth, within what limits is it proper to urge a reassessment? What are the ways in which fieldworkers can return value to the community, appropriate to its economic circumstances and with appropriate attention to its needs and interests? Given that resources (both temporal and monetary) of fieldworkers are also limited, how do they prioritize tasks to make sure that their obligation to the language, its speakers and their community is discharged with the greatest benefit? Such questions are not just questions for individual fieldworkers, but to an extent also for their disciplines. What is the nature and extent of the obligation of academic disciplines to address the needs of impoverished communities which host the linguistic, social or cultural objects of our studies, and what should we be doing as disciplines to address these obligations? Grenoble, Rice and Richards (Chapter 11) examine some of these issues from the perspectives of three linguists with extensive experience in endangered language communities in a variety of economic circumstances. Finally, the chapter by Aristar Dry (Chapter 12) gives a concrete example of one type of technological resource of particular importance which, placed at the disposal of language communities whose language is in peril, can help them to maintain it or, failing that, to preserve a record for a posterity that may wish reclaim their heritage, ideally in more prosperous times.

Note

1. For more recent treatments of this debate, see Edwards (1979) and Thanasoulas (2001).

References

Abley, M. (2003) _Spoken Here: Travels Among Threatened Languages_. Boston, MA: Houghton Mifflin.

Ammerlaan, T., Hulsen, M., Straating, H. and Yagmur, K. (eds) (2001) _Sociolinguistic and Psycholinguistic Perspectives on Maintenance and Loss of Minority Languages_. Münster/New York: Waxmann.

Bradley, D. and Bradley, M. (2002) _Language Endangerment and Language Maintenance_. London: Routledge/Curzon.

Crystal, D. (2000) _Language Death_. Cambridge: Cambridge University Press.

Dalby, A. (2003) _Language in Danger: The Loss of Linguistic Diversity and the Threat to Our Future_. New York: Columbia University Press.

Edwards, J. (1979) _Language and Disadvantage_. London: Edward Arnold.

Engelmann, S. (1970) How to construct effective language programs for the poverty child. In F. Williams (ed.) _Language and Poverty_ (pp. 102–122). Chicago, IL: Markham.

Fishman, J. (ed.) (2001) _Can Threatened Languages be Saved?_ Clevedon: Multilingual Matters.

Grenoble, L. and Whaley, L. (eds) (1998) _Language Loss and Community Response_. Cambridge: Cambridge University Press.

Grenoble, L. and Whaley, L. (2006) _Saving Languages: An Introduction to Language Revitalization_. Cambridge: Cambridge University Press.

Grin, F. (ed.) (1996a) Economic approaches to language planning. Special issue of _International Journal of the Sociology of Language_ 121.

Grin, F. (1996b) Economic approaches to language planning: An introduction. _International Journal of the Sociology of Language_ 121, 1–16.

Grin, F. (1996c) The economics of language: Survey, assessment, and prospects. _International Journal of the Sociology of Language_ 121, 17–44.

Grin, F. and Vaillancourt, F. (1997) The economics of multilingualism: Overview and analytic framework. _Annual Review of Applied Linguistics_ 17, 43–65.

Grin, F. and Vaillancourt, F. (1999) _The Cost-effectiveness Evaluation of Minority Language Policies: Case Studies on Wales, Ireland and the Basque Country_. Monograph Series No. 2. Flensburg: European Centre for Minority Issues.

Hale, K., Krauss, M., Watahomigie, L.J., Yamamoto, A.Y., Craig, C., LaVerne Masayevsa, J. and England, Nora C. (1992) Endangered languages. _Language_ 68, 1–42.

Harrison, K.D. (2007) _When Languages Die: The Extinction of the World's Languages and the Erosion of Human Knowledge_. New York: Oxford University Press.

Hinton, L. and Hale, K. (eds) (2001) _The Green Book of Language Revitalization in Practice_. San Diego, CA: Academic Press.

Nettle, D. and Romaine, S. (2000) _Vanishing Voices: The Extinction of the World's Languages_. Oxford: Oxford University Press.

Sproul, A. (1996) Regional economic development and minority language use: The case of Gaelic Scotland. _International Journal of the Sociology of Language_ 121, 93–118.

Thanasoulas, D. (2001) Language and disadvantage. *ELT Newsletter* (August 2001). On WWW at http://www.eltnewsletter.com/.

Williams, F. (ed.) (1970a) *Language and Poverty: Perspectives on a Theme*. Chicago, IL: Markham.

Williams, F. (1970b) Some preliminaries and prospects. In F. Williams (ed.) *Language and Poverty: Perspectives on a Theme* (pp. 1–10). Chicago, IL: Markham.

Part 1

Poverty as a Factor in Language Maintenance and Language Death

Chapter 2

Poverty as a Crucial Factor in Language Maintenance and Language Death: Case Studies from Africa

HERMAN M. BATIBO

Introduction

The complex interconnection between language and poverty has long been recognized (Nettle & Romaine, 2000; Robinson, 1996; Watson, 1994). On the one hand, poverty affects language survival, as communities will always look for a medium that gives them access to the most viable socioeconomic opportunities. On the other hand, language frequently helps to determine economic status, prestige and access to resources or power. Many communities, especially those that are socioeconomically disadvantaged and speak minority languages, are therefore caught up in this critical dilemma, as they have to choose between survival of their languages and access to economic and social benefits or resources (Batibo, 2001, 2005b).

This paper discusses the phenomena of language shift and language death, which continue to constitute a critical problem in all five continents of the world. The problem has caused much alarm and preoccupation among linguists, ethnographers, language planners and even national governments, particularly after the revelation of statistics that by the turn of the century as many as 90% of the world's languages will have become extinct (Krauss, 1992). The main thrust of the paper is that poverty is a crucial factor in language maintenance, as speakers of any language tend to identify themselves with the most socioeconomically prestigious language. In this study, it will be demonstrated that many minority language speakers in Africa are progressively shifting to the dominant languages, in their quest for education, job opportunities, social services and wider communication. This paper argues that one way of arresting this trend is to empower the minority languages and their speakers by instituting viable codification measures and improving the socioeconomic well-being of the speakers.

Language Maintenance Measures

Auburger (1990) proposes five measures for the maintenance of a minority language where such a language is in contact with a major language. First, there must be a strict diglossic use of the minority and majority languages, in such a way that each language is confined to its own domains of use. Usually the majority language would be used as a language of wider communication, serving in public domains like government business, local administration, education, judiciary, social services as well as private industry, while the minority languages would be used mainly in intraethnic communication, family interaction and cultural expression. Usually the majority language will be used in the secondary or public domains and the minority language in the primary domains. Second, the minority language must be used in a written mode. The written medium will enhance the oral mode and boost the self-esteem and confidence of the speakers. Third, the minority language speakers must have an emotional attachment to their language. As a result of this attachment, they will develop sensitivity to correctness and purity. They will want, as much as possible, to maintain the original forms of the language. Fourth, there must be a successful process of learning the minority language with sustainable proficiency. Parents will ensure that the children not only learn the language correctly, but also maintain appropriate use of its structure. Lastly, in order to ensure continued use of a minority language, there must be a process of reinforcement by immigration of speakers from the main source of the language. This usually happens when a small community of speakers has regular contacts with the main language group, as is the case of the Nama speakers in the Matlhatlhaganyane Ward in Tsabong due to many factors, one being their regular contacts with the much larger Nama (Khoekhoegowab) community in Namibia (Batibo & Tsonope, 2000).

In order to make such measures effective and sustainable, the communities in question must, ideally, live in an environment which is economically sustainable, sociopolitically supportive and culturally vibrant, so as to maintain pride and strong loyalty to their language and culture. It is in quest of a better life that communities abandon their languages. Most communities equate better living with access to resources. The resources in this case imply any benefits of economic or social value which contribute to the economic well-being or social satisfaction of the people. These benefits include job opportunities, business attractions, education, health care, land (including arable areas, water places, fauna and flora) and spiritual freedom. It is when the speakers of a language find better economic or social prospects in another language community that they abandon their language and shift to the new one. Usually the new language is taken to have a higher status, is more socioeconomically privileged and is more technically developed. Hence, language maintenance is vulnerable where socio-economic attractions to another language are high.

Factors That Are Likely to Affect Language Maintenance

Detachment from traditional socioeconomic way of life

Where communities have detached themselves either voluntarily or by force from their traditional socioeconomic way of life, their levels of language maintenance have been affected. This is because, in most cases, they have become dependent on the communities that are well-established in the new socioeconomic lifestyle. Hence, hunter-gatherer or nomadic pastoralist groups, who often abandon their traditional socioeconomic ways of life to become sedentary farmers because of the effect of natural disasters like drought or cattle diseases which threaten their economies, often succumb to the languages of the farming communities that have more sustainable economies. However, there are cases where the hunter-gatherer communities have been forced to change their lifestyle because of lack of adequate land to sustain their lifestyle or because of the introduction by government of land laws that impinge on their rights to use their traditional land. This is the case of the Central Game Reserve in Botswana, where traditionally the land belonged to the hunter-gather communities and they were able to roam freely in this extensive land. But, with the encroachment of the Bantu-speaking populations in the area and the decision by the Botswana government to declare the land a game reserve, their traditional way of sustaining their living was greatly affected. Most of them were removed from the area and relocated in other settlements outside the reserve. As a result, they were forced to abandon much of their traditional socioeconomic way of life and to depend almost entirely on state-based provision of livelihood. This state of deprivation of their traditional land and dependence on the state brought them a lot of frustration and many started to abuse alcohol (Selolwane, 1995). Similar cases have been cited from Namibia, where hunter-gatherer communities lost large tracts of land. In 1970, following the Odendaal Commission Report, the Ju/'hoansi people lost 70% of their previous foraging territory and all but one of their permanent waters. They were left with about 6000 square kilometers of land, enough to support only about 170 residents by hunting and gathering (Biesele *et al.*, 1991).

Cases of detached communities that have lost their original languages have been cited in Eastern, Central and Southern Africa (Crawhall, 2005). Typical examples are the Hadza and Ongamo in Tanzania; Elmolo, Yaaku and Okiek in Kenya; Khomani and Kora in South Africa; Boni in Somalia; Nyang'i, Singa and Kooki in Uganda; and the Khoesan communities, such as Deti-Khwe, Korana, //Xegwi, Xiri, Seroa and /Xam, which were once spoken in Southern Africa as described by Traill (1995).

Effects of urbanization

Urban centers often attract populations from rural areas because of their many socioeconomic charms, which they offer in the form of job opportunities, self-propelled businesses, amenities, modern lifestyle and leisure. Usually the minority language speakers, who tend to be the most poverty-stricken members of many societies, are the ones who are most attracted to these urban places. But in most urban centers, it is the indigenous lingua franca or a pidginized form of the ex-colonial language that will be used as a common interethnic medium.

Most children born in an urban setting grow up without knowledge of their minority languages. With the fast growth of urbanism in Africa, which is estimated at 50% by 2020 (Peralta, 2006), more and more young people who are born in urban settings will grow up without any or reasonable proficiency in their mother tongues. In fact, many of the urban children have generally developed negative attitudes towards their ethnic languages, as they consider them to be linked to rural and low income or subsistence living.

Migration

Migrations are of at least two types: a minority language community may move into an area settled by a majority group or a large majority language group may move into an area where a minority language is spoken. The result in both cases is the doom of the minority language, as in either case the type of language contact is superordinate. That is, a dominant language is imposing itself on a minority language (Batibo, 2005a).

Often, small communities move into large communities for economic survival. This is the case of the San groups which have been absorbed by the mainly Tswana agriculturalists as herders, abandoning their languages in Central Botswana. Such moves have been considered strategies for survival or linguistic suicides (Dorian, 1977). A classical case of group strategy, in which people abandon their original language so as to integrate in a new environment for socioeconomic reasons, is that of the Hungarian immigrants in Austria who, after their settlement and integration in the new land in the 1940s, completely abandoned their original Hungarian language (Gal, 1979). Also, many minority groups have migrated into more fertile lands during droughts, abandoning their languages in the process, as they have found themselves intermingling with larger and more socioeconomically established groups.

On the other hand, the expansion of the major groups, particularly the agriculturalist and pastoralist groups, has caused linguistic and cultural suffocation of the smaller groups. A number of cases have been cited, especially in East Africa, where groups such as the Sonjo, the Akie, the Kwavi and the Aasax have abandoned their languages in favor of the expanding pastoralist Maasai groups (Nurse, 2000). Similar cases have been recorded of the Zinza and Shubi groups, who are fast abandoning their languages in favor of the powerful agro-pastoralist language, Sukuma, which is dominant in the area (Batibo, 2005b).

Policies on resource allocation

The tendency in most economies of the world, particularly those that have embraced the capitalist ideology, is to invest in areas with the most returns. This principle has also been followed by a number of countries in Africa, which have tended to focus their development efforts in the most viable areas or communities. Such moves have been motivated by the global economic principles of maximizing returns and optimizing results at as little cost as possible. This philosophy has tended to favor areas with developed economic networks, fertile zones or places with natural resources, at the expense of the less favored areas that often are the areas occupied by the minority language speakers. It is only in the now-unpopular egalitarian philosophies of the socialist system that some equilibrium would be sought. Thus, resources have been allocated in the more developed communities because of the already existing infrastructure and skilled human resources. The areas inhabited by the minority language speakers, which are often situated in remote, hardly accessible and usually less developed parts of the country, are neglected. As a result, they are further left behind. This is the situation in the arid and densely forested areas of Central and Southern Africa, where the indigenous people, namely the San and the Pygmies, are so economically and sociopolitically marginalized that they have to move into the larger communities for socioeconomic survival. One should note that before the arrival of the agro-pastoral Bantu speakers and the introduction of government laws, these original groups were able to sustain their lifestyles through nomadic living and environmentally sensitive conservational methods.

On the other hand, where the government has endeavored to promote local economies by creating new settlements with attractive infrastructure or initiating economic activities, this has attracted speakers of the mainstream languages who have then moved into the areas. The incoming majority language speakers marginalize the minority groups and force them to adopt their languages. One example of this effect is the case of the /Gwi and //Gana in the Central Kalahari part of Botswana (Nthomang, 2006).

Successes have only been noted where the stimulation of local economies has been based on the indigenous knowledge of the minority groups, and when these groups have been fully involved in the planning and running of their economic and social activities. Successes of such an approach have been noted among Naro speakers in Ghanzi, the Western part of Botswana, where communities have been trained through home-language based literacy with the local indigenous knowledge as a foundation (Visser, 2000).

Societal multilingualism

Societal multilingualism is often considered a curse, as it is taken to negatively impact a country's unity, identity and social coercion/harmony. Most societies or countries would prefer a state of monolingualism and monoculturalism. In fact, this way of thinking was very prevalent in Europe during the time of state formation, so much that English, French and Spanish were promoted in their respective states at the expense of the minority languages which were equally spoken in those countries. Equating multilingualism with socioeconomic underdevelopment has recently been supported by some scholars, such as Robinson (1996) and Watson (1994), who argue that although no causal relationship has been established between linguistic diversity and economic development, it has been observed that the highest concentrations of language diversity are found in the less economically developed countries.

In other words, the poorest countries of the world, including those of Africa, are found in areas with the highest concentration of languages. Many reasons could be given for this coincidence, but one legitimate reason would be that in most multilingual countries, not all languages are given equal status or privilege. The speakers of the less privileged languages are usually the ones who become socioeconomically disadvantaged. As multilingualism is a reality in Africa, where countries like Nigeria, Cameroon and the Democratic Republic of Congo have more than 200 languages each (485 in Nigeria alone), it is important to design language policies which ensure that the linguistic diversity becomes a developmental asset rather than a liability.

Where countries have adopted monolingualism and a monocultural approach (e.g. Botswana, Tanzania, Somalia and to some extent Kenya and Ethiopia), or a limited number of languages as official languages, for pragmatic reasons such as South Africa, all other languages have been marginalized, causing their speakers to focus more attention on the nationally privileged languages. In fact, if realistic language policies were to be established in Africa with optimal utility planning philosophies, all languages could be promoted to various degrees, according to their relative utility, taking into account: the number of speakers, their vitality levels, the speakers' attitudes and costs involved in the promotion process (Hachipola, 1996).

Political and ethnic conflicts

Conflicts, especially in Africa, constitute an important factor linked both to poverty and to language shift or death. Most conflicts in Africa are fueled by political or ethnic misunderstandings. The root problems are poverty, exploitation and domination between groups or political tendencies. Where such conflicts have been rampant, as has been the case in Sierra Leone, Liberia, the Democratic Republic of Congo, Rwanda and Burundi, many ethnic groups have been forced to flee into other areas, thus scattering or mixing in with other communities. In the process, many groups have been made poorer and economically dependent on the host groups. This, in turn, has compelled them to be absorbed linguistically and culturally into the host groups.

A typical example is to be found in Tanzania, where the refugees from Rwanda and Burundi, who have been in the country for many decades, have been totally assimilated into the local way of life. Most members of the younger generations speak only Kiswahili, the national language of Tanzania. Similar situations have been reported in countries with many refugees, like Zambia, Chad, Kenya, Uganda, Guinea, Sudan and the Democratic Republic of Congo, where refugees from neighboring countries have been forced to learn local languages and have become totally dependent on the local economy for their subsistence. Moreover, a number of African countries have experienced internal displacement of people due to sociopolitical conflicts. A number of groups have found themselves being forced to depend on other groups for land and livelihood, thus learning new languages and often abandoning their own. The countries in Africa with the highest number of internally displaced people include Sudan, Angola, the Democratic Republic of Congo, Sierra Leone, Uganda, Rwanda, Burundi, Somalia, Ethiopia and Eritrea (Clover, 2002).

The promotion of major indigenous languages

After the attainment of independence, African countries were faced with two options: adopt an exoglossic policy by promoting the ex-colonial language as the national or official language, or adopt an endoglossic policy that promotes an indigenous language as the national and/or official language. Most countries chose the first option.

Those countries which adopted the option of promoting an indigenous language usually promoted the indigenous lingua franca to take on new roles such as the language of education, administration, judiciary, legislature, social welfare, trade and mass media. The use of these languages in the secondary domains has made such languages more prestigious both politically and socioeconomically. As a result, they have attracted many speakers from the minority languages, who now see their languages as economically unviable. This is the case with Kiswahili (Tanzania and Kenya), Amharic (Ethiopia), Afrikaans (South Africa, during Apartheid), Chichewa (Malawi, during Kamuzu Banda's regime), Setswana (Botswana) and Sango (Central African Republic). As observed by Heine (1990) and Batibo (2005b), the major powerful lingua francas of Africa are causing the most minority language deaths on the African continent. Thus, the most vicious language killers in Africa are not the ex-colonial languages (as they are in Asia, Australia and the Americas), but the major powerful indigenous languages. As these languages tend to acquire high prestige and status, due to their use in socioeconomic and political spheres, the speakers of the minority languages would progressively be attached to them at the expense of their own languages, hence the beginning of the process of language shift and death.

Information and contact barriers

Minority language speakers are grossly disadvantaged because they happen not to have sufficient proficiency in the widely used languages. They have no access to vital information regarding their lives, particularly in socioeconomic advancement or social welfare, in their local languages. In most African countries, reports, newspapers and radio broadcasts are prepared either in the ex-colonial languages or the major national lingua francas. Thus, minority language speakers are not aware of any new insecticides, new breeds of seeds for their gardens, new fertilizers for their farms, new sprays for cow diseases, new skills for food preservation and many other new developments in their society. A recent study carried out in Botswana by Batibo and Mosaka (2000) revealed that many of the people in the rural areas do not read government reports or newspapers. Nor do they listen to radio announcements about developmental issues or social hazards, such as HIV/AIDS, alcohol, drug abuse and terrorist acts.

Minority language speakers are unable to participate in literacy activities that are often carried out in the major national lingua francas. This is the case in countries such as Kenya, Tanzania, Ethiopia, Botswana, Mali and the Central African Republic, where only the national lingua francas are used in literacy activities. The few exceptional countries where literacy activities are carried out in most languages of the country include Namibia and Zambia. But, even in these countries, speakers of the very small languages have to rely on the orthographies of the larger neighboring or related languages.

Finally, the lack of proper knowledge of the major lingua franca by the minority language speakers is a significant handicap for them because they cannot be good entrepreneurs in business or trade, due to their limited communicative competence in it. They cannot succeed in important bargains or advertise their goods properly. This is often the case in many Tanzanian open markets, where people with limited knowledge of Kiswahili (such as the Sukuma, Haya, Ha and Nyakyusa), are outwitted by mother tongue speakers of the language.

A Case Study of Language Empowerment from Western Botswana

One typical case in which a minority language has been empowered is that of Naro, a Khoesan language spoken by about 9000 people in Western Botswana in the Ghanzi District. Naro is one of the 26 minority languages in the country. As is the case with most minority languages in

Botswana, especially those of Khoesan origin, Naro was threatened by extinction as the speakers shifted to Setswana, the national language, and Shekgalagarhi, the dominant zonal language in the area.

A group of NGOs and members of the Dutch Reformed Church established a center in the area more than 20 years ago. The center, known as Kuru Development Trust, was concerned with the educational, economic and sociopolitical empowerment of the Naro people. The center carried out its empowerment process at three levels. The first involved linguistic empowerment. Realizing that the best way to revitalize a language is to use it in writing and institute literacy in the community, the Kuru Development Trust, with the help of missionaries from the Dutch Reformed Church, made a comprehensive description of Naro. Extensive fieldwork culminated in the publication of a dictionary, a grammar and a phonological sketch of the language. This process was followed by the establishment of a standard orthography for the language and the production of literacy materials, including story books, newsletters, reports and translated Bible passages (Visser, 2000: 199).

The center initiated literacy classes in Naro for both children and adults. The mere publication of reading materials in the language instilled pride and self-esteem among the Naro speakers. It also created positive attitudes and strong loyalty towards the language, as its speakers realized that Naro was as good as the other languages spoken in the area (Setswana, Shekgalagarhi and English). In fact, they were no longer embarrassed by the click sounds, which they had previously thought to be peculiar, given that they did not exist in the more dominant languages, such as Setswana and Shekgalagarhi. Many Naro speakers, especially the youth, enrolled in the literacy classes. The language was also used in the preschool system in Naro-speaking areas. Parents were so enthusiastic about the language that they now encouraged their children to learn and speak Naro.

The next level of empowerment was in the sociopolitical sphere. The Kuru Development Trust, an NGO, established community councils to deal with matters relating to leadership and social welfare in the Naro villages. These committees were also responsible for executing educational and literacy programs. A training center, known as Bokamoso ('the future'), was established to train young teachers who would teach in the various preschools and adult literacy programs (Batibo, 2004). The fact that the Naro people were able to run their own affairs built tremendous self-confidence among them and they became proud of their language. This enabled a sustained and active intergenerational transmission of the language.

The third level of empowerment was in the economic sphere. Naro speakers were trained in ways of generating their own income. The center used the already existing indigenous knowledge as a base to promote economic activities. The Naro people had a tradition of painting and producing artifacts such as crafts, sculptures, jewelry, decorations and pottery. These skills were developed so that the Naro could produce higher quality and more diverse products. They were taught how to make this artistic production a sustainable source of income. They established cooperative shops to sell their goods. This attracted cultural tourism in the area, as the Naro also initiated other activities, such as traditional dances and musical performances. Moreover, they were trained to improve their income-utilization methods. The earlier tendencies of squandering money or abuse of alcohol were discouraged. Jobs were created for the young people and recreational facilities were established. Hence, most Naro speakers learned to utilize their time profitably.

As a result of this holistic empowerment process, the per-capita income of the Naro has increased substantially, and many of them are able to make an independent living. The number of youth reaching higher education has increased, as the younger generation has not only a solid educational base in the mother-tongue-medium preschool, but also self-confidence. They are therefore able to compete on equal ground with the speakers of the major languages. The functional literacy among the Naro has increased, and many of them are excited to read books, pamphlets and newsletters in their mother tongue.

The Naro are now able to live a healthier lifestyle because of access to information about health and social hazards. At the same time, it has been reported that with a solid mother tongue base, they are able to learn the other languages like Setswana, Shekgalagarhi and English more easily. Also, they are now ready to co-operate with the majority groups in matters of nation building as they see themselves being valued and respected.

As a result of these developments, the Naro people have cultivated a very positive attitude towards their language. This has slowed, if not completely reversed, the process of language shift towards Setswana or Shekgalagarhi. In fact, the empowerment of Naro language speakers has encouraged speakers of other minority languages like /Gwi and //Gana to become bilingual in Naro, and even to start shifting towards it (Hasselbring, 2000). Naro is now considered a dominant language in the Ghanzi zone (Batibo, 2005: 52).

Conclusion

It is essential that the alarming trend of language shift from disadvantaged minority languages to privileged major languages be reversed by empowering the smaller language speakers educationally, economically and sociopolitically. This holistic empowerment can only work by involving the communities themselves. No speech community, however poor, will abandon its language to become mute. Communities abandon their languages because they are already bilingual and see socioeconomic benefits in the other language that are absent in their own language. Such people will normally have developed negative attitudes towards their language and will encourage their children to learn the more prestigious language because of the opportunities that it can offer. In this case, we can say that poverty is relative: however developed a community may be, it would still be attracted to another community, and hence another language, if there are more gains to be obtained from the other community or language.

Poverty itself is an ill that is a result of underdevelopment. Underdevelopment, on the other hand, is caused by lack of viable resources, the inability to manage and develop them properly or the deprivation of the means to manage them. Many minority language groups, especially in Africa, are lacking in resources because of the hostile habitat where they are located, lack of means (skills or capital) to exploit the resources or the ability to manage resources adequately. As a result, they find themselves migrating into larger and more organized communities or urban centers for better opportunities, thus abandoning their languages. The promotion of the major indigenous languages to become national or official languages has aggravated the situation, as it has widened the gap and increased the socioeconomic gradient. Thus, language endangerment has become more critical in countries like Tanzania, Kenya, Ethiopia, Mali, Malawi, Zimbabwe and South Africa, where dominant languages have been elevated to national or official languages.

References

Auburger, L. (1990) Linguistic minority relations. *Sociolinguistica* 4, 169–190.

Batibo, H. (2001) The empowerment of minority languages for education and development. In R. Trewby and S. Fitchat (eds) *Language and Development in Southern Africa: Making the Right Choices* (pp. 123–135). Windhoek: Gamsberg Macmillan.

Batibo, H. (2005a) The marked bilingualism model and its relevance to Africa. *Malawian Journal of Linguistics* 4, 1–32.

Batibo, H. (2005b) *Language Decline and Death in Africa: Causes, Consequences and Challenges*. Clevedon: Multilingual Matters.

Batibo, H.M. (2005) Transmitting local and indigenous knowledge in a diminishing bio-cultural environment: Some case studies from Botswana and Tanzania. Paper presented at the International Conference of Safeguarding the Transmission of Indigenous Knowledge, Aichi, Japan, 14–17 April.

Batibo, H.M. and Mosaka, N. (2000) Linguistic barriers as a hindrance to information flow: The case of Botswana. In H.M. Batibo and B. Smieja (eds) *Botswana: The Future of the Minority Languages* (pp. 95–104). Frankfurt: Peter Lang.

Batibo, H.M. and Tsonope, J. (2000) Language vitality among the Nama of Tsabong. In H.M. Batibo and J. Tsonope (eds) *The State of Khoesan Languages in Botswana* (pp. 12–35). Gaborone: Tasalls.

Biesele, M., Hubbard, D. and Ford, J. (1991) Land issues in Nyae Nyae: A communal areas example in Namibia. National Conference on Land Reform and the Land Question, Windhoek, 25 June to 1 July. Vol. 1. Research papers and addresses, and consensus document, Office of the Prime Minister, ed., (pp. 517–544). Windhoek, Namibia, Government of the Republic of Namibia.

Clover, J. (2002) *Situation Report: Refugees and Internally Displaced Peoples in Africa*. On WWW at http://www.iss.co.za/AF/current/Refugees_IDPs.html.

Crawhall, N. (2005) Hunter-gathers in Africa: Threats and opportunities – cases of South Africa, Tanzania and Gabon. A paper presented at the UNESCO Expert Meeting 'Safeguarding the Transmission of Local and Indigenous Knowledge of Nature', Aichi Prefectural University, Nagoya, Japan, 14–15 April.

Dorian, N.C. (1977) The problem of the semi-speaker in language death. In W.U. Dressler and R. Wodak-Kodotter (eds) *Language Death* (pp. 23–32). (*Journal of the Sociology of Language* vol. 12). Paris: Mouton.

Gal, S. (1979) *Language Shift: Social Determinants of Linguistic Change in Bilingual Austria*. New York: Academic Press.

Hachipola, S.J. (1996) *Survey of the Minority Languages of Zimbabwe*. Harare: Departments of African Languages and Literature, University of Zimbabwe.

Hasselbring, S. (2000) *A Socio-linguistic Survey of the Languages of Botswana* (Vol. 1). Gaborone: Tasalls.

Heine, B. (1990) Language policy in Africa. In B. Weinstein (ed.) *Language and Political Development* (pp. 167–189). Norway: Ablex.

Krauss, M. (1992) The world's languages in crisis. *Language* 68, 4–10.

Nettle, D. and Romaine, S. (2000) *Vanishing Voices: The Extinction of the World's Languages*. Oxford: Oxford University Press.

Nthomang, K. (2006) Basarwa development at crossroads: Contradictions and resistance-critical insights from the CKGR relocations. *Pula* 20 (1), 53–65.

Nurse, D. (2000) *Inheritance, Contact and Change in Two East African Languages* (Language contact in Africa 4). Koeln: Ruediger Koeppe Verlag.

Peralta, C. (2006) *Urban Growth Threatening Africa's Cities*. On WWW at http://www.planetzen.com/node/21376.

Robinson, C.D.W. (1996) *Language Use in Rural Development: An African Perspective*. The Hague: Mouton de Gruyter.

Traill, A. (1995) The Khoesan languages of South Africa. In R. Mestrie (ed.) *Language and Social History: Studies in South African Societies* (pp. 1–18). Cape Town: David Philip.

Visser, H. (1994) Literacy in Naro. In S. Sangestad and T. Tsonope (eds) *Developing Basarwa Research and Research for Basarwa Development* (pp. 25–29). (Report from a Workshop held at the University of Botswana, 17–18 September 1993.) Gabarone: University of Botswana, National Institute of Developmental Research.

Visser, H. (2000) Language and cultural empowerment of the Khoesan people: The Naro experience. In H.M. Batibo and B. Smieja (eds) *Botswana: The Future of the Minority Languages* (pp. 193–221). Frankfurt: Peter Lang.

Watson, K. (1994) Caught between Scylla and Charybdis: Linguistics and the educational dilemma facing policy makers in pluralist states. *International Journal of Education* 37, 70–94.

Chapter 3

Language Diversity and Poverty in Africa

MATTHIAS BRENZINGER

Introduction

Languages and poverty are related in many ways and on quite different levels. Poverty in its most severe manifestations of hunger and disease jeopardizes the lives of millions of Africans. Not only natural disasters and diseases, but also warfare, forced migration, bad governance and illiteracy are among the factors causing widespread poverty on the African continent. The survival of entire communities, and with them their cultures and languages, is threatened by poverty. Strategies aiming at poverty reduction must tackle these intertwined causes that produce and perpetuate poverty. The active involvement of the people concerned is a central aspect in the implementation. African languages are relevant in that they must be employed in order to reach the poor. As such, African languages play an important role in activities that aim to counter poverty.

The main focus of this discussion of language diversity and poverty is, however, the links between relative poverty and language choices. In this discussion, the notion of relative poverty should emphasize low quality-of-life in contrast to threats to physical survival. The latter is referred to as absolute poverty. Two main features of relative poverty are exclusion from symbolic and material markets and denial of access to tangible or intangible resources. This type of poverty relates mainly to social issues, such as education and well-being, and less to the physical features of poverty, such as short life-expectancy and severe malnutrition. Social and economic phenomena of deprivation and marginalization, as experienced by members of ethnolinguistic minorities, fall mainly within this characterization of relative poverty. Poverty as such will not be discussed, merely its impact on language choices as threats to language diversity.

Language choices are considered insofar as they relate to the maintenance or abandonment of African languages, i.e. choices which safeguard or threaten the existing language diversity. In the discourse on language endangerment, scholars quite regularly employ metaphors such as language death, killer languages and language murder and suicide, evoking pictures in which languages themselves are alive or dead. Languages are portrayed by these terms either as suffering victims or as aggressive offenders, prior to any scholarly analysis. More technical terms, such as language shift and displacement, replacing and abandoned languages, language and linguistic diversity, seem more fitting and will be applied in discussing the relationship between poverty and language diversity.

The more general relationship between languages and poverty will be addressed first, before the impact of relative poverty on language diversity.

Absolute Poverty and African Languages

No matter which indexes one chooses to scale different levels of poverty, African countries always seem to end up at the bottom. Poverty has many faces, and in its absolute, existential form it kills, or at least precludes a long and healthy life. Hunger is among the most prominent characteristics of absolute poverty, and was considered separately in 1948 in Article 25 of the Universal Declaration of Human Rights: 'Everyone has the right to a standard of living adequate for the health and well-being of himself and his family, including food'. Natural disasters and diseases, such as droughts and malaria, are common causes of malnutrition and lack of food in Africa.

Humanitarian disasters causing hunger are very often man-made: civil war and violent conflicts, in addition to widespread bad governance and mismanagement. Genocide wipes out entire communities along with their cultures and languages. With regard to language diversity, the Sudan is one of the most heterogeneous countries in Africa. Since the late 1980s, the army has dispersed local communities in the Nuba Mountains and killed hundreds of thousands, and as a consequence, many distinct Nubian languages have vanished. In more recent years, the army has extended its terror to the Darfur region. The forceful spread of Arabic and Islam, called 'Sudanization', aims for the reduction of ethnic multiplicity – even to the extent of wiping out entire nationalities. In Sudan, as in other African countries with cruel regimes, the very survival of the people is endangered. To mention the threats to languages here seems to be awkward. The endangerment of the languages and cultures should not be disregarded in these contexts, however, as the reason these ethnolinguistic minorities are oppressed is precisely their distinct cultures and languages.

In 2005, according to the Global Information and Early Warning System (GIEWS) on food and agriculture of the Food and Agriculture Organization (FAO) of the United Nations, one out of two sub-Saharan African countries required emergency food aid, and 206 million hungry people lived in this part of the world. Applying the Global Hunger Index, which has been developed by International Food Policy Research Institute (IFPRI) in Washington, DC, the 10 countries that scored worst in 2006 are all in sub-Saharan Africa. The Global Hunger Index combines three indicators: child malnutrition, child mortality and estimates of the proportion of people who are calorie-deficient. Some of the poorest countries, such as Somalia, could not even be considered in the survey due to lack of data (IFPRI, 2006: 1). The Human Development Index (HDI) of the United Nations includes more variables, such as economic performance, quality of health and educational systems and life expectancy. With regard to the HDI, African countries again rank lowest, with Mali as the third last, followed in ascending order by Sierra Leone and Niger.

Sub-Saharan Africa is home to most of the world's hungry. With 60% of the people living with HIV – more than 25 million – it is also the global epicenter of the AIDS pandemic (UNAID, 2006). HIV/AIDS and poverty are intertwined in a vicious circle. AIDS increasingly shows its negative effects, and the HDI drops even further in African countries for that reason. Poverty increases vulnerability to HIV infections, and AIDS boosts economic and social pressure on the already poor. Families lose their income earners or food producers, while others have to stay at home to care for sick relatives. Today, hundreds of thousands of AIDS orphans struggle to survive without parental care, and most of them live with relatives as additional dependents on already poor income earners. The relationship between AIDS and poverty is manifold, but there is no one-to-one correlation. The countries in Southern Africa are the most economically developed on the continent, yet they show the world's highest HIV prevalence.

There is no easy answer to the question of how to reduce poverty in Africa, but there is no doubt about the fact that the AIDS pandemic must be addressed as one of the key issues in the search for strategies aimed at reducing poverty. The use of African languages can make a difference in health education and awareness programs. In campaigns, people must be addressed in their own languages in order for them to reach a thorough liberated understanding of the conditions of exposure and risks of HIV infections. Genuine comprehension within one's own symbolic system may result in desired behavioral changes and may finally lead to a reduction of infection, and with that of poverty. African languages are indispensable in these processes, as most Africans do not speak the languages of their countries' former colonizers (Brenzinger & Harms, 2001).

Even more important is the role of African languages in building up effective public education systems. The relevance of mother tongue education has been widely acknowledged and is implemented in many African countries. Mother tongue education is an essential component of strategies aiming at eradicating poverty, but it is not essential for safeguarding Africa's language diversity. While mother tongue education generally fosters the use and status of minority languages, and with that supports their survival in the context of national states, the opposite outcomes can be observed in many language-shift situations of subnational contexts in Africa. Mother tongue education on the African continent means – with very few exceptions – that dominant African languages become the media of instruction. Thus, students from ethnolinguistic minorities are rarely taught in their own languages, but are instead instructed in regionally or nationally dominant languages. With this so-called mother tongue education, a relatively small number – maybe up to 20% – of the African languages gain governmental support in the educational sector. This imbalance creates a dilemma for language workers and linguists, as any attempt to use African languages in formal education needs their support. However, this inadvertently helps to threaten languages of the ethnolinguistic minorities, as they are generally not included as media in mother tongue education (Brenzinger, 2001: 106–108).

Productive and responsible democratic societies can only develop with the active involvement of the majority of their educated citizens. Such stable political and economic conditions are prerequisites for the eradication of poverty. In order to reach economic integration and ethnic stabilization, which is the only way to overcome poverty, educational policies must reach the majorities. For this goal to be reached, the choice of African languages as media of instruction is crucial. The most promising strategies are to promote stable multilingualism: spread of proficiency in European languages among all people in addition to use of African languages.

Why Still So Many African Languages?

On the whole, the extent of endangerment of the world's linguistic diversity reflects the distribution of languages on our planet. A significant concentration of countries with very high numbers of languages are located near the equator, including Papua New Guinea, India, Mexico, as well as the countries of Central and Western Africa. The highest density of endangered languages exists in the linguistically heterogeneous parts of the world; obviously, languages can only disappear where they still exist.

Home to about one third of the world's languages, the African continent is among the linguistically richest areas. More than 2000 African languages are still spoken, and these represent a significant part of the world's linguistic diversity, also comprising a great deal of typological variation. At the same time, poverty is prevalent on that very continent, and African countries are among the poorest on a worldwide scale, as mentioned earlier.

This complementary correlation is not accidental: the discrimination of the majority of Africans from national development contributed to the maintenance of African languages. Deserted infrastructures, low percentages of school enrollment, lack of political representation and participation, and meager public health care services are among the conditions that hinder the economic and social progress of African majorities. This exclusion of entire communities in rural Africa has fostered the use of more than 2000 languages and, with that, conserved an important part of the world's linguistic heritage. In this sense, marginalization, or relative isolation, rather, and relative poverty, have 'saved' large numbers of African languages.

Today, the poorest African countries are not necessarily also the linguistically richest, and vice versa. For example, some of the poorest countries like Rwanda, Burundi and Somalia, are monolingual with one common African language. Similarly, Nigeria may be considered rich with respect to its oil resources, and with about 500 languages, also on linguistic grounds. Language diversity is obviously not a result of underdevelopment and poverty. On the contrary, the large number of African languages reflects the longest oral intellectual tradition of humanity. African language diversity records the entire language history from the eve of human speech to modern times.

Language maintenance relies on language choice of individuals and is a rather complex issue in itself, as poverty is. In discussing the relationship between the two, language choice and poverty in Africa, communal and individual language behaviors both need to be looked at. Oral, unwritten languages, i.e. the vast majority of African languages, can only exist and survive as everyday media of speech communities. Many African rural communities are still excluded from processes that allow for economic and social upward mobility in a national context. They live mainly on subsistence economy with very little cash income. Under these conditions, family and neighbors are crucial for the physical and social survival of any individual. Language is the most common device for maintaining and perpetuating distinct ethnic and linguistic identities on the community level. Thus, cultural and linguistic proficiency is key to being treated as a member of the community. Ultimately, competence in the community language is critical for survival under such conditions.

Language choices, the crucial factor that determines the fate of languages, are individual decisions. Those African people who can make their living only in and with their communities, in most cases pass their communities' languages on to their children. Language-use patterns are stable within such community contexts. However, migration and urbanization are rapidly expanding and changing living conditions in most parts of the continent. Individual language choices in these new settings are far more complex and no longer controlled by one speech community. Urban citizens have various options and quite different communication needs. Most African minority languages do not allow access to modern life and are very often abandoned under such conditions. Migration and urbanization in Africa result from attempts by people to escape poverty, and they create unfavourable conditions for the transmission of minority languages.

Language Choices in the Face of Poverty

Does language choice really exist? Can people really decide to maintain or abandon their languages? These basic questions have been extensively discussed by scholars. Edwards (1984: 292) and Tsunoda (2005: 74–75), for example, conclude that circumstances determine this kind of fundamental language choice; thus, people themselves have, *de facto*, no choice. Coulmas (2005), in contrast, emphasizes the fact that speakers cannot avoid constantly making language choices. Of course, all choices are made in certain contexts, and thereby are constrained in many ways. How does poverty affect language choices? Minorities in liberal countries can choose their linguistic identity more or less freely. They usually do not die of hunger or genocide and enjoy at least basic human rights. Many minorities in African countries are in quite different positions, as mentioned earlier.

In Africa, increasing numbers of speakers and entire speech communities abandon their own less useful languages and shift to more useful languages. More useful languages might be labeled as prestigious, economically advanced and politically more powerful, bigger or simply stronger. All these terms, however, are meaningless without reference to specific contexts. A small-community language may have none of these fancy assets of the larger ones, but can still allow its speakers to survive in a community. Basic questions are: who is in control of the social and economic environment of a speech community, and which value systems do the community members share? The globally or even nationally most prestigious and powerful language might not be useful for a person in a rural setting. In fact, the most powerful language of all, English, might turn out to be without any value for a subsistence farmer.

The threats to African language diversity will be looked at with a focus on value systems that underlie judgments of language choices. New value systems employed by African communities can be the globally prevailing ones that are brought to their attention through mass media, formal education, religious mission work, etc. English, and to a much lesser extent French, are associated with these new values. Even though these languages hold high prestige and promise social and economic opportunities, African speech communities have not yet abandoned their heritage languages in favor of them. The loss of speakers in one African language is typically still the gain of speakers of another African language. The bold statement that African languages are not replaced by the prestige languages, such as English and French, must be evaluated against two different backgrounds.

First, it is predominantly the approximately 100 African languages, spoken by more than 1 million people, which face a challenge in relevant domains. All of these languages are safe, as they are widely transmitted as first languages. Individuals from such large speech communities may be raised in 'foreign' languages, but this does not reduce the vitality of these major African languages. The vast majority of African languages have stable speech communities of thousands of speakers, and foreign languages have not yet entered the home domain in most cases. If language shift occurs at all, it will take a long time, and major African languages are at present the more likely replacing languages.

Second, members of the roughly 200–300 small ethnolinguistic minorities are generally not exposed to these 'foreign' languages and do not speak them in their daily lives. In fact, most cannot speak the foreign languages at all. Small African languages, however, are of utmost importance for linguistic diversity, as many of them are unclassified language isolates. These small communities are vulnerable to external and internal threats, and they are marginalized and poor. The smaller an

African speech community is, the smaller the potential threat by 'foreign' languages. Other African languages are in closer contact and more attractive in these contexts.

Language shift on the African continent occurs on different levels. On a local level, language shifts co-occur with shifts to value systems of other African communities. During the past decades, numerous cases have been observed in which former hunter-gatherers have assimilated and taken on the language of a pastoral society. In pastoral society, the only possession that matters is livestock, and hunter-gatherers are looked down upon as people without cattle. Many formerly hunting-gathering communities, such as the Yaaku, Aasax and Akie (some speakers are still left in the case of the latter) have abandoned their heritage languages and adopted the Maa language along with a pastoral way of live. The young generations of these former hunter-gatherers are pastoralists and now share the prejudice against 'poor people without cattle', i.e. against their own ancestors and even elders.

For example, bridewealth inflation led the formerly foraging Yaaku to change first their subsistence patterns, and finally their ethnic and language identity: 'When Yaaku girls began marrying neighboring pastoralists, the parents received livestock as bridewealth, not only beehives as was the Yaaku custom. This made it necessary for young Yaaku men to acquire cattle too since Yaaku fathers demanded cattle as bridewealth from then on' (Brenzinger, 1992a: 300–301). Hunter-gatherers were considered poor, and in order to found families, young Yaaku men had to become pastoralist and take on the Maa language.

In similar contexts, small communities are currently adopting the languages of immediate neighbors, languages that are often themselves spoken by small speech communities only. In Southern Ethiopia, for example, 'Ongota is replaced by Ts'amakko (Ts'amay), Kwegu (Koegu) by Mursi, Shabo by Majang and Harro by Bayso. In small communities, language is the main indicator for group identity. 'Ongota people today survive as Ts'amay, and in order to become Ts'amay, 'Ongota were obliged to speak Ts'amakko and to abandon their former language.

On a national level, ethnolinguistic minorities are not in a position to resist outside pressures when, for example, loyalty to the nation is associated with speaking the national language. Communities may change their ethnic and language loyalty when they can no longer make a living. Numerous communities are replacing their heritage languages with those of the national dominant media, such as Setswana in Botswana, Swahili in Tanzania or the National varieties of Arabic in the Maghreb region. Where members of minorities are given a chance to participate and progress in national developments, they are often confronted with the fact that modernization and upward social mobility demand from them the sacrifice of their cultural and linguistic identities.

On an international level, African languages of wider communication are quite frequently replacements for minority languages via their spread as languages of trade and religion or as a consequence of urbanization. In such processes, Bambara in Mali, Hausa in Nigeria and Niger, and Swahili in Eastern Africa have gained speakers at the expense of smaller languages. For example, communities may change their language affiliation along with a change in religious faith. Economically disadvantaged communities in West African countries may be better off as part of a wider, Hausa-speaking or Dyula-speaking Muslim society. Poverty may trigger changes in religious faith and a shift to the languages associated with these new religions.

People choose languages not only under certain conditions, but also on various grounds. Coulmas (2005) distinguishes between symbolic and utilitarian criteria for language choices. Symbolic values are most relevant to social identity and other matters of well-being, while pragmatic considerations involve, among other things, economic issues. In most African contexts, language choice is less a matter of choosing an ethnic identity than of searching for the best path to physical survival. Language choices are made on both grounds, more on symbolic ones among the rich, while the poor are forced to decide for their mother tongue on utilitarian criteria.

Many communities experience a loss of essential material, spiritual or intellectual resources required for their past livelihood, such as foraging grounds, ancestral beliefs or hunting techniques. With such losses, they become poor and deprived within their own traditional value system. 'We lost everything!' is what the young Khwe Chief, Kipi George, stated shortly before he passed away. Back in the 1970s, the phrase 'we are dying of hunger' became the commonly used greeting among his formerly foraging communities in the Caprivi Strip of Namibia and in the northern part of Botswana. Before then, as Khwe elders frequently remember, the bush provided them with an abundance of everything they needed. In their old way of life, they never felt poor. In their highly mobile lives without permanent housing, there was no place for commodities other than those that one could carry on one's body. Nowadays, Khwe are poor in almost all respects even by their own estimation. No longer allowed to hunt and possessing no alternative means of sustaining a livelihood, these former hunter-gatherers are impoverished and experience the lowest life expectancies, the lowest school enrolment rates and the lowest levels of cash income in Namibia. However, Khwedam, their Central Khoesan language, is still vital among the Namibian Khwe communities. Deprived of their former resources and excluded from national developments, they nevertheless take pride in their past as the autochthonous people of the region. The language is maintained as the community's daily medium for communication because no matter how poorly, Khwe in Namibia can only physically and socially survive within their own social network.

In contrast to that, many Khwe children in neighboring Botswana grow up speaking the national language, Setswana, as their first language, and some never acquire Khwedam. Khwe in Botswana are much better off than their Namibian relatives, and the proficiency in Setswana does allow them access to formal education, public health services and the job market. This striking difference in language choice by the same people in the two countries illustrates the dominance of pragmatic considerations under poor living conditions.

As demonstrated by the earlier examples, communities may develop desires for new assets that they did not have in the past, such as domestic animals, farms and houses, consumer items and access to mass media and modern means of communication. Such aspirations are felt within the framework of new value systems, and in the framework of empowerment relations of domination and marginalization. External threats may be physical, such as famine and war, but more often they are such abstract factors as increased mobility, the spread of cash economy, formal education or diminishment of natural resources. Small communities are increasingly unable to respond to such challenges and opt to change their ethnic and language loyalty. In such cases, communities take over the language and identity of their immediate neighbors, a national identity and language, or a regional identity and language of wider communication. Overcoming poverty by assimilating even linguistically is among the main motives for language shifts in Africa.

Poverty and the Future of Linguistic Diversity

The crucial observation made by Nettle and Romaine (2000) is that 'access to economic resources is, in modern times, probably the fundamental determinant of language shift and language death'. This phenomenon has various implications for the future of linguistic diversity on the African continent. Poverty is a growing threat to languages spoken by ethnolinguistic minorities, and may in the near future develop into the prime criteria for abandoning one's own language. Even rural communities in remote areas on the African continent no longer live on their own, and very few probably did in the past.

Only a few major African languages stand to gain in the context of modern economic development. In at least some African states, major African languages compete with and counter the domination of the languages of the former colonial powers. Such major African languages give their speakers access to material and symbolic resources, and therefore may be considered well-established and 'safe' for the time being.

The majority of African languages are not involved in modern economic contexts and their speakers are widely excluded through political processes. Small speech communities will abandon their own languages with great ease when opportunities are opened to them to participate and make progress in modern economic and sociopolitical life. Because poverty and marginalization have been key factors for language maintenance on the African continent, strategies that are applied to support language maintenance in other parts of the world may actually work against maintenance efforts of endangered languages there. 'Mother tongue' education, generally a well-established tool to foster language vitality, in most African contexts means education in the mother tongue of the national or subnational dominant African language. Instead of supporting all African languages, this well-meant practice puts further external pressures on the language use of the minority communities.

Citizens in many African countries democratically elect their governments, and with continued efforts and good fortune, sub-Saharan African nations as a whole will further progress. With these developments, the national states will become the dominant frames of reference for minorities and their cultures on the African continent. Respect and appreciation of cultural and linguistic diversity as assets rather than obstacles to national unity are essential to further the use and maintenance of heritage languages among minority communities in African states. Nevertheless, proficiency in nationally and internationally dominant languages will gain importance throughout the world and will also continue to spread on the African continent. These developments do not necessarily require the sacrifice of other languages, i.e. mother tongues of ethnolinguistic minorities, as most societies have always been multilingual. In order to counter the processes that point towards a monolingual world imposed by the dominant nations of the 'first world', linguists need to support the development of multilingual alternatives in education and national communication. With a promising language management program, South Africa is on its way to establishing a thoroughly multilingual society, which may be a model for other African states.

A reduction of poverty, and progress in building up liberal societies with individual rights and fair chances for the neglected masses, will increase pressure on small African languages. There will be no future for languages that are considered a hindrance to the economic and social progress of and by their speakers. Communities will abandon their heritage languages as soon as opportunities are opened for them to make progress in modern economic and sociopolitical life if these languages are not made economically and socially valuable. Strategies need to be developed to actively employ such languages in tackling issues related to overcoming poverty. Ultimately, in order to maintain and perpetuate the world's language diversity, speakers must find good economic and cultural reasons for keeping their ancestral languages as vital media in natural everyday communication with their offspring. Instead of being obstacles for job opportunities, etc., these languages should become treasures in themselves with an economic value, as well as an important means by which to overcome marginalization and poverty.

References

Brenzinger, M. (1992a) Patterns of language shift in East Africa. In R. Herbert (ed.) *Language and Society in Africa* (pp. 287–303). Johannesburg: Witwatersrand University Press.

Brenzinger, M. (1992b) Lexical retention in language shift: Yaaku/Mukogodo-Maasai and Elmolo/Elmolo-Samburu. In M. Brenzinger (ed.) *Language Death* (pp. 213–254). Berlin, New York: Mouton de Gruyter.

Brenzinger, M. (1996) Language displacement and language shift. In F. Coulmas (ed.) *The Handbook of Sociolinguistics* (pp. 273–284). Oxford: Blackwell.

Brenzinger, M. (1998) Various ways of dying and different kinds of deaths: Scholarly approaches to language endangerment on the African Continent. In K. Matsumura (ed.) *Studies in Endangered Languages: Papers from the International Symposium on Endangered Languages Tokyo, November 18–20, 1995* (pp. 85–100). Tokyo: Hituzi Syobo.

Brenzinger, M. (2001) Language endangerment through marginalization and globalization. In O. Sakiyama (ed.) *Lectures on Endangered Languages: 2* (pp. 91–116). ELPR Publication Series C002.

Brenzinger, M. (2005) The endangerment of language diversity: Responsibilities for speech communities and linguists. *Al-Maghrib al-Ifrîqî* (Université Mohammed V – Souissi, Rabat) 6, 63–80.

Brenzinger, M. (2006) Language maintenance and shift. In K. Brown (ed.) *The Encyclopedia of Language and Linguistics* (2nd edn), Vol. 6, R. Mesthrie (ed.) *Society and Language* (pp. 542–548). Oxford: Elsevier.

Brenzinger, M. and de Graf, T. (2006) Language documentation and maintenance. In *Encyclopedia of Life Support Systems* (EOLSS), UNESCO. (On-line encyclopedia: http://www.eolss.net/.)

Brenzinger, M., Dwyer, A. and Yamamoto, A.Y. (2003) Safeguarding of endangered languages. *The Endangered Language Fund Newsletter* 7 (1), 1–4.

Brenzinger, M. and Harms, G. (2001) *HIV/AIDS Threat and Prevention in Marginalised Ethnic Groups*. Eschborn: GTZ.

Coulmas, F. (2005) *Sociolinguistics. The Study of Speakers' Choices*. Cambridge: Cambridge University Press.

Edwards, J. (1984) Language, diversity and identity. In J. Edwards (ed.) *Linguistic Minorities, Policies and Pluralism* (pp. 277–310). London: Academic Press.

FAO (2006) World hunger increasing. FAO Head calls on world leaders to honour pledges. FAO Newsroom. (www.fao.org/newsroom/en/news/2006/1000433/index.html)

Tsunoda, T. (2005) *Language Endangerment and Language Revitalization. An Introduction*. Berlin, New York: Mouton de Gruyter.

UNAIDS (2006) Report on the global AIDS epidemic: Executive summary. UNAIDS. (data.unaids.org/pub/GlobalReport/2006/2006_GR-ExecutiveSummary_en.pdf)

Part 2

Language as a Determinant of Access to Resources

Chapter 4

The Impact of the Hegemony of English on Access to and Quality of Education with Special Reference to South Africa

NEVILLE ALEXANDER

Introductory Remarks

To the best of my knowledge, there are no studies in the African context that deal directly with the relationship between language-medium policy and practice in education and poverty. At best, we have general reports on the relationship between failure rates, drop-out rates or/and repeater rates and the language-medium issue. The fundamental reason for this lacuna is, of course, the difficulty of isolating or, at least, weighting, language medium as a factor or a variable in the educational performance of individual learners. In this essay, I approach this matter in a preliminary manner with specific reference to work in progress in South Africa by educationists, economists and statisticians. It should, therefore, be taken as the beginning of a larger research program that will unfold in the course of the next few years. This task is particularly pertinent because of the diverse poverty eradication and poverty alleviation initiatives that are currently being punted in South Africa by both governmental and nongovernmental institutions. The contrast is significant in sociopolitical terms. Further afield, the international rhetoric around the *Make Poverty History* campaign compels all scholars to examine their particular disciplines in terms of the ways in which their practices and their theoretical positions *a priori* either exacerbate or alleviate poverty in the world or in their relevant spaces.

In order to make the analysis and understanding of the South African dynamic as precise as possible, I spend considerable time on the big picture, beginning with our views about the global relation of forces as manifest in the global, regional and national linguistic hierarchies that have evolved over time. In this context, we must keep in mind the kind of caveat that Mufwene (2002: 191) issues when he reminds us that as language planners, we have to take into account the ecologies that make it possible for languages to thrive in their given state. For, as he puts it, if we are going to get the speakers of affected (endangered) languages to change their behavior,

> ...we must convince them of the benefits that humanity, especially the affected populations, can derive by changing their behaviors. As both languages and cultures are dynamic and constantly (re)shaping themselves through the behaviors of the populations with which they are associated, bemoaning ancestral traditions alone will not do the job.

Researching the Historical Background

Whatever the point of departure and philosophical assumptions of the numerous studies on colonial language policy and practice in Africa under British rule, there is complete agreement on the fact that in all of the affected territories, proficiency in the English language came to be seen by would-be men and women of substance as the most important key to social, economic and political success. Along this trajectory, it is on the issue of the hegemony of English as a global language that we ought to do many more in-depth studies of individual countries. Of particular significance would be analyses that enhance our understanding of which African individuals and which social conditions were decisive in establishing not the dominance[1] but the hegemony of English. It would be important to identify the historical moment when there was what the Afrikaans poet and writer, Van Wyk Louw, called 'a balance of arguments' such that the alternative choice(s) made by these decisive individuals (or groups of individuals) would have initiated a totally different social and historical path of development.[2] How, to give a practical example, did the situation arise where a black South African medical doctor could say, at the turn of the 19th century:

> The question naturally arises which is to be the national language. Shall it be the degraded forms of a literary language, a vulgar patois; or shall it be that language which Macaulay says is "In force, in richness, in aptitude for all the highest purposes of the poet, the philosopher, and the orator inferior to the tongue of Greece alone?" Shall it be the language of the "Kombuis" [kitchen, NA] or the

language of Tennyson? That is, shall it be the Taal [Afrikaans, NA] or English?... (cited in Alexander, 1989: 29)

As a significant footnote to the history of Africa, it should be recorded that in the Union of South Africa, it was eventually decided by the representatives of the white minority to have both English and Afrikaans (until 1925, Dutch) as the official, i.e. 'national', languages.

A second area for research on the historical background to the current linguistic landscape on the continent of Africa concerns the contradiction between articulated language policy understandings and the *de facto* policies of the leadership cadres of the nationalist and/or avowedly socialist movements of national liberation and political independence in the period between 1945 and 1975, more or less, when most of the continent was rid of formal rule by its colonial overlords. Works by Laitin, among others, have dealt with some of the issues involved in a generalized form, but, as important and useful as these are, we still need detailed studies of individual countries. Such studies are important in terms of determining the potential of language planning for the initiation and consolidation of counterhegemonic strategies for the establishment or, in some instances, the re-establishment of African languages in 'the controlling domains of language'.[3] This, in turn, is an essential condition of the success of the core projects of the African Academy of Languages (ACALAN), to which I shall return at the end of this essay.

Post and neocolonial language policies in Africa have, quite naturally, received much more attention from scholars.[4] However, with a few notable exceptions, very little work has been done in terms of paradigms such as world systems theory or of the social reproduction approach of Pierre Bourdieu, in which the economic, including the class, aspects of specific language policies become manifest and explicable. For each of the African (or other) countries concerned, it would be of inestimable value if we could demonstrate how the situation came about and was perpetuated where, in the original formulation of Pierre Alexandre:

> ... (on) the one hand is the majority of the population, often compartmentalized by linguistic borders which do not correspond to political frontiers; this majority uses only African tools of linguistic communication and must, consequently, irrespective of its actual participation in the economic sectors of the modern world, have recourse to the mediation of the minority to communicate with this modern world. This minority, although socially and ethnically as heterogeneous as the majority, is separated from the latter by that monopoly which gives it its class specificity: the use of a means of

universal communication, French or English, whose acquisition represents truly a form of capital accumulation. But this is a very special kind of capital, since it is an instrument of communication and not one of production. It is nevertheless this instrument, and generally this instrument alone, which makes possible the organization of the entire modern sector of production and distribution of goods. (Alexandre, 1972: 86)

A Note on the Political Economy of Language in Contemporary Africa

Any consideration of the impact of language policy on access to and quality of education in modern Africa, as elsewhere, has to begin by posing a few critical questions about the relationship between language policy, language use and economic and political power. Given the structure of the linguistic markets inherited by the African ruling strata from the colonial era, how do language policies or, more pertinently, *de facto* language policies, tend to reinforce or to counter the all-too-evident social inequalities of the postcolonial system? The character of the postcolonial state is, naturally, the key to finding the appropriate answers to this question, in spite of the fact that most analyses of these peripheral *neo*colonial states never even mention, much less discuss, the language issue.[5]

Difficult though it might be, it is essential that students of the political sociology of language attempt to establish the causal connection between the objective imperatives of administering polities where, on the one hand, there had been little or no disruption of socioeconomic patterns of interaction or of the transactions and relations of daily life for the vast majority of the population and, on the other hand, the apparent certainty of their leadership about the benevolent effects of virtually unchanged language and, usually, other social policies. In particular, it is necessary to trace the chain of reasoning that led political and cultural leaders to argue from the alleged neutrality of the languages of the former colonial powers in terms of the nation-building project, to the perpetuation of what, after a decade or more of 'independence', was palpably a policy of perpetuating class stratification and discrimination, one that deepened and complicated the very ethnic divides that the original policy of officializing the respective European languages was intended to avoid. Another way of addressing this question is to ask what the degree of consciousness of 'elite closure'[6] of the new rulers is.

In order to approximate a satisfactory analysis of the political economy of language in contemporary Africa, it is necessary to have recourse to something like the amended version of world systems theory, which Clayton (2000) calls 'constructive structuralism'. In line with world systems theory, this approach begins by stressing the fact that language dispensations in specific polities or regions of the world are impacted upon by the global ecology of languages, which, stated diachronically but crudely, is itself the product of mass migrations caused by either natural disasters or historical conflicts. Abram de Swaan, in a recent economics-based analysis of the linguistic world order, provides an abstract synchronic description as follows:

> ... (The) worldwide constellation of languages is an integral part of the "world system". The population of the earth is organized into almost two hundred states and a network of international organiza- tions – the political dimension of the world system; it is coordinated through a concatenation of markets and corporations – the economic dimension; it is linked by electronic media in an encompassing, global culture; and, in its "metabolism with nature", it also constitutes an ecological system. ... (The) fact that humanity, divided by a multi- tude of languages, but connected by a lattice of multilingual speakers, also constitutes a coherent language constellation, as one more dimension of the world system, has so far remained unnoticed. (de Swaan, 2001: 1–2)

Because of the constraints of space, it suffices to state that the current 'constellations' of 'languages', i.e. the super and subordinate relations that reflect the status of specific languages on local, national, regional and global levels, are the consequence of the 'evolution' of linguistic markets (in Bourdieu's use of this concept), which themselves are a reflection of power relations among the social strata that constitute the respective entities. As indicated earlier, this particular complex has been studied satisfactorily at a general level of analysis. Clayton's contribution to the complexity of our understanding of what he refers to as the 'shaping of hegemony' is the role of agency in general and of subaltern groups or strata in particular. Specifically, he contends that the general- ization in terms of which 'European' language[7] comes to dominate the controlling domains of language does not hold universally, i.e. that under given conditions, it serves the interests of the colonizers better to enhance the status and increase the powerful functions of local or vehicular (or cross-border) languages. In the African context, there are very few relevant cases. Kiswahili and, with some qualifications, Amharic, are perhaps the best African candidates for the status of the exceptions that prove the rule.[8]

A recent strand of analysis that attempts to view the political economy of language in terms of functional multilingualism in economic life runs the risk, in my opinion, of promoting a kind of economic diglossia where the 'minority' languages are confined as instruments of communication in the processes of production, exchange and distribution to the so-called informal sector, as against the nationally dominant languages (in Africa, these are almost without exception languages of European origin) that perform these powerful functions in the 'formal' economy.[9] This approach to the issue derives from a dual-economy paradigm that has a long history but, even if it had been useful in earlier times, is particularly irrelevant and misleading in the era of globalization. Ultimately, it may do no more than serve as an apologetic justification for the perpetuation of existing social stratification. In Africa specifically, the languages of the majority of the people have to become the dominant languages, in whatever combinations, in the respective economy, taken as a whole, of the individual countries. Only if this happens will the danger of a two-tier citizen-subject social model be countered in favor of a democratic system where all are citizens and all have similar life chances. Djité (2005) has written a useful analytical essay on the subject from the point of view not of minorities in Europe, North America and elsewhere, but from that of the 'third world', where the 'informal economy' is often the major contributor to the GDP or the main source of employment (Djité, 2005: 15).

Both Djité (2005) and Edwards (2005) in mercifully jargon-free essays have demonstrated how in economically more developed countries, this informal sector constitutes a set of niche markets in which, necessarily, local languages are essential for lubricating the economic processes. Edwards also points to the fact that these niche markets are often rapidly occupied by the products of multinational firms. In so doing, she gives one more indication that the 'dual economy' is no more than an abstraction. Both authors also insist that the economic benefits of multilingualism should be transferred to the central economies. In respect of Africa, Djité (2005: 22) concludes with unerring logic that:

> Communication facilitated in the local languages will remove the inefficiencies introduced by the selection and promotion of the official language, and policies that promote growth with equity are necessary to achieve socio-economic inclusion for all.

Edwards (2005: 164) similarly warns against the establishment of economic diglossia or ghettoization of the 'minority languages' by stating clearly that:

English may be the language of global trading, but the ability to speak other languages none the less ensures a competitive edge. The multilingual populations of inner-circle countries are a valuable resource, which we overlook at our peril. Their contribution to international business is becoming increasingly evident in areas such as China and the Middle East. . . . Initiatives that target minorities rely heavily on the knowledge and experience of minority-language speakers. . . . Bilinguals are a marketable commodity; the ability to speak other languages opens up a far wider range of better-paid employment opportunities than might otherwise be the case.

Language Medium Policy, Educational Access and Quality: The Case of Postapartheid South Africa

Against this background, a general overview of the impact of language policy and language practice on social inequality acquires much more significance. Ayo Bamgbose, Emeritus Professor for Linguistics and African Languages at Ibadan University, Nigeria, who is also the most senior African scholar in the fields of Applied Linguistics and the Sociology of Language, has written an authoritative study on precisely this subject. In his elegantly written thesis,[10] he provides us with incisive analyses of the many different ways in which languages have been and are used in order to exclude groups and classes of people as well as individuals. Echoing the elite-closure thesis, he arrives at the general conclusion that:

> The included are a major stumbling block in the use of African languages in a wider range of domains. Apart from lack of political will by those in authority, perhaps the most important factor impeding the increased use of African languages is lack of interest by the elite. They are the ones who are quick to point out that African languages are not yet well developed to be used in certain domains or that the standard of education is likely to fall, if the imported European languages cease to be used as media of instruction at certain levels of education. Hence, a major part of the non-implementation of policy can be traced to the attitude of those who stand to benefit from the maintenance of the status quo. (Bamgbose, 2000: 2)

His analyses highlight the fact that in Africa, language policy has, generally speaking, reinforced the creation of a numerically small class of citizens and a majority class of non-citizens.[11] Because of the importance of education in the global knowledge economy, it is, naturally, the pivot on which 'development' depends. And it is precisely in this crucial domain that language policy in postcolonial Africa, with hardly any exception, has been an unmitigated disaster. Bamgbose discusses in detail the centrality of mother tongue education for the vast majority of African children as the only option for effective quality education against the background of the widespread social pathology of what I have called the static maintenance syndrome[12] that has undermined all education in postcolonial Africa.

One of the most recent examinations of this complex, by a former Director of the UNESCO Regional Office for Africa (in Dakar, Senegal), Professor Pai Obanya, concludes that if education is to become accessible to all, and not only to the privileged elite, it is essential that, at the very least, the 'Ife-appeal' of six years of mother tongue instruction[13] should be implemented throughout the country. And a comprehensive report to African Ministers of Education compiled by the Association for the Development of Education in Africa (ADEA), the Deutsche Gesellschaft für Technische Zusammenarbeit (GTZ) and the UNESCO Institute for Education refers to 'the colossal failure of the educational system' so far in Africa and goes to the logical extent of proclaiming unequivocally that:

> ... (the) use of African languages as MOI (media of instruction N.A.) throughout multilingual educational models is viewed as a realistic solution for the improvement of education in Africa. It is one which requires initial investment, but it is also one which will show promising economic, educational and social returns. (ADEA, 2005: 30)

By way of example, I shall consider the South African case in terms of access to, and quality of, school education. Extrapolation to the tertiary educational level would simply reinforce the findings of the research that has been done in connection with the school system if one makes allowance for the fact that those who reach the tertiary institutions are usually the 'best' in terms of the existing norms and standards.[14]

A University of Cape Town M. Phil. mini dissertation on the subject of *Medium of Instruction and its Effect on Matriculation Examination Results in 2000 in Western Cape Secondary Schools* hypothesized that:

> ... African language speaking learners in the Western Cape will tend to do badly in the matriculation examination largely because the medium of instruction and assessment is not the mother tongue, but a second or third language. (October, 2002: 5)

The dissertation, among other things, compares the results of Afrikaans L1 and English L1 students with those of Xhosa L1 students in key subjects and confirms the hypothesis. The actual statistics are, in the context of the 'new' South Africa, ironic and extremely disturbing because they demonstrate all too clearly some of the avoidable continuities between apartheid and postapartheid education. Probably the most significant finding of this study is that the only 'learning area' in which all the matriculation candidates performed at comparable levels was the First Language (Higher Grade) subject, i.e. English, Afrikaans, and isiXhosa First Language (Higher Grade). This was, for the Xhosa L1 speakers the only subject in which they were taught and assessed in their mother tongue. Ironically, the results for isiXhosa First Language (Higher Grade) are better than for the other two languages! (see October, 2002: 76–77).

These findings have been reinforced by a recent, much larger survey of matric results by Simkins and Patterson (2005). Although their point of departure for their inquiry into *Learner Performance in South Africa* is, pedagogically speaking, somewhat conservative, as its preferred model appears to be a transitional bilingual one, they nonetheless arrive at the conclusion in respect of the causal significance of the language of teaching (medium of instruction) factor that:

> ... social and economic variables at the individual household level do not play an enormous role in determining performance, with the exception of the language variables. Pupils whose home language is an African language are at a considerable disadvantage in the language of instruction by the time they reach Grade 11[15] if the language of instruction is never spoken at home. This can be offset somewhat if the language of instruction is spoken sometimes at home and it can be offset considerably if the language of instruction is spoken often at home. (Simkins & Patterson, 2005: 33)

They also claim that competence in the language of instruction is crucial for performance in mathematics. 'Every extra per cent earned in the language test is associated with an addition of one sixth of a percent in the mathematics test in Grade 9 and one third of a percent in Grade 11' (Simkins & Patterson, 2005: 34).[16] Their study, although limited and preliminary in many respects, has advanced the argument for mother tongue based education, whether single- or dual-medium is irrelevant in this context, from postulating a correlative (October) to demonstrating a causal relationship between educational success and language medium.[17] As such, it has already given rise to a shift in the perceptions of the political and cultural leadership who, in recent months, have begun speaking more openly and frequently in public about the virtues and benefits of mother tongue education.

One of South Africa's most prominent educational analysts and researchers who, until recently, was at best skeptical about the virtues and practicality of mother tongue education, remarked recently in response to a question about fundamental changes between apartheid and postapartheid education that:

> ... we haven't made much progress in realizing the potential of poor children in terms of giving them quality schooling. ...The legacy of apartheid-era education is seen in the poor education of black teachers who, generally, teach black children. The (Joint Education) trust's research shows that the average mark a sample of grade three teachers in 24 rural schools in SA achieved on a grade six test in their subject was 55%. Teachers are shaky in terms of the subject they are teaching, and this is exacerbated by the language problem. They are not teaching in their own tongue. He praises Education Minister Naledi Pandor for her promotion of mother tongue education, at least in the earlier years of school... (Blaine, 2005: 17)

In the Western Cape province of South Africa, the government is firmly committed to the implementation of mother tongue based bilingual education for a minimum of seven years of primary schooling and is investigating the financial and training implications of extending the system into the secondary school.

The Extra-mural Environment

Unless African languages are given market value, i.e. unless their instrumentality for the processes of production, exchange and distribution is enhanced, no amount of policy change at school level can guarantee their use in high-status functions and, thus, eventual escape from the dominance and the hegemony of English (or French or Portuguese where these are the relevant postcolonial European languages). In the South African context, we have understood for many years that the language-medium policy caused cognitive impoverishment and, consequently, necessitated investment in compensatory on-the-job training by the private sector in order to enhance the 'trainability' of the just-from-school recruits. This wastefulness would be completely avoidable if there were a national development plan in which reform of education and economic development planning were integrated. This would mean that fundamental changes in the language-medium policy would be directly related to the increased use of the African mother tongues, where relevant, in the public service and in the 'formal' economy. An articulated program of job creation and employment on the basis of language proficiencies would, in the South African context, also serve as an organic affirmative action program, one that would not have the unintended consequence of perpetuating and entrenching divisive racial identities inherited from the apartheid past.

Moves in this direction are now increasingly evident, even though they are still offset by negative attitudes in respect of African languages.[18] My former student, Michellé October, who has become a colleague, is researching this area. Preliminarily, she has discerned a definite move on the part of major economic players, such as the banking sector, parastatal communications firms and the public service administration, towards increased use of African languages at the workplace, in their administration and especially at the interface with customers. One of the country's biggest banks, for example, has made available on their autobank screens instructions in isiZulu and Sesotho, not only in English and Afrikaans, as was the case in the past. According to their latest data, just under 30% of their customers use the two indigenous African languages. They intend to make this facility available in all of the 11 official languages of the country. The parastatal South African Broadcasting Corporation found that during the financial year 2003–2004, they had a jump in revenue because of the increased provision of local content programs in African languages (M. October, personal communication). It is clear that if this trend continues in all the different economic sectors and large institutions, including especially the educational system, the market potential of the languages will be enhanced in ways that cannot now be anticipated.

By way of conclusion, I should like to refer to the continental activities of the African Academy of Languages (ACALAN), which is now recognized as a specialized cultural agency of the African Union with responsibility for language policy and planning. This organization reflects a profound change that is taking place in the postcolonial landscape. Largely because of the abysmal failure of education, some countries are considering the introduction of mother tongue based bilingual education as the probably most effective alternative to the transitional and subtractive bilingualism models that have been the norm in Africa since the 1960s. ACALAN has taken on itself the task of planning and coordinating the implementation of a continent-wide program of language development and status planning with a view to making a fundamental contribution to the solution of the conditions that produce, and reproduce, poverty on the continent.[19] The year 2006–2007 was proclaimed the Year of African Languages by the Heads of State of the African Union, meeting in Khartoum (Sudan) on 23–25 January 2006, although the actual activities of the Year turned out to be fairly low-key events, except in South Africa, Mali, Ethiopia and Cameroon, it nonetheless raised the profile of the language issue on the continent. This will undoubtedly contribute towards reshaping of hegemony and is already having major knock-on effects not only in South Africa, but elsewhere on the continent.

Notes

1. The dominance of English was the result of colonial conquest and the subsequent language of administration policies of the British rulers.
2. In modern social science jargon, this is a suggestion for more careful studies of the intersection of structure and agency in concrete historical situations.
3. See Sibayan (1999: 448–450).
4. See, among many others, Bamgbose (2000), Heine (1982), Herbert (1992), Prah (1995) and Scotton (1990).
5. For an overview of the most recent and useful analyses of the postcolonial state in Africa, see Chapter 1 of Leonard and Straus (2003). Also see Chapters 3 and 4 of Okumu (2002).
6. This concept is described by its author as 'a tactic of boundary maintenance. It involves institutionalizing the linguistic patterns of the elite, either through official policy or informally established usage norms in order to limit access to socioeconomic mobility and political power to people who possess the requisite linguistic patterns' (Scotton, 1990: 27). She also makes it clear that in sub-Saharan Africa, we are invariably dealing with cases of 'strong elite closure', where the social gap between the elites and the masses is deepened by the dominant position of foreign, i.e. European, languages in which more than half of the population do not have adequate proficiency (Scotton, 1990: 27–28).
7. Clayton's study refers to the relationship between Vietnam and Cambodia, but the principles on which his analysis is based hold true for any other comparable situation. As a critique of Phillipson's theses on 'linguistic imperialism' as well as of development aid in respect of education, Clayton's work is useful and raises important issues, but it is not immediately relevant in the present context.
8. de Swaan (2001) has an excellent chapter on 'language, culture and the unequal exchange of texts' as well as a useful chapter on the persistence of the 'colonial' languages in Africa. His chapter on the South African case is, however, less insightful.
9. See Stroud and Hyltenstam (2005) for an introduction to the field.
10. Bamgbose, A. (2000) *Language and Exclusion. The Consequences of Language Policies in Africa*. Münster/Hamburg/London: LIT.

11. This language-based analysis is symmetrical in its consequences with Mamdani's portrayal of the colonially generated categories of 'citizens' and 'subjects' (see Mamdani, 1996).
12. This means simply that most African people are willing to maintain their primary languages in the primary contexts of family, community, primary school and religious practice, but they do not believe that these languages have the capacity to develop into languages of power. In terms of Bourdieu's paradigm, their consciousness reflects the reality of the linguistic market and they have become victims of a monolingual habitus, in spite of the fact that most African people are proficient in two or more languages.
13. In the Nigerian context, this includes the use of a 'language of the immediate community' if for any reason the L1 of the child cannot be used.
14. In spite of this, however, South Africa still has to record an average drop-out rate of 40% of university students tracked over a four-year period and a 20% drop-out of all first-year university students (see National Assembly (2005) Question 619).
15. In South Africa, the school-leaving (matriculation) examination is taken at Grade 12.
16. However dubious such number-crunching might be, the authors have grappled, with a large measure of success, with the issue of relative weighting of causal factors, which October (2002: 77) had been forced to leave in abeyance. Their statistical methods for weighting the effects of different relevant variables are explained in Chapter 3 of the study.
17. Other important variables such as a good meal once a day and a favorable home literacy environment are essential, of course, but for the first time in postapartheid South Africa, the language medium has been demonstrated to be a central cause of academic success or failure.
18. This is largely a function of the fact that proficiency in African languages continues to be inadequately remunerated except at the highest levels of translation and interpreting.
19. For a full discussion of the ACALAN program of action, see Alexander (2005).

References

ADEA, GTZ, UIE and Commonwealth Secretariat (2005) *Optimizing Learning and Education in Africa – The Language Factor*. A Stock-taking Research on Mother Tongue and Bilingual Education in Sub-Saharan Africa. Working Document. Draft 22/07/2005. Association for the Development of Education in Africa; Deutsche Gesellschaft für Technische Zusammenarbeit; UNESCO Institute for Education and Commonwealth Secretariat.

Alexander, N. (2002) Linguistic rights, language planning and democracy in postapartheid South Africa. In S. Baker (ed.) *Language Policy: Lessons from Global Models* (pp. 116–129). Monterey, CA: Monterey Institute of International Studies.

Alexander, N. (ed.) (2005) *The African Academy of Languages and the Intellectualisation of African Languages*. Cape Town: Praesa.

Alexandre, P. (1972) *An Introduction to Languages and Language in Africa*. London: Heinemann.

Bamgbose, A. (2000) *Language and Exclusion*. Hamburg: LIT-Verlag.

Blaine, S. (2005) Losing the legacy of apartheid education. *Business Day* (20 Years Anniversary Edition Supplement), August 23, p. 17[MSOffice1].

Bourdieu, P. (1991) *Language and Symbolic Power*. Edited and introduced by J.B. Thompson (G. Raymond and M. Adamson, trans.). Cambridge: Polity Press.

Castells, M. (1997) *The Power of Identity: The Information Age – Economy, Society and Culture* (Vol. II). Oxford: Blackwell Publishers.

Clayton, T. (2000) *Education and the Politics of Language. Hegemony and Pragmatism in Cambodia, 1979–1989*. Hong Kong: Comparative Education Research Centre.

Cooper, R. (1996) *Language Planning and Social Change*. Cambridge: Cambridge University Press.

De Swaan, A. (2001) *Words of the World. The Global Language System*. Cambridge: Polity Press.

Djité, P. (2005) Multilingualism and the economy. Unpub. mimeo.

Edwards, V. (2005) *Multilingualism in the English-speaking World*. Oxford: Blackwell.

Heine, B. (1990) Language policy in Africa. In B. Weinstein (ed.) *Language Policy and Political Development* (pp. 167–184). Norwood, NJ: Ablex.

Leonard, D. and Straus, S. (2003) *Africa's Stalled Development: International Causes and Cures*. Boulder, CO and London: Lynne Rienner.

Mufwene, S. (2002) Colonisation, globalisation and the future of languages in the twenty-first century. *International Journal on Multicultural Societies* 4 (2), 162–193.

Myers-Scotton, C. (1990) Elite closure as boundary maintenance: The case of Africa. In B. Weinstein (ed.) *Language Policy and Political Development* (pp. 25–42). Norwood, NJ: Ablex.

Obanya, P. (2002) *Revitalizing Education in Africa*. Lagos: Stirling-Horden.

October, M. (2002) *Medium of Instruction and its Effect on Matriculation Examination Results for 2000 in Western Cape Secondary Schools*. Praesa Occasional Papers No. 11. Cape Town: Praesa.

Okumu, W. (2002) *The African Renaissance: History, Significance and Strategy*. Trenton, NJ and Asmara: Africa World Press.

Republic of South Africa (2005) *National Assembly, Internal Question Paper No 13-2005. Question 619*. On WWW at http://www.gov.education.za.

Sibayan, B. (1999) *The Intellectualization of Filipino*. Manila: The Linguistic Society of the Philippines.

Simkins, C. and Patterson, A. (2005) *Learner Performance in South Africa: Social and Economic Determinants of Success in Language and Mathematics*. Cape Town: HSRC Press.

Weinstein, B. (ed.) (1990) *Language Policy and Political Development*. Norwood, NJ: Ablex.

Chapter 5

Econolinguistics in the USA

JOHN BAUGH

Introduction

I first encountered the phrase 'Language and Poverty' in a volume by that title edited by Frederick Williams (1970), and it changed my life. It was there that I first read Labov's (1969) classic article, 'The Logic of Nonstandard English'. His diligent analyses were consistent with my own life experiences in inner-city African American communities in New York, Philadelphia and Los Angeles. The vast majority of brilliant people known to me as a child were fellow African Americans. Racial segregation was such during my childhood in the 1950s and 1960s that I did not know many White people other than schoolteachers, and they derided my use of English along with that of most of my African American peers. I suffered the early indignity of being tracked into low reading groups as I tried very hard to hear differences in the pronunciation of *pin* versus *pen*, or *tin* versus *ten*, a distinction not shared by many European Americans, even in parts of the South. The dialect demanded of me at school did not match the one we used in my home community.

My ear was attuned to the linguistic differences that mattered to people in my neighborhood. Growing up in a middle-class African American community, I fared far better than my peers whose parents did not graduate from college. My mother was only 17 and my father only 20 when I was born. Dad took advantage of the GI Bill and attended Pratt Institute in Brooklyn (the city of my birth), and completed his education at Drexel University in Philadelphia, where both he and my mother had been born and raised. Because my linguistic awareness and competence were nurtured in African American contexts, I was mindful of linguistic differences between my home, my peers, my teachers at school and the polite rhetoric of elders at church. Television was in its infancy in my youth, but because my father worked at RCA, where the first color televisions were produced, our family had the distinction in our community of being among the first to own a color television. This point is significant in my case because it exposed me to linguistic norms that were not used in our neighborhood.

At the time, I did not associate the language in our community with that of 'the poor', simply because I was very much aware of the relatively favorable circumstances in which I lived compared to children two blocks away living in public housing. Because both my parents worked, I attended a public school where childcare was available on campus. My first exposure to Whites occurred in public school, where about 15% of the students were White but not from affluent backgrounds. They did not speak like people on television, and neither did some of the White teachers, whose speech was frequently laced with vernacular expressions from their own cultural heritage, be it Irish, Italian or Yiddish.

Although our teachers, all of whom were White, did not sound exactly like Whites on television, they made it clear to Black students that our vernacular speech was inferior and must be avoided if professional 'success' was our ultimate objective. These messages were conveyed in both subtle and overt ways through praise, admonition and linguistic sanctions in the classroom. The first and only time I encountered an African American teacher in my K-12 public education was in the fifth grade, when we moved to Los Angeles. This teacher was clearly an advocate for me, and she encouraged me to represent my classroom on the student council. She encouraged me in ways that I had not known previously, but I did not attribute her encouragement to our common racial heritage. My parents had always preached colorblind social equality, knowing quite well that racial prejudice still existed. However, their example of selfless hard work, combined with their attempts to shield me from racism, at least within the confines of our home, led me to believe that my fifth-grade teacher simply had the wisdom to recognize my underutilized talents and abilities. I simply saw her as a 'better' teacher, because race was not yet a strong social construct to me. I had been taught that teachers, doctors, the clergy and the police were professional authorities who had my best interest at heart. I was not cynical, nor did I draw explicit racial inferences from day-to-day social encounters.

Whereas my life as a young child in the 'Germantown' neighborhood of Philadelphia was primarily restricted to African Americans, with rare exceptions at school or during service encounters with my parents, Los Angeles exposed me to a wide array of low-income English language learners among first- and second-generation immigrant families from China, Japan and Mexico. Some elderly Whites still resided in our multiracial Los Angeles community, but they were few, and African

Americans were but one among many racial minorities I encountered on a daily basis. My early communicative competence exposed me to the social stratification of English among urban and rural Blacks, because my grandparents were entrepreneurs who operated successful businesses primarily serving a Black clientele. I would visit their stores from time to time, and I observed vast differences in communication styles among Black people, consistent with the diversity described by Gates (1994).

Unlike my linguistic experiences in Philadelphia, where Black styles of English were strongly criticized in school, in Los Angeles I discovered that I had considerable linguistic advantages in comparison to my classmates for whom English was not native (ENN). They were struggling to learn a new language at the same time that I was trying to learn all of the Standard English substitutions for the word *ain't*. Although I found my own linguistic barriers between Standard English and African American vernacular English (AAVE) to be considerable, it was clear that my linguistic circumstances differed greatly from fellow students who had previously learned to read and write Chinese or Japanese. The linguistic tables turned dramatically when my parents purchased a home in the Western San Fernando Valley, where we were only the second African American family to move onto our block. As a Boy Scout earning my 'Firemanship' merit badge, I was required to interview local firemen about any previous fires in my neighborhood. There had only been one fire reported on my street; the other African American family that had moved onto the block before we arrived had been greeted by burning crosses on their lawn. My parents were unaware of this when they purchased the home, and I was taunted with racial slurs from a handful of upper-middle-class Whites who routinely told me that I was the first Black person they had ever met. Some of these racial slurs were intentionally hurtful, while other painful barbs were the result of ignorance and the prevalence of racial bigotry at the time. These personal reflections are intended to shed light on my linguistic research, providing impressions of how I first encountered language and poverty in the USA.

A Brief Account of the Emergence of English as the Dominant Language in the USA

Most Americans take for granted that English is the national language. However, the evolution of English language usage and diversity in America is long and complicated. For the purpose of these remarks, looking at the relationship between language and poverty, let it suffice to say that residents of this country who lacked English proficiency, regardless of racial background, have tended to be poorer than typical native speakers of Standard American English. These remarks are intentionally simplistic, focusing on linguistic details at the exclusion of other historical evidence regarding those who were enslaved or the vast numbers of indigenous Native Americans who were displaced from their native land in order to make room for White settlers in pursuit of 'Manifest Destiny'. There can be little question that the ultimate rise of English as the most influential language in the USA ascended at the expense of numerous 'home-grown' native languages that are now extinct, or soon to be extinct. Obviously, European languages did not take root in either North or South America until colonists established their early settlements, and distant monarchs eager to expand their growing empires laid claim to the wealth of natural resources and products that could be extracted here through slavery.

It was under these special historical circumstances that the English, Spanish, Dutch, Portuguese and French languages traveled across the Atlantic, resulting in various linguistic combinations. The ensuing decline of indigenous languages in America coincided with the rise of Pidginization and Creolization among enslaved Africans, as diverse bilingual communities spawned and fluctuated between heritage languages from afar and the emerging dominant colonial languages.

Although many of the early settlers to Plymouth, Philadelphia and Jamestown were seeking religious freedom, they departed England speaking different varieties of British English. Indeed, many of the highly distinctive regional dialects spoken by long-standing, upper-class residents of the Eastern USA are the historical remnants of their colonial ancestors who first settled these regions. Unlike the social stratification that was well entrenched in Europe, voluntary immigrants to the English colonies were, in many instances, capable of amassing huge fortunes, often with the knowledge, support and blessing of the Crown. King George had it within his authority to grant favors, including vast tracts of land, providing the foundation of many family fortunes, and slave labor only enhanced the wealth of those who exploited the involuntary labor of Black captives from Africa.

The colonial linguistic stew that gave rise to the current social stratification of English in the USA was the creation of political circumstances that have very little to do with language per se. However, because language usage among the wealthy, who had access to literacy and education, differed substantially from language usage among the poor, a broad array of linguistic stereotypes began to emerge that perpetuated the myth that those with greater economic means (i.e. those considered to be 'well spoken') also tend to be more intelligent and academically gifted than their less fortunate, 'poorly spoken' counterparts. Political might has always determined linguistic dominance throughout history, but folk conceptions of wealth and intelligence tend to conceal the sociopoliticial circumstances that establish dominant-to-subordinate linguistic norms (Zentella, 1997).

Some Observations Regarding the Social Stratification of English Fluency in the USA

Labov's (1966) study of the social stratification of English in New York City provides a useful lens through which to view the social stratification of English more broadly throughout the USA. Regional standards tend to embody local provincial linguistic norms regarding 'standard' usage, compared to nonstandard varieties that thrive in close geographic proximity. In some instances, these dialect differences will be lexical (e.g. *soda* versus *pop*, *bag* versus *sack*), while many other distinctive dialect differences will be based on pronunciation (e.g. *bof* rather than *both*, or *dat* in contrast to *that*).

Although linguists attend to the minutia of these differences, including important differences in phrasing (e.g. Standard English 'What did you say?' versus AAVE 'Say what?'), perceptions of the relative 'standard' or 'nonstandard' status of a dialect are the result of impressions derived from a collectivity of dialect attributes. Thus, the perception that one sounds haughty, aloof, inattentive or assertive will depend fundamentally on the interpretation of those listening.

Madison Avenue and Hollywood have joined forces to perpetuate national linguistic stereotypes. Advertisers routinely employ British accents to imply high quality projects or German-accented English when selling automobiles and other products that call for precise engineering. 'Good Old Boys' with down-home country accents are used to sell pick-up trucks, while Martha Stewart takes great care to project the linguistic image of a well-educated American hostess. Maurice Chevalier, Carmen Miranda and Ricardo Montalban have all shown that some varieties of accented English are highly marketable in America, while other nonstandard varieties have not fared quite so well. Lippi-Green (1997) observed that many Disney films tend to reinforce negative stereotypes associated with African American English (as depicted by the black crows in *Dumbo*) or Arabic-sounding English (as spoken by the villain Jafar in *Aladdin*). Numerous other examples could be cited to illustrate how films and mass media reinforce and perpetuate linguistic stereotypes and linguistic standards throughout the nation.

It is also rare to find minority news broadcasters who preserve any trace of Nonstandard English, with the noteworthy exception of former athletes who obtain jobs broadcasting sports. However, minorities who do not have fluent command of Standard English do not obtain primary broadcast responsibilities.

Most professional contexts in the USA vividly display the social stratification of local linguistic diversity, based on the proportion of white-collar to blue-collar employees onsite. Thus, the social stratification of linguistic diversity on a large urban construction site will differ substantially from that found in a bank or among a hospital staff. Individuals who are well-educated and are perceived to be well-spoken users of American (or British) English are likely to fare well professionally in the USA, while those who cannot easily employ standard linguistic norms in academic or professional contexts are not. However, Standard English fluency is a poor gauge of human potential. Many talented individuals seeking employment are often overlooked because their true abilities are not perceived by decision makers who are intolerant of colleagues, customers, clients or students who lack fluency in Standard American English.

Some Educational Consequences Resulting from the Social Stratification of English Fluency in the USA

Those who have been educated outside the USA rarely understand the decentralized nature of our public education system, which is under the jurisdiction of state and local regulations. While federal funding and support are vital to many educational programs throughout the nation, the USA does not have a central ministry of education governing instruction. The linguistic relevance of this observation is that school districts and states vary greatly in the ways in which they identify, classify and educate students from different linguistic backgrounds.

Inspired by the ways in which professionals are educated in medicine and law, Shulman (1994) developed case study procedures regarding teacher preparation and teaching that, in the opinion of this author, exposed evidence of educational malpractice, especially regarding the classification of language minority students, or the development of effective language arts pedagogy for students who are either ENN or native speakers of AAVE (Baugh, 1999). The Ebonics controversy that erupted in Oakland over 10 years ago has never been fully resolved, and ballot propositions to abolish or retract bilingual education in California, Arizona and other states are indicative of the tumultuous state of language arts education for low-income students who lack fluency in Standard American English.

All too often, critics of Nonstandard English are unaware of the historical, linguistic or sociopolitical circumstances that have placed ENN and AAVE students at an educational disadvantage in comparison to their peers who have mastered Standard American English. Moreover, these linguistic circumstances tend to exceed considerations of race and expose fundamental flaws in the concept of race as a social science construct (Baugh, 2003, 2005, 2006, 2007; Baugh & Alim, 2007).

Some General Observations Regarding Language and Poverty

Although most of the examples that I have cited thus far are drawn from the context of the USA, parallels regarding the social stratification of linguistic diversity abound throughout the world. In general terms, a nation will embody one or more official language, and those languages will in turn reflect a distribution of dominant-to-subordinate languages and/or dialects. Centers of political or commercial power are likely to attract influential speakers of the dominant dialect(s) of the dominant language(s), whereas those who reside beyond the parameters of the dominant languages and/or dialects may be more or less stigmatized, depending on local historical and sociopolitical circumstances.

Wealth is relative; it depends upon, among other things, where you are in the world, along with the combination of linguistic and cultural experiences you bring to any communicative event. Many years ago, Brown and Gilman (1960) observed that speakers of French modified their use of *tu* or *vous* depending on their corresponding power relationship or solidarity with their interlocutor. Hymes (1974) observed that this kind of 'communicative competence' reflects the integration of linguistic competence with an awareness of communicative norms within a given culture.

Native speakers of the dominant dialects or languages in most advanced industrialized societies tend to represent the linguistic elite in their respective speech communities. Native speakers of non-dominant dialects or languages tend to be associated with less affluent segments of society. In addition to native members of any given speech community are those who do not share their competence and fluency. Second language learners vary greatly in their competence and fluency, and this fluency, or lack thereof, may or may not correspond with wealth. That is to say, once wealth or poverty and language are compared beyond the dominant languages in any given speech community, one cannot merely assume that those who lack fluency in the dominant language also lack wealth. Tourists, for example, may in fact be quite wealthy, with sufficient resources to hire others to take care of linguistic transactions that exceed their personal abilities. As a result of these variable personal circumstances, in the following sections I propose a model of linguistic relativity that can be applied to individuals in diverse caste-like communities (Ogbu, 1978).

Linguistic Capital and Linguistic Relativity in Global Perspective

My thoughts regarding linguistic capital have been shaped greatly by Bourdieu (1983). His observations regarding the demographic distribution of 'social capital' and 'cultural capital' are more comprehensive to the human communicative enterprise than the more narrow interpretation of linguistic capital of which I now speak. Awareness of linguistic norms and conventions may or may not coincide with comparable knowledge of cultural and social norms in a given speech community (Hymes, 1974).

The 'linguistic relativity' previously mentioned coincides with personal variability in 'linguistic capital'. Speakers of dominant dialects or languages are likely to have the highest linguistic capital in their native speech communities. The amount of linguistic capital one can have in a non-native speech community will depend on the combination of linguistic and communicative competence one possesses, along with the relative receptivity of natives within the speech community to outsiders. Moreover, not all outsiders are viewed equally; some are seen as desirable while others are not. Controversies in various countries regarding the value of immigrants also correspond closely with linguistic stereotypes associated with these groups.

The Sociolinguistic Inertia of Language and Poverty: Some Policy Implications

Most industrialized societies in the world tend to reflect three major linguistic groupings:

(1)   Native 'standard' speakers of the dominant language(s).
(2)   Native 'nonstandard' speakers of the dominant language(s).
(3)   Those for whom the dominant language(s) is/are not native.

In the USA, 'Standard American English' is the dominant language, although that term allows for considerable regional variability. Educated Parisian French represents the dominant language in France and Mandarin as spoken by well-educated speakers represents the dominant linguistic standard in China. Other examples are readily available, and in each instance the proportion of speakers that are distributed within these three groups varies. For example, Standard American English is the dominant linguistic norm in the USA, and it is spoken natively by millions of Americans, whereas Standard South African English is the dominant linguistic norm in South Africa, although few South Africans are native speakers of English.

As previously mentioned, dominant linguistic norms are determined by political circumstances, and those who hold political power typically reinforce their might through policies that bolster their native language. As political circumstances change, so too might linguistic priorities. For example, under the political domination of the former Soviet Union, citizens in Poland, Hungary, Romania and East Germany (among others) were strongly encouraged, if not coerced, to learn Russian. Changing political circumstances introduced modified linguistic priorities and attempts to elevate the status of established European languages that languished under Soviet rule.

Canada and Switzerland have more than one official national language. Their example suggests that other nations could function quite effectively with more than one official language, but linguistic policies throughout the world tend to protect and perpetuate the dominant linguistic norms rather than provide mechanisms whereby immigrant languages can become coequal with long-standing linguistic norms.

Numerous policy implications abound as a result of the trifurcation of most speech communities into dominant, nondominant and non-native groupings. But policy considerations do not conform to a 'one size fits all' model. South Africa, after the fall of apartheid, adopted a national policy sanctioning 11 official languages, taking care to include English and Afrikaans, despite a history of racial oppression where Whites were once the only native speakers of those languages. Some politicians within the USA have attempted to dismantle bilingual education, based on assumptions that doing so would force immigrant students to learn English more rapidly while preserving English as the primary national language. In France, the Académie Française carefully guards against foreign linguistic borrowings (such as 'le weekend') through formal introduction of officially approved French alternatives, frequently without success. This diversity of linguistic circumstances throughout the world might otherwise complicate policy considerations, but my approach to this matter reflects a personal bias, because it is my hope that linguists and linguistic science may be employed to help advance social justice and equality. It is my fervent hope that enlightened policy-makers throughout the world will do two things: (1) provide educational opportunities to learn the dominant linguistic norms and (2) be more accepting of those who are not yet fluent speakers of the dominant language(s). In many instances, linguistic barriers are used to maintain the status quo, thereby thwarting prospects to advance equal opportunities in education, employment and justice. These linguistic tasks may prove to be arduous and daunting, but they may help us break down the barriers typically associated with language and poverty throughout the world.

References

Baugh, J. (2003) Linguistic profiling. In S. Makoni, G. Smitherman, A.F. Ball and A.K. Spears (eds) *Black Linguistics: Language, Society, and Politics in Africa and the Americas* (pp. 155–168). London: Routledge.

Baugh, J. (2005) Conveniently Black: Self-delusion and the racial exploitation of African America. *Du Bois Review* 2 (1), 1–14.

Baugh, J. (2006) It ain't about race: Some lingering (linguistic) consequences of the African slave trade and their relevance to your personal historical hardship index. *Du Bois Review* 3 (1), 145–159.

Baugh, J. (2007) Plantation English in America: Nonstandard varieties and the quest for educational equity. *Research in the Teaching of English* 41 (4).

Baugh, J. and Alim, H.S. (eds) (2007) *Talking Black Talk: Language, Education, and Social Change.* New York: Teachers College Press.

Bourdieu, P. (1983) Ökonomisches Kapital, kulturelles Kapital, soziales Kapital. In R. Kreckel (ed.) *Soziale Ungleichheiten (Soziale Welt, Sonderheft 2)* (pp. 183–198). Goettingen, Germany: Otto Schartz.

Brown, R. and Gilman, A. (1960) The pronouns of power and solidarity. In T. Sebeok (ed.) *Style in Language* (pp. 235–276). Cambridge, MA: MIT Press.

Gates, H.L. (1994) *Colored People.* New York: Knopf.

Hymes, D. (1974) *Foundations in Sociolinguistics: An Ethnographic Approach.* Philadelphia, PA: University of Pennsylvania Press.

Labov, W. (1966) *The Social Stratification of English in New York City.* Washington, DC: Center for Applied Linguistics.

Labov, W. (1969) The logic of nonstandard English. In F. Williams (ed.) *Language and Poverty: Perspectives on a Theme* (pp. 153–190). Chicago, IL: Markham.

Lippi-Green, R. (1997) *English with an Accent: Language, Ideology, and Discrimination in the United States.* New York: Routledge.

Ogbu, J. (1978) *Minority Education and Caste.* New York: Academic Press.

Shulman, J. (ed.) (1994) *Diversity in the Classroom.* Hillsdale, NJ: Lawrence Erlbaum.

Williams, F. (ed.) (1970) *Language and Poverty: Perspectives on a Theme.* Chicago, IL: Markham.

Zentella, A.C. (1997) *Growing up Bilingual: Puerto Rican Children in New York.* Malden, MA: Blackwell.

Chapter 6

Where in the World is US Spanish? Creating a Space of Opportunity for US Latinos

OFELIA GARCÍA and LEAH MASON

Introduction

In the USA, Spanish is often characterized as the language of the conquered, the colonized and the immigrants; that is, as a *language of poverty*. But in the context of economic globalization in the 21st century, Spanish in the USA is slowly being *negotiated* as a language with economic value.[1]

This chapter starts out by examining the US Spanish language ideology[2] that minoritizes Spanish and that constructs it as a language of poverty. It then goes on to examine the perspective gained from constructing US Spanish through a global angle. This global Spanish language ideology positions Spanish not as a *characteristic* of the poor, but as a *negotiable resource* for US bilinguals. The struggle between a language ideology that characterizes US Spanish as a language of poverty and one which constructs it as a negotiable resource is further examined as it plays out in US Spanish language education policies and practices.

The chapter concludes by arguing that as a result of language education policies and practices that characterize US Spanish as a language of poverty, US Latinos[3] are being excluded from the possibility of negotiating Spanish as a resource for themselves. Thus, US Latinos are in a double bind. Robbed of educational spaces in which their bilingualism could be nurtured, many shift to English at a rapid pace. As English speakers, they then continue to lag behind Anglo-English speakers in educational outcomes and economic rewards. But as English speakers, they are also left out of the growing Spanish/English bilingual market for which literacy in Spanish, as well as English, is a requirement.

US Spanish as a Characteristic of Poverty

Three cases as contextualization

That Spanish is minoritized[4] in the USA is evident in the ideology expressed by statements of three people – a US professor in an academic journal, a comic in a US mainstream publication and a US judge in his courtroom. In a 2004 article entitled 'The Hispanic Challenge', Samuel P. Huntington, a professor at the Department of Government at Harvard University, said:

> The persistent inflow of Hispanic immigrants threatens to divide the United States into two people, two cultures, and two languages. Unlike past immigrant groups, Mexicans and other Latinos have not assimilated into mainstream US culture, forming instead their own political and linguistic enclaves – from Los Angeles to Miami – and rejecting the Anglo-Protestant values that built the American dream. ...There is no *Americano* dream. There is only the American dream created by an Anglo-Protestant society. Mexican Americans will share in that dream and in that society only if they dream in English. (Huntington, 2004: 1)

That speaking Spanish is to remain in the shackles of poverty – economic, social, moral and intellectual – is echoed by the words of satirical advice columnist Dame Edna. In a 2003 *Vanity Fair* column, and in response to a reader's question regarding whether or not she should begin to learn Spanish, Dame Edna said:

> Forget Spanish. There's nothing in that language worth reading except Don Quixote... There was a poet named Garcia Lorca, but I'd leave him on the intellectual back burner if I were you. As for everyone's speaking it, what twaddle! Who speaks it that you are really desperate to talk to? The help? Your leaf blower? (Dame Edna, 2003: 116)

Dame Edna's response portrays Spanish as academically unimportant, its contributions to literature insignificant and Spanish speakers as servants and gardeners for upper- and middle-class English-speaking families. Perspectives conveyed in mainstream media, whether written as the remarks of a serious advice columnist or a satirical advice columnist, draw attention to real issues in society and the internalization of these stereotypes. The linking of Spanish speakers as employees of the service industry also drew national interest in the 1995 custody suit of Martha Laureano and her five-year-old daughter. In Amarillo,

Texas, District Court Judge Samuel C. Kiser ruled that Martha Laureano's decision to speak Spanish to her daughter was child abuse and ordered her to speak only English to her daughter. Reprimanding her conduct, the judge further commented that if she did not speak to her daughter in English then her daughter would be condemned to life as a maid (Baron, 2001). These three examples represent and link ideas about Spanish, with poor people of low social status who are unworthy of respect. In the following sections, we discuss the ways in which Spanish has been minoritized in the USA, linking it to the following characteristics:

- the language of the conquered and the colonized;
- the language of immigrants;
- the language of many;
- the language of the uneducated and poor;
- a racialized language.

Spanish as the language of the conquered and the colonized

According to Heinz Kloss (1977), Spanish in the USA could be said to have special rights because it was spoken by what he calls *'solitary original settlers'*, that is, Spaniards arrived in what today is Florida and the US Southwest before the Anglo-Saxons. It is important to point out that the position of Spanish then was the opposite of what it is today in the USA. Spanish was, and continues to be today in many Latin American countries, the language of the conqueror and the powerful, devastating the linguistic and cultural resources of many Indigenous groups. Speaking of the US context, Kloss (1977) claims that the languages of solitary original settlers are entitled to be held in higher esteem than those of groups who might have arrived later. And yet, although none of the languages other than English in the USA have fared well in the face of English hegemony, it is Spanish that has suffered the most minoritization. This has to do with its status as the language of *the conquered* in what was then Mexico and is today the US Southwest, and as the language of *the colonized* in Puerto Rico.

The Treaty of Guadalupe Hidalgo (1848) which ended the Mexican American War ceded nearly half of the Mexican territory to the USA (what today is California, Arizona, Texas, New Mexico, Nevada, Utah and parts of Colorado and Wyoming). Article IX of the Treaty guaranteed that Mexicans would enjoy 'all the rights of citizens of the United States... and in the meantime shall be maintained and protected in the free enjoyment of their liberty and property and secured in the free exercise of their religion without restriction' (quoted in Crawford, 1992: 51). Initially, Spanish was used in legislation, education and the press, but slowly its importance was eroded and its use limited, as Spanish was minoritized.

When California became a state in 1850, it was decreed that 'all laws, decrees, regulations and provisions emanating from any of the three supreme powers of this State, which from their nature require publication, shall be published in English and Spanish' (del Valle, 2003: 13). But in 1855, English was declared the only language of instruction, the publication of state laws in Spanish was suspended, and court proceedings were required to be in English (Castellanos, 1983: 18).

In 1850, the territory of New Mexico (including present day Arizona and New Mexico) was added to the Union. When 13 years later Arizona and New Mexico were separated as territories, the population of New Mexico was around 50% Spanish speaking. New Mexico wasn't admitted to statehood until 1912 when more Anglos had moved in and the majority was English speaking. The pressure to linguistically assimilate was carried out, in part, by repressing schooling in Spanish and replacing it with schools in English only. For example, in 1874, 70% of the schools were in Spanish, 33% were bilingual and only 5% were in English only. Fifteen years later, in 1889, 42% of the schools were in English only, whereas only 30% of the schools were conducted in Spanish and 28% remained bilingual (del Valle, 1983). By 1891, a New Mexico statute required all schools to teach in English.

A report of the Pew Hispanic Center counts 26,784,268 Latinos of Mexican descent in the USA in 2005. Of these, 16 million have been born in the USA. Latinos of Mexican descent make up 64% of all US Latinos, linking Spanish to its characteristic as *the language of the conquered*.

The end of the Spanish American War in 1898 granted the US Congress complete authority to decide the political status and civil rights of the inhabitants of Puerto Rico (García *et al.*, 2001). From 1898 to 1948, without the consent of the Puerto Rican people, English became the official language of public schools in Puerto Rico (García *et al.*, 2001; Language Policy Task Force, 1992). Although the Jones Act of 1917 made Puerto Ricans citizens of the USA, it did not confer them full civil and political rights. Commonwealth, the term used to describe the status of Puerto Rico since the 1950s, did not change the political, economic and social relationship between the island and the USA (Trías Monge, 1997). During the post-Second World War decade (1945–1955), approximately 50,000 Puerto Ricans migrated to the USA. Today there are 3,794,776 Puerto Ricans in the USA (Pew Hispanic Center, 2006), constituting the second most numerous Latino group and 9% of the US Latino population. The Spanish that Puerto Ricans have brought to the USA has also been minoritized, as it became characterized as the *language of colonized people*.

Spanish as the language of immigrants

In 1965, the *Immigration and Naturalization Services Act of 1965* (also known as the *Hart Celler* or the *INS Act of 1965*) abolished the national origin quotas[5] that had been established by the *National Origins Act of 1924* (also known as the *Johnson-Reed Act*). As a result, an unprecedented number of immigrants from Latin America, as well as other non-Western nations, entered the USA. Although in 1942 the *Bracero Program* had brought short-term Mexican contract laborers for agricultural work, after 1965 a large number of immigrants from Mexico and Latin America started to join Latinos of Mexican descent.

Table 6.1 shows the number of immigrants from 1850 to 2000, according to the official US Census. Immigration from Latin America has increased sharply, especially since 1970 when it accounted for 1/5 of the immigrants. By 2000, immigrants from Latin America constituted more than one half of all immigrants in the USA. According to the US 2000 Census, there were 16,916,416 foreign-born Latin Americans in the USA, and approximately 15 million of them spoke Spanish.

In a recent tabulation of Hispanics at mid-decade, the Pew Hispanic Center (2006) reported that out of the 41,926,302 US Latinos, 25 million are native born and almost 17 million are foreign born. That is, approximately 40% of the US Latino population is foreign born. According to another study conducted by the Pew Hispanic Center (Passal, 2006), there are approximately 11.1 million unauthorized Latino migrants as of March 2006. Spanish is also thus characterized as *the language of immigrants*, sometimes undocumented.

Spanish as the language of many

In 2005, one out of every seven people in the USA was Latino. And rising birth rates will make this number even higher (Jelinke, 2005). But given the fact that the shift to English among Latinos is comparable to that of other immigrants (see next section), how many Latinos actually speak Spanish? Table 6.2 shows that according to the 2000 US Census, there are almost 25 million Latinos who speak Spanish at home, that is, 78% of the US Latino population.

The USA is the fifth largest Spanish-speaking country, after Mexico, Argentina, Colombia and Spain. There are seven states in the USA with

Table 6.1 Region of birth of the foreign-born population: 1850–2000

	1850	1870	1890	1910	1930	1960	1970	1980	1990	2000
Europe	92.2%	88.8%	86.9%	87.4%	83.0%	75.0%	61.7%	39.0%	22.9%	15.8%
Asia	0.1%	1.2%	1.2%	1.4%	1.9%	5.1%	8.9%	19.3%	26.3%	26.4%
Africa	–	–	–	–	0.1%	0.4%	0.9%	1.5%	1.9%	2.8%
Oceania	–	0.1%	0.1%	0.1%	0.1%	0.4%	0.4%	0.6%	0.5%	0.5%
Latin America	0.9%	1.0%	1.2%	2.1%	5.5%	9.4%	19.4%	33.1%	44.3%	51.7%

Table 6.2 Language spoken at home by US Latinos*

Language spoken at home	Number	% Language spoken
Speak only English	6,764,744	21.4%
Speak Spanish	24,636,215	78.0%
Speak other language	168,617	0.5%
Total	31,569,576	100.0%

*US Census (2000) SF3, PCT11

more than 1 million Latinos – California (12.5 million), Texas (7.8 million), Florida (3.4 million), New York (3.0 million), Illinois (1.8 million), Arizona (1.6 million) and New Jersey (1.3 million) (Pew Hispanic Center, 2006, Table 10). And there are seven states where approximately one fifth or more of the population is Latino – New Mexico (43.9%), California (35.5%), Texas (35.4%), Arizona (28.9%), Nevada (23.5%), Florida (19.8%) and New York (19.7%) (Pew Hispanic Center, 2006, Table 12). There are also 10 US cities with more than 1 million Latinos. In fact, after Mexico City, Los Angeles has the most Mexicans; after Habana, Miami has the most Cubans; and after San Juan, New York has the most Puerto Ricans. Spanish is characterized as the *language of too many* in the USA.

Spanish as the language of the uneducated and poor

The educational achievement of the Latino student population is poor in comparison to its White and Black counterparts. According to the 2000 US Census, only 64% of Latinos between the ages of 18 and 24 years have completed high school compared to 92% of Whites and 84% of Blacks in the same age group. While the dropout rate for 16- to 24-year-olds who are out of school and do not have a high school or GED diploma is 7% for Whites and 13% for Blacks, the percent for Latinos is greater than the combined total for their White and Black peers, at 28%.

The relationship between educational achievement and the economic status of Spanish speakers is evident in the large gap between poverty levels of Latinos and White non-Latinos. According to the 2000 US Census, Latinos comprised 12% of the US population, yet the poverty rate among Latinos was 21.8%, more than double the percentage of White non-Latinos who live in poverty. Latino men earn 63% of the earnings of White men, while Latinas earn only 54% of the amount White women earn. Whereas the median personal earnings of US Latinos in

2005 was $20,000, it was $30,000 for White non-Latinos (Pew Hispanic Center, 2006, Table 25). In 2002, the median net worth of Latino households was $7932; that is, 9% of $88,651, the median wealth of White households at the same time (Kochhar, 2004).

Racialized Spanish

US Latinos have been racialized in the USA. Urciuoli (1996: 15) explains the concept of *racialization* saying:

> When people are talked about as a race..., the emphasis is on natural attributes that hierarchize them and, if they are not White, make their place in the nation provisional at best. When groups are seen in racial terms, language differences are ideologically problematic. ...Racializing is defined by a polarity between dominant and subordinate groups, the latter having minimal control over their position in the nation-state... Racialized people are typified as human matter out of place: dirty, dangerous, unwilling, or unable to do their bit for the nation-state.

Spanish, as a language of racialized people, has also undergone the same process. Urciuoli (1995: 35) continues:

> Whenever English speakers complain about the "unfairness" of hearing Spanish spoken in public spaces or in the workplace, they racialize Spanish by treating it as matter out of place. ...Language varieties that evolve in colonized circumstances are unprotected from judgment unless and until they are approved by, for example, an elite language academy representing a nation-state.

That Spanish speakers, as well as Spanish, have been racialized in the USA, is also evident in the official governmental categories to which US Latinos are assigned. *Hispanic* became a US Census category in 1980, replacing 'Persons of Spanish Mother Tongue' (1950 and 1960) and 'Persons of Both Spanish Surname and Spanish Mother Tongue' (1970) (Rodriguez, 1989: 63). But Hispanic in itself became a racial category, excluding the possibility that Hispanics may be White or Black. It was 2000 when, for the first time, Hispanics were asked for a racial identification, including claiming to be of two races. But perhaps learning the lessons that they had been taught for years in the USA, approximately 42% of Latino respondents in the 2000 US Census indicated that they were not White, nor Black nor Asian, but of another race.

The Construction of US Spanish as a Problem

The minoritization of the Spanish of US Latinos is constructed through two processes:

- the conflation of ethnicity and language;
- the insistence in seeing Spanish and English as oppositional categories without the possibility of Spanish-English bilingualism.

Both of these respond to two of the three semiotic processes that Irvine and Gal (2000: 36) have identified as crucial in the operation of language ideologies – *iconization* and *erasure*.

The conflation of ethnicity and language

Because so little attention is paid to languages other than English in the USA, most analyses rely on ethnic characteristics. And thus, it is mostly impossible to differentiate between US Latinos who are English monolinguals, those who are bilingual and those who are Spanish monolinguals. As a result, Spanish is often blamed as the culprit when there may be other factors responsible for the social differences with other US groups.

An example of how the conflation of Spanish language and Latino ethnicity hides other factors is the way in which status dropout rates[6] are estimated. The 2000 US Census only reported that the status dropout rate for 16- to 24-year-old Latinos was 28%, significantly higher than the 7% dropout rate for Whites and 13% for Blacks. But if we break down these figures further and consider only Latinos born in the USA who are, of course, all English speakers, the status dropout rate is still higher than that for both Whites and Blacks. Among the second generation there is a 15% dropout rate, while there is a 16% dropout rate among the third generation. Clearly, something else is happening here besides the Spanish language, for those US Latinos born in the USA who speak English are still doing more poorly than Whites and even Blacks.

The same can be said of income. Although in 2005 the median income of US Latinos was $36,000 compared to $50,000 for White, English-speaking non-Latinos, native-born US Latinos, who also speak English, are not doing better than Whites. In fact, their median income was $39,000, higher than foreign-born Latinos ($34,000) but very much lower than that of White non-Latinos (Pew Hispanic Center, 2006).

The negation of Spanish-English bilingualism

Although Spanish is *a* language of Latinos, it is not *the* language of Latinos. In fact, we can say that it is Spanish-English bilingualism that is the language of Latinos.

The US Census asks those who speak Spanish how well they speak English. As Table 6.3 indicates, it turns out that 89% of US Latinos are indeed bilingual.[7]

But although we have information about the English of US Latinos, we have little information about their Spanish, for the census never asks how they speak that language. Spanish-English bilingualism has always been portrayed as a problem, rather than as a resource, and thus, bilingualism is never assessed and Spanish language education policies and practices work against the development of that bilingualism. Although Spanish-English bilingualism characterizes the language use of US Latinos, research on language and income for US Latinos mostly focuses on English-language ability or on Spanish monolingualism, without considering the impact of their bilingualism.

Since 1980, the National Commission for Employment Policy (NCEP) has sponsored economic research on the relationship between English language ability and income differentials for Latinos. All of the studies reiterate that a deficiency in English language abilities is one of the primary roadblocks for Latinos in the labor market. This was the result of a report sponsored by NCEP in 1982, which added that the lack of English fluency affects not only the labor market position of Latinos, but also their educational achievement and their social stigmatization.

Table 6.3 English proficiency of U.S. Latinos*

Speak English "very well"	11,874,405	48.2%
Speak English "well"	5,323,330	21.6%
Speak English "not well"	4,675,560	19.0%
Total Bilingual	21,873,295	88.8%
Speak English "not at all"	2,762,920	11.2%
Monolingual Spanish Speakers	2,762,920	11.2%

*US Census, (2000). SF3, PCT11

The gap in income differentials between Latinos who speak only Spanish and Latinos who speak English, which exists despite comparable levels of education and experience between the two groups, was also the subject of a study by Bloom and Grenier (1996), who found that that in comparison to English speakers, Spanish-speaking Latinos suffered a penalty of 8–15% in the case of men, and 6% in the case of women.

The limited English proficiency of Latinos is viewed as a negative outweighing the value of their asset, Spanish-English bilingualism, which Latinos bring to the labor market. The disparities in income supported when comparing Spanish monolinguals with those who speak English, as if there are two opposing categories, promote the gradual construction and association of English as a language of economic opportunity and Spanish as one of limited opportunity and poverty. But most importantly, this makes Spanish-English bilingualism nonexistent as a category of analysis, erasing it and excluding the possibility of using bilingualism as a resource.

Linguistic consequences: Shift to English

As a result of the way in which US Spanish is constructed, giving economical value and social status only to English, US Latinos shift to English. The language shift of US Latinos has been widely documented and continues at an unrelenting pace even today (Alba & Nee, 2003; Alba *et al.*, 2002; Bills, 1997; Hernández-Chávez, 1993; Portes & Rumbaut, 2001). According to the 2000 US Census, 16% of Latinos born in Latin America are monolingual speakers of English. Third generation Latinos speak English only, and the second generation shows a strong preference for English over Spanish. Bilingualism then becomes merely transitional. Bills explains this rapid language shift to English by stating:

> The finding of clear associations between using Spanish and low socioeconomic status is repeated in study after study. Furthermore, these associations are transparent to everyone in the society, and the clarity of the evidence to Hispanic youth and young adults surely pushes the process of the shift. (Bills, 1997: 280)

Economic consequences: Privileging English-only speakers

The Swiss economist, François Grin (2003) has explained that if one language is promoted to prominent status, then its native speakers will have social and economic advantages precisely because of the competence in the prestigious language.

By constructing Spanish as a language of poverty and Spanish-English bilingualism as nonexistent, White English monolinguals enjoy privilege while excluding US Latinos.

We will turn to this again later.

Deconstructing US Spanish within the Context of Bilingualism

A changing perspective from English only to one of Spanish-English bilingualism has begun to emerge. Although most studies compare Latinos who speak English with those who do not in economic measures, researchers have begun to ask – How do Latinos who speak English only fare with regards to those who are bilingual?

In a 1990 study, García found that English monolingualism had no effect whatsoever on income, especially for Cuban Americans in Miami-Dade County, where Spanish had negotiated for itself a role not only for communication, but also for economic value (García, 1995). These findings were confirmed by Boswell (2000: 422), who claimed that for both Florida and Miami-Dade County: 'Hispanics who speak English very well and speak Spanish have higher incomes, lower poverty rates, higher educational attainment, and better-paying jobs than Hispanics who only speak English. The differential in mean income is especially apparent'. In Miami-Dade County, Spanish-English bilingualism has begun to emerge as a valuable economic resource.

Linton (2003: 24) has also found that there is a 'positive relationship between upward mobility and bilingualism'. The development of this positive relationship is described through Portes and Rumbaut's (1996, 2001) model of *selective acculturation*. The selective acculturation model is an additive model that allows a person to adapt to the majority culture while still holding on to elements of their origin. Selective acculturation explains that when ethnic networks and strong communities (such as that of the Cuban American population in Miami-Dade County) support children to deal with prejudice, navigate the education system and find a place in the labor market for the ethnic language, bilingualism can bring equal, if not greater, benefits. In the case of the Cuban population in Miami, the Spanish-speaking community has embraced bilingual schooling and invested in the local market to build institutions run by bilingual citizens. This has promoted bilingualism as an asset, a tool and a resource, which is a benefit to the entire community.

Portes and Rumbaut's (1996, 2001) new model of 'segmented' assimilation suggests that participation in the subeconomy of the ethnic economic enclave requires fluency in the ethnic language and bilingualism. Affirming the value of Spanish-English bilingualism, Massey (1995: 648) has said: 'Increasingly the economic benefits and prospects for mobility will accrue to those able to speak both languages and move in both worlds'.

Spanish as a Global Resource

If the USA constructs Spanish as a language of poverty, in the last three decades Spain has promoted Spanish as a global resource. The words of Álvarez Martínez (2001) are indicative of this language ideology:

> *Cuando afirmamos, pues, que el español está de moda, lo que estamos diciendo es que ahora nuestra lengua, lengua oficial de veintiún países, es el centro de atención de gran parte del mundo.*
> [When we say that Spanish is fashionable, what we're saying is that now our language, official language of twenty-one countries is the center of attention of a great part of the world.]

One of the most evident indications of this new Spanish language ideology promoted by Spain is the establishment of *Instituto Cervantes* on 11 May 1990, with the purpose 'Agrupar y potenciar los esfuerzos en la defensa y promoción del español en el extranjero' [To bring together and empower the efforts to defend and promote Spanish outside of Spain] (Sánchez, 1992: 60). By 2006, there were 66 Instituto Cervantes Centers all over the world, with four in the USA – Albuquerque, Chicago, New York and Seattle.

In promoting Spanish as a global language that is fashionable and that people all over the globe would want to speak, Spain promotes its characteristics as an important demographic presence and status of economic profitability and global influence.

Spanish as an Important Demographic Presence

The demographic strength of Spanish is evident in the number of its native speakers, the number of its speakers and the number of countries in which it is spoken.

Table 6.4 shows that in 1996, Spanish ranked fourth in terms of native speakers (Grimes, 1996) and its ranking is expected to hold by 2050, according to predictions made by Graddol (1997).

With regard to the number of Spanish speakers worldwide, Spanish again is ranked fourth, with between 400 and 425 million speakers, after Chinese, English and Hindi-Urdu (Graddol, 1997). According to

Table 6.4 Number of native speakers in millions

Grimes (1996)	Graddol (1997) in 2050
1. Chinese: 1123	1. Chinese: 1384
2. English: 322	2. Hindi/Urdu[a]: 556
3. Russian: 288	3. English: 508
4. Spanish: 266	4. Spanish: 486

[a]In Graddol's analysis, Hindi and Urdu were counted as one language

Ethnologue (2005), there are over 322 million speakers of Spanish worldwide (Gordon, 2005).

Spanish is also official in 21 countries. Only English, French and Arabic hold official status in more than 21 countries. In 1997, Spanish was the language of 77 international organizations, putting it in third place behind English (181 international organizations) and French (165 international organizations) (Graddol, 1997).

On the Internet, Spanish is also acquiring a presence. Wallraff (2000) reports that of the 56 million people who use a language other than English on the Internet, Spanish represents nearly a quarter (cited in Mar-Molinero, 2004).

Spanish as having Global Influence

It is often said that although Spanish is demographically powerful, it is economically weak. But, increasingly, Spanish is recognized for its economic profitability as well as for its global influence. Table 6.5 presents the estimations of *Gross National Product of Languages* given to us by Graddol (1997). In Graddol's analysis, Spanish has a gross national product (GNP) of $610 billion and ranks sixth, after English, German, French, Chinese and Japanese.

Graddol (1997) has also developed an *Index of Global Influence*, which is based on what he calls the *Engco Model*. The Engco Model includes three major components:

- demographics (numbers, age and rate of urbanization);
- economics (GNP and opening to international trade);
- UN development indices (combines quality of life with literacy and education).

Table 6.5 Gross national product of languages in $US billions

Language	GNP
1. English	$2338
2. German	$1196
3. French	$803
4. Chinese	$803
5. Japanese	$700
6. Spanish	$610

Using the Engco model, Spanish receives a score of 31 when English is 100. In fact, Spanish is in fifth place behind English, German, French and Japanese.

Spanish and Economic Profitability: The USA

Although Spanish competes in global influence, its potential for economic profitability in the USA is what makes Spanish an important resource (Carreira, 2002; Pomerantz, 2002; Villa, 2000). But it is interesting that this potential is maximized in the country where Spanish is precisely marked as the language of poverty. Understanding the economic potential of Spanish in the US market is important for any who would wish to change the characterization of Spanish from being the 'language of the poor' and to renegotiate it as a potential resource of US Latinos.

The Spanish-speaking market in the USA has grown, and continues to grow significantly. In 2003, the Latino population controlled $653 billion in consumption power, and that figure is expected to reach $1 trillion by 2008 (Selig Center for Economic Growth, 2003). This represents *more than three to four times the buying power* of the rest of the Spanish-speaking world (Carreira, 2002; Villa, 2000). In fact, the US Latino purchasing power is growing at a triple rate compared to that of the overall US population (Franco, 2004).

The rapid growth of the Spanish-speaking market is even better understood when taking into account the fact that Latinos comprise approximately 13% of the US population and in 2003 contributed to 23% of the buying power of the nation (Carreira, 2002). This may have to do with the undocumented, but it is also clear that Spanish has buying power in the USA. The Spanish-speaking market is growing eight times faster than the rest of the English-speaking market, surpassing that of

African American and Native Americans. From 1990 to 2002, the buying power of Latinos doubled. In addition, the spending patterns of the young Latino population (35% of the Hispanic population in 2000 was under the age of 18) will dictate the success or failure of youth-oriented products and services (Franco, 2004).

The earnings in Spanish language ads have increased more than seven times since 1990. Although the earnings were $14.3 million in 1970, they reached $111 million in 1990 and $786 million in 2002. Spanish is clearly turning from being a language which restricts access to the US economy, to one which is part of a growing Spanish-speaking market in the USA itself, as well as a language capable of opening up access to the world economy.

US Spanish Language Education Policies and Practices

At the same time as Spanish-English bilingualism is acquiring value in the global market today, the USA is restricting bilingualism. In teaching Latino students, the focus in US classrooms is on the teaching of English. Not enough attention is paid to the basic academic preparation of Latinos, regardless of language –something that has a marked effect on their possibilities for employment and their income potential. At the same time, there is little attention given to the advantages of developing Spanish-English bilingualism.

There are two important educational programs that target different aspects of the education of Latinos (1) bilingual education and (2) the teaching of Spanish as a heritage language. The first one, bilingual education, is an educational effort mostly at the elementary level, but also at the secondary level, focusing on using both Spanish and English. This is implemented primarily with the goal of developing the English language skills of Latino immigrants, and in very few cases to develop their bilingualism.[8] The field of teaching Spanish as a heritage language developed at the secondary and tertiary level, and focused on developing the Spanish of Latino students. As we will see, whereas the first one focuses mostly on English, the second one targets only Spanish, leaving little room for the development of Spanish-English bilingualism that is necessary for negotiation of Spanish as a resource of US Latinos.

Bilingual Education

Perhaps no other educational policy reveals as much the struggle between an ideology that views Spanish as the language of poverty and one that glimpses the possibility of negotiating Spanish-English bilingualism as a resource than bilingual education.

Since the passage of the Bilingual Education Act in 1968, bilingual education has been mostly a path towards Anglification. In the 1974 reauthorization, bilingual education was clearly defined as *transitional*:

It is instruction given in, and study of, English and (to the extent necessary to allow a child to progress effectively through the education system) the native language of the children of limited English speaking ability... (quoted in Castellanos, 1983: 120)

But from the beginning, some bilingual education programs valued bilingualism and attempted to develop Spanish also. The 1984 reauthorization specifically approved *developmental bilingual education* in which students can maintain their languages after learning English. These programs, however, have always been rare. With the 1984 reauthorization, funding also became available for English-only programs as special alternative instructional programs (SAIPs), and these programs were expanded in the 1988 reauthorization (Crawford, 2004; E. Garcia, 2005).[9] The 1988 reauthorization also imposed a three-year limit on participation in transitional bilingual education programs. Congress reauthorized Title VII in 1994 for the last time, substituting the title of Bilingual Education Act for *Improving America's Schools Act*. Although it gave increased attention to two-way bilingual education programs, the quota for the SAIPs in which English only is used was lifted.

Even transitional bilingual education came under attack in the last two decades of the 20th century. The most effective attack against bilingual education was spear-headed by a Silicon Valley software millionaire, Ron Unz. *Proposition 227* (California Education Code, Section 305–306), which was introduced in 1998 as 'English for the Children' and required that 'all children in California public schools shall be taught English by being taught in English' (quoted in Del Valle, 2003: 248), was passed by 65% of the California voters. A year after California's *Proposition 227* was passed, Unz took his efforts to Arizona. In 2000, 63% of the Arizona voters approved *Proposition 203* (Arizona Revised Statutes 15-751-755), which banned bilingual education. In 2002, the proposition in Massachusetts (Question 2, G.L. c. 71A) to replace transitional bilingual education with Structured English Immersion programs for English language learners passed by 68%. But in that same year, Amendment 31 to Colorado's state constitution that would have made bilingual education illegal was defeated with 56% of voters opposing it. The campaign to defeat the amendment focused on the possibility that non-English-speaking children would be in the same classrooms as other children. A TV commercial warned that Unz' initiative would 'force children who can

Table 6.6 The silencing of the word 'bilingual'

Original name	Modified name
Office of Bilingual Education and Minority Languages Affairs (OBEMLA) →	Office of English Language Acquisition, Language Enhancement and Academic Achievement for LEP students (OELA)
National Clearinghouse for Bilingual Education (NCBE) →	National Clearinghouse for English Language Acquisition and Language Instruction Educational Programs (NCELA)
Title VII of Elementary and Secondary Education Act: The Bilingual Education Act →	Title III of No Child Left Behind, Public Law 107–110: Language Instruction for Limited English Proficient and Immigrant Students, 2001

barely speak English into regular classrooms, creating chaos and disrupting learning'. As Crawford (2004: 330) says, the approach used could be described as 'If you can't beat racism, then try to exploit it'.

As many have remarked, the word 'bilingual' (what Crawford has called 'the B-Word') has been progressively silenced (Crawford, 2005; Garcia, 2003, 2006; Hornberger, 2006). The names of offices, clearing-houses and laws have been changed to omit any reference to a bilingual reality. García (2008) portrays this silencing of the word 'bilingual'; some examples are presented in Table 6.6.

As the last row of Table 6.6 indicates, in 2001 *No Child Left Behind* (NCLB) was passed, containing Title III (Public Law 107–110) which is titled, *Language Instruction for Limited English Proficient and Immigrant Students*. The purpose of Title III is 'to ensure that children who are limited English proficient, including immigrant children and youth, attain English proficiency'. Although it is still possible to obtain funding for bilingual education programs, NCLB requires mandatory, high stakes tests in English for all children, leading Crawford (2005: 336) to call the Act 'No Child Left Untested'.

Spanish as a Heritage Language

In 1978, Guadalupe Valdés held a National Endowment for the Humanities Institute to encourage thinking about teaching Spanish for Spanish speakers in contrast to existing approaches of teaching Spanish as a foreign language, an approach to which US Latinos had long been subjected in secondary and tertiary education (Valdés, 1997). Since then, attention to this field has increased, although its growth has been slow and insufficient (for more on this see Fishman *et al.*, 2006; Valdés, 1997). In 1999, Russ Campbell of the University of California in Los Angeles organized the first conference of *Heritage Languages in the United States*. Attempting to include those US Latinos who are no longer speakers of Spanish, the field has renamed itself 'Spanish as a Heritage Language'. However, as García (2005) has remarked, the choice of words is problematic. On the one hand, as the 17-year-old Dominican García (2005) quotes, heritage language sounds a lot like something old, something that is not a viable resource in the USA. On the other hand, focusing only on the heritage language ignores the possibility of Spanish-English bilingualism, the true resource for US Latinos.

Why?

Ideological space for Spanish-English bilingualism in the USA has been closed by the common assumption that the Spanish language itself is to blame for the poverty of its speakers. Speaking of US language policy, Wright (2004) reminds us that this is consistent with other US behavior toward language. Says Wright (2004: 163, 165)

> Some of the most robust resistance to globalization comes from within the United States itself... The US government is able to guard its sovereignty and autonomy in the classic manner of the nation states... [W]e appear to be witnessing asymmetric developments within globalization: loss of economic autonomy and political sovereignty for many states; continuing economic autonomy and political sovereignty together with the survival of some elements of traditional "one nation, one territory, one language" nationalism for the United States.

But as this US space has closed, a space for Spanish-English bilingualism and biliteracy has been opened globally, in which Spanish may be considered an economic resource for those who are educated and bilingual. Given the lack of interest displayed by US schools in educating bilingual citizens, the possibilities for negotiating Spanish as a global and economic resource will remain in the hands of the Spanish and Latin American elite, robbing Latinos, one more time, of the possibility that their Spanish be an instrument for acquisition of economic power.

If we consider the possibility for Spanish to be a negotiable resource of US bilingual Latinos, and the educational establishment's work against such bilingualism, the question that we must pose is why – Why are we afraid of educating bilingual and biliterate US Latinos, capable of negotiating for all of us, as well as for themselves, Spanish/English bilingualism as an economic and social resource? Cameron (1995: 216–217) speaks of what she calls 'verbal hygiene'; that is, a way of advancing particular agendas by controlling language use. She explains:

> Arguments about language [have] provided a symbolic way of addressing conflicts about class, race, culture and gender. It is true that this symbolic deployment of language tends to obscure the true source of disagreement and discomfort.

In a chapter called 'Accumulation by Dispossession' Harvey (2005: 181) provides what may be a reason for the disagreement and discomfort:

> Hegemonic state power is typically deployed to ensure and promote those external and international institutional arrangements through which the asymmetries of exchange relations can so work as to benefit the hegemonic power.

By dispossessing US Latinos of Spanish-English bilingualism, the USA ensures that only those who speak English only can benefit and continue to accumulate capital and other resources.

But what are the costs involved in this dispossession? François Grin (2003) has said, in the context of the European Union, that English is worth learning, but that restricting foreign/second language acquisition to English only would be a very short-sighted policy. How short-sighted is our present policy of restricting the Spanish-English bilingualism of US citizens? Will we pay a price in a globalized world? We cannot foresee the future, but it is clear that for now, US Latinos are paying a price.

Notes

1. We are aware that the only value of language is not simply economic. Fishman (1999: 19) upholds the nonmaterial value of language and says that by focusing so much on power, it misses 'the real elephant' and 'reduces human values, emotions, loyalties and philosophies to little more than hard cash and brute force'. The topic of this book, however, is poverty. Thus, we focus here on the economic value of Spanish.
2. Language ideology has been defined by Irvine (1998: 52) as the linking 'of ideas and interests through which people interpret linguistic behavior', and more specifically as the linking of 'ideas about language with ideas about social rank, respect and appropriate conduct'.
3. Throughout this chapter, we use 'Latino' to refer to all Spanish speakers of Latin American descent. We prefer this term to 'Hispanic', the term used by the US Census.

4. We use 'minoritized' and not 'minority' to signal the role of power as it was exerted.
5. The quota was 2% of the number of people from that country who were already living in the USA in 1890.
6. The status dropout rate refers to those who are out of school and have not earned a high-school diploma or GED.
7. In our analysis, we consider those who 'speak English very well, well or not well' as bilingual, using a minimalist definition of bilingualism, as that of Diebold (1964).
8. Of course, not all bilingual education programs are of the transitional kind. There are a few developmental bilingual education programs, and there are also two-way bilingual education programs. These two other kinds of bilingual education programs develop bilingualism, but there have always been few of these in the USA.
9. For more on this entire history, see especially http://www.ncela.gwu.edu/policy.1_history.htm.

References

Alba, R., Logan, J. and Stults, B. (2002) Only English by the third generation: Loss and preservation of the mother tongue among the grandchildren of contemporary immigrants. *Demography* 39 (3), 467–484.

Alba, R. and Nee, V. (2003) *Remaking the American Mainstream: Assimilation and Contemporary Immigration.* Cambridge, MA: Harvard University Press.

Álvarez Martínez, M.A. (2001) El español como lengua extranjera en las universidades españolas. II Congreso Internacional de la Lengua Española, Valladolid, Spain (October). Centro Virtual Cervantes. On WWW at http://cvc.cervantes.es/obref/congresos/valladolid/ponencias/activo_del_espanol/1_la_industria_del_espanol/alvarez_m.htm. Accessed 1.10.06.

Baron, D. (2001) Language legislation and language abuse: American language policy through the 1990s. In R.D. Gonzalez and I. Melis (eds) *Language Ideologies: Critical Perspectives on the Official English Movement* (pp. 5–29). Mahwah, NJ: Lawrence Erlbaum.

Bills, G.D. (1997) Language shift, linguistic variation, and teaching Spanish to native speakers in the United States. In M.C. Colombi and F.X. Alarcón (eds) *La enseñanza del español a hispanohablantes* (pp. 263–282). Boston, MA: Houghton Mifflin.

Bills, G.D., Hernández-Chávez, E. and Hudson, A. (1995) The geography of language shift: Distance from the Mexican border and Spanish language claiming in the southwestern U.S. *International Journal of the Sociology of Language* 114, 9–27.

Bloom, D. and Grenier, G. (1996) Language, employment, and earnings in the United States: Spanish-English differentials from 1970 to 1990. *International Journal of the Sociology of Language* 121, 45–68.

Boswell, T. (2000) Demographic changes in Florida and their importance for effective educational policies and practices. In A. Roca (ed.) *Research on Spanish in the United States: Linguistic Issues and Challenges* (pp. 406–431). Somerville, MA: Cascadilla Press.

Cameron, D. (1995) *Verbal Hygiene.* London: Routledge.

Carreira, M. (2000) Validating and promoting Spanish in the United States: Lessons from linguistic science. *Bilingual Research Journal* 24, 333–352

Carreira, M. (2002) The media, marketing and critical mass: Portents of linguistic maintenance. *Southwest Journal of Linguistics* 21 (2), 37–54.

Castellanos, D. (1983) *The Best of Two Worlds. Bilingual-bicultural Education in the U.S.* Trenton, NJ: New Jersey State Department of Education.

Crawford, J. (ed.) (1992) *Language Loyalties: A Sourcebook on the Official English Controversy.* Chicago, IL: University of Chicago Press.

Crawford, J. (2004) *Educating English Learners: Language Diversity in the Classroom* (5th edn). (Formerly Bilingual Education: History, Politics, Theory, and Practice). Los Angeles, CA: Bilingual Educational Services.

Dame Edna (2003, February) Ask Dame Edna. *Vanity Fair*, 116.

Del Valle, J. (2006) U.S. Latinos, *la hispanofonía*, and the language ideologies of high modernity. In C. Mar-Molinero and M. Stewart (eds) *Globalisation and the Spanish-speaking World* (pp. 27–46). London and New York: Palgrave.

Del Valle, S. (2003) *Language Rights and the Law in the United States.* Clevedon: Multilingual Matters.

Diebold, A.R. (1964) Incipient bilingualism. In D. Hymes (ed.) *Language in Culture and Society* (pp. 495–511). New York: Harper and Row.

Fishman, J.A. (1991) *Reversing Language Shift. Theoretical and Empirical Foundations of Assistance to Threatened Languages.* Clevedon: Multilingual Matters.

Franco, L. (2004) *The Hispanic Market in 2010.* The Conference Board. On WWW at http://www.conference-board.org/publications/describe.cfm?id = 884. Accessed 8.11.06.

García, E. (2005) *Teaching and Learning in Two Languages: Bilingualism and Schooling in the United States.* New York: Teachers College Press.

García, O. (1995) Spanish language loss as a determinant of income among Latinos in the United States: Implications for language policy in schools. In J. Tollefson (ed.) *Power and Inequality in Language Education* (pp. 142–160). Cambridge: Cambridge University Press.

García, O. (2005) Positioning heritage languages in the United States. *Modern Language Journal* 89 (4), 601–605.

García, O. (2008) Teaching Spanish and Spanish in teaching in the USA: Integrating bilingual perspectives. In C. Hélot and A-M. de Mejía (eds) *Forging Multilingual Spaces: Integrated Perspectives on Majority and Minority Bilingual Education.* Bristol: Multilingual Matters.

García, O., Morín, J.L. and Rivera, K. (2001) How threatened is the Spanish of New York Puerto Ricans? Language shift with vaivén. In J.A. Fishman (ed.) *Can Threatened Languages be Saved? Reversing Language Shift Revisited* (pp. 44–73). Clevedon: Multilingual Matters.

Gordon, R.G., Jr. (ed.) (2005) *Ethnologue: Languages of the World* (15th edn). Dallas, TX: SIL International. On WWW at http://www.ethnologue.com/. Accessed 8.11.06.

Graddol, D. (1997) *The Future of English.* London: British Council. On WWW at http://www.britishcouncil.org/learning-research-futureofenglish.htm. Accessed 1.9.06.

Graddol, D. (2006) *English Next.* London: British Council. On WWW at http://www.britishcouncil.org/learning-research-englishnext.htm. Accessed 1.10.06.

Grimes, B.F. (2000) *Ethnologue: Languages of the World* (14th edn). Dallas, TX: SIL International.

Grin, F. (1995) The economics of foreign language competence: A research project of the Swiss National Science Foundation. *Journal of Multilingual Multicultural Development* 16 (3), 227–231.

Grin, F. (2001) English as economic value: Factos and fallacies. *World Englishes* 20 (1), 65–78.

Grin, F. (2003) *Language Policy Evaluation and the European Charter for Regional or Minority Languages.* Basingstoke: Palgrave.

Grin, F. and Daftary, F. (eds) (2003) *Nation-building, Ethnicity and Language Politics in Transition Countries.* Budapest: Local Government and Public Service Reform Initiative of the Open Society Institute.

Harvey, D. (2005) *The New Imperialism.* Oxford: Oxford University Press.

Hernández-Chávez, E. (1993) Native language loss and its implications for revitalization of Spanish in Chicano communities. In B.J. Merino, E.T. Trueba and F.A. Samaniego (eds) *Language and Culture in Learning: Teaching Spanish to Native Speakers of Spanish* (pp. 45–57). London: The Falmer Press.

Hornberger, N.H. (2006) Nichols to NCLB: Local and global perspectives on US language education policy. In O. Garcia, T. Skutnabb-Kangas and M.E. Torres-Guzmán (eds) *Imagining Multilingual Schools: Languages in Education and Globalization* (pp. 223–237). Clevedon: Multilingual Matters.

Huntington, S.P. (2004, April) *The Hispanic Challenge.* On WWW at http://www.foreignpolicy.com. Accessed 1.9.06.

Irvine, J. (1998) Ideologies of honorific language. In B.B. Schieffelin, K.A. Woolard and P.V. Kroskrity (eds) *Language Ideologies: Practice and Theory* (pp. 251–262). New York: Oxford University Press.

Irvine, J. and Gal, S. (2000) Language ideology and linguistic differentiation. In P.V. Kroskrity (ed.) *Regimes of Language: Ideologies, Polities, and Identities* (pp. 35–84). Santa Fe, NM: School of American Research Press.

Kloss, H. (1977) *The American Bilingual Tradition.* Rowley, MA: Newbury House.

Kochhar, R. (2004, October) *The Wealth of Hispanic Households: 1996 to 2002.* Washington, DC: Pew Hispanic Center. On WWW at http://www.pewhispanic.org/files/reports/34.pdf. Accessed 1.11.06.

Language Policy Task Force (1992) English and colonialism in Puerto Rico. In J. Crawford (ed.) *Language Loyalties* (pp. 63–71). Chicago, IL: University of Chicago Press.

Linton, A. (2003) Is Spanish Here to Stay? Contexts for Bilingualism Among U.S.-born Hispanics. Center for Comparative Immigration Studies Summer Institute, University of California, San Diego.

Mar-Molinero, C. (2004) Spanish as a world language: Language and identity in a global era. *Spanish in Context* 1 (1), 3–20.

Massey, D.S. (1995) The new immigration and ethnicity in the United States. *Population and Development Review* 2 (3), 631–662.

National Commission for Employment Policy (1982) *Hispanics and Jobs: Barriers to Progress.* Washington, DC: National Commission for Employment Policy.

Ogbu, J.U. (1998) Voluntary and involuntary minorities: A cultural-ecological theory of school performance with some implications for education. *Anthropology and Education Quarterly* 29 (2), 155–188.

Passal, J.S. (2006, March) *Size and Characteristics of the Unauthorized Migrant Population in the U.S.* Washington, DC: Pew Hispanic Center. On WWW at http://pewhispanic.org/reports/report.php?ReportID = 61. Accessed 8.11.06.

Pew Hispanic Center (2006, September) *Statistical Portraits of the Hispanic and Foreign-born Populations at Mid-decade.* Washington, DC: Pew Hispanic Center. On WWW at http://pewhispanic.org/reports/middecade/. Accessed 8.11.06.

Pomerantz, A. (2002) Language ideologies and the production of identities: Spanish as a resource for participation in a multilingual marketplace. *Multilingua* 21, 275–302.

Portes, A. and Rumbaut, R.G. (1996) *Immigrant America: A Portrait* (2nd edn). Berkeley, CA: University of California Press.

Portes, A. and Rumbaut, R.G. (2001) *Legacies: The Story of the Immigrant Second Generation.* Berkeley, CA: University of California Press.

Rodriguez, C.E. (1989) *Puerto Ricans: Born in the U.S.A.* Boston, MA: Unwin Hyman.

Sánchez, A. (1992) Spanish language spread policy. *International Journal of the Sociology of Language* 95 (1), 51–69.

Selig Center for Economic Growth (2003) *The Multicultural Economy.* Athens, GA: University of Georgia.

Trías Monge, J. (1997) *Puerto Rico: The Trials of the Oldest Colony in the World.* New Haven, CT: Yale University Press.

Urciuoli, B. (1996) *Exposing Prejudice: Puerto Rican Experiences of Language, Race, and Class.* Boulder, CA: Westview Press.

US Census Bureau (2000) *US Census Bureau Report 2000.* Washington, DC: US Government Printing Office.

Valdés, G. (1997) The teaching of Spanish to bilingual Spanish-speaking students: Outstanding issues and unanswered questions. In M.C. Colombi and F.X. Alarcón (eds) *La enseñanza del español a hispanohablantes* (pp. 263–282). Boston, MA: Houghton Mifflin.

Valdés, G., Fishman, J.A., Chavez, R. and Perez, W. (2006) *Developing Minority Language Resources. The Case of Spanish in California.* Clevedon: Multilingual Matters.

Villa, D. (2000) Languages have armies, and economies, too: The presence of U.S. Spanish in the Spanish-speaking world. *Southwest Journal of Linguistics* 19, 143–154.

Wallraff, B. (2000, November) What Global Language? *The Atlantic Monthly* (digital edition). On WWW at http://www.theatlantic.com/issues/2000/11/wallraff.htm. Accessed 8.11.06.

Wright, S. (2004) *Language Policy and Language Planning. From Nationalism to Globalization.* Hampshire and New York: Palgrave Macmillan.

Zentella, A.C. (1997) Spanish in New York. In O. García and J.A. Fishman (eds) *The Multilingual Apple. Languages in New York City* (pp. 167–201). Berlin: Mouton de Gruyter.

Chapter 7

Perpetuating Inequality: Language Disadvantage and Capability Deprivation of Tribal Mother Tongue Speakers in India

AJIT K. MOHANTY

Introduction: Poverty as Capability Deprivation

Eminent welfare economist and Nobel laureate Amartya Sen conceptualizes poverty as 'capability deprivation' and 'unfreedom' (Dreze & Sen, 2002; Sen, 1982, 1985). Capability, in his view (Dreze & Sen, 2002), 'refers to the ultimate combinations of functionings from which a person can choose' (35) and freedom is 'the range of options a person has in deciding what kind of life to lead' (35–36). Thus, curtailment of capabilities and lack of real social opportunity, rather than the conventional indicators such as low income or impoverishment of life conditions, are relevant to understanding the nature and causes of poverty. Sen explores the cyclic nature of the relationship between social discrimination, lack of opportunities, lack of freedom, capability deprivation and poverty, stressing that 'the crucial role of social opportunities is to expand the realm of human agency and freedom, both as an end in itself and as a means of further expansion of freedom' (Dreze & Sen, 2002: 6).

The emphasis on 'capability' has been seen as a powerful interdisciplinary approach to deal with the questions of poverty and the well-being of marginalized communities (Robeyns, 2006). Robeyns (2006) suggests that, in dealing with the problems of such communities, it is necessary to identify capability inputs and obstacles to the realization of capabilities. Education, which plays a crucial enabling role in Sen's view of economic development, can be seen as a major capability input. Illiteracy is 'unfreedom' and a major obstacle imposing severe limitations to economic opportunities. Besides directly enhancing economic opportunities through easier access to jobs and income, school education adds to social and cultural freedom and empowers persons for adequate participation in the exercise of political rights. Inequality of opportunities is related to distributional aspects of freedom – inequalities in respect of freedom, participation and development. This is particularly crucial for Indian society where social divisions, based on such distinctions as caste, class, culture, language and religion, are pervasive. Dreze and Sen (2002) speak of the substantial problem of 'voicelessness' of the disadvantaged groups in India, particularly the Scheduled Tribes (ST),[1] arising out of the large-scale illiteracy and lack of education, both of which impede economic development.

Thus, education is seen as the most crucial input necessary for development out of poverty. Lack of education for the disadvantaged in India, according to Dreze and Sen (2002), is not due to parental indifference or due to the purported large-scale participation of children in the labor force (a claim which they show to be unsubstantiated). They attribute large-scale nonattendance and school drop out[2] to lack of interest (of parents as well as children) and to a host of 'discouragement effects' due to alienating curricula, inactive classrooms, indifferent teachers and social discrimination in the classroom (Dreze & Sen, 2002: 158). Although Dreze and Sen (2002) do not analyze the roots of the discouragement effects, linguistic and cultural discrimination and disadvantages, arising out of prevalent inequalities due to such discriminatory treatments, are central to the vicious circle of illiteracy, educational failure, lack of freedom, capability deprivation and poverty.

This paper focuses on the relationship between the languages of the tribal people and their poverty and shows how multiple layers of discrimination – in Indian constitution and governance, low instrumental vitality of tribal languages, exclusion and nonaccommodation of minority mother tongues in education and inequalities in the relationship between power and languages – severely restrict their freedom of choice and access to resources, leading to illiteracy, educational failure and capability deprivation. While education is the enabling factor for economic development, language is the enabling factor for access to quality education.

Indian Multilingualism and the Cycle of Language Disadvantage

Linguistically, India is one of the most diverse countries of the world. There are 300–400 major languages belonging to five language families. The Census of India (1961) recorded 1652 extant mother tongues. The number is much larger – 3000–4000 according to some estimates – if one goes by unclassified census declarations. There are 22 official languages recognized by the Constitution of India (VIIIth Schedule) along with English, which has an associate official language status.[3] The complex presence of a large number of languages in different public spheres makes Indian multilingualism distinct, with several features very different from the dominant monolingual societies (Mohanty, 1994a). Grass-root level bilingualism is widespread, with most of the people using two or more languages in different domains of daily life. In fact, bilingualism of the individuals and communities at the regional levels has been viewed 'as constituting the first incremental step towards concentric layers of societal multilingualism' (Mohanty, 2006: 263). In face of the widespread mutual contact of bilingual communities, languages tend to be maintained. This is possible because languages complement each other with a smooth functional allocation into different domains of use. I use my mother tongue, Oriya, in my home, English in my workplace, Hindi in the marketplace and for viewing television programs, Bengali for communication with my domestic help (and for others who speak the language), Sanskrit for my religious activities and some Kui with the tribal informants for my research with the (Kond) tribal community. Languages complement each other in my life as they do those of other Indians without any mutual conflict. This, as well as fluidity of perceived boundaries between languages, is also associated with the multiplicity of linguistic identities which forms a part of early multilingual socialization (Mohanty *et al.*, 1999) in India.

The features of Indian multilingualism combine to make it a positive force for the individuals and communities. Our studies (see Mohanty [1994a, 2003a] for discussion and Skutnabb-Kangas [1995] for a review) have shown cognitive and social benefits associated with multilingualism and mother tongue maintenance. A review of cross-cultural studies on bilingualism (Mohanty & Perregaux, 1997) shows that the Indian research has contributed to the findings of a positive psychological and social role of multilingualism. All these features add to making multilingualism a positive force in India where common people accept the presence of multiple languages as necessary aspects of life.

Despite such positive features and the much talked of maintenance norms, nearly 80% of Indian languages are endangered, most of them tribal languages. While many languages coexist and are maintained in the multilingual mosaic, languages are also victims of discrimination, social and political neglect and deprivation. There is a wide gap between the statuses of languages; while some are privileged with access to power and resources, others are marginalized and disadvantaged. Indian multilingualism is characterized as a 'multilingualism of the unequals' (Mohanty, 2004).

Formal Bases of Linguistic Discrimination

Linguistic discrimination and inequalities are rooted in the statutory and political processes of governance. Constitutional recognition of only 22 of the languages as official languages means that most of the Indian languages are effectively kept out of the power domains. Languages are also specifically recognized for many other public purposes, such as for promotion of culture and literature, as well as state level recognition for use in limited spheres of governance. The constitutional and governmental recognitions are reflections of the political power of the linguistic groups. In December 2003, Parliament of India passed the 100th Constitutional Amendment Bill to include four languages (Bodo, Dogri, Maithili and Santali) in the VIIIth Schedule of official languages. This recognition came to these languages after prolonged movements and political lobbying. Maithili was earlier classified in the Census within Hindi (which, in fact, has 20 mother tongues grouped under it with over 1 million speakers). With the Constitutional amendment of 2003, two tribal languages – Bodo and Santali – were recognized as official languages. It was the first time since the adaptation of the Constitution that such recognition was accorded to a tribal language. This came as a result of assertive language maintenance movements by the two tribal language communities. Other less powerful languages and mother tongues are often dubbed as 'dialects' and weak voices for recognition are suppressed in the political and power dynamics. Even in the official Census figures, mother tongue declarations are reclassified and grouped under major languages due to various quasipolitical considerations. The Census of 1991 listed 216 mother tongues (with a large number of mother tongues clubbed together under each 'mother tongue') with an arbitrary cutoff criterion of a minimum of 10,000 speakers. The mother tongues declared by less than 10,000 persons were grouped under the *'other mother tongues'* category, which included nearly 9 million speakers. Thus, more than 900 mother tongues spoken by nearly 1% of the population remained unlisted. Education is another major basis of institutionalized inequality. As I will show later, only a few of the languages are used for school instruction. Most of the tribal and minority languages have no place in the schools and literacy programs. Pervasive discrimination and neglect in all spheres of governance limit the scope of democratic participation and effectively deny equality of opportunity to the linguistic minorities.

Marginalization of Languages and the Cycle of Disadvantaged

The ethos of language maintenance and large-scale contact bilingualism, in which dominant contact languages are adopted by linguistic minorities along with maintenance of native languages, enhance chances of survival for minor, minority and tribal languages. This, however, does not ensure equality of power and opportunities and access to resources. Ironically, the very processes of maintenance are also associated with marginalization of languages, particularly the tribal and minority languages (Mohanty, 2004, 2006). These languages are pushed out of major domains of power and development, such as official, legal and other formal use, education, trade and commerce. This, in effect, creates shift pressures from the dominant contact languages threatening their survival. In face of such threats, the speakers of these languages adopt what I have characterized as 'anti-predatory strategies' (Mohanty, 2004, 2006) to ensure survival by a passive withdrawal into domains of lesser power and visibility. In effect, language shift does not occur; but there is considerable domain shrinkage with languages barely maintained mostly in the domains of home and in-group communication. The 'natural' bilingualism among the tribal and other linguistic minority speakers is part of the maintenance strategy also ensuring smooth social functioning and intergroup relations, 'but the cost of such survival and maintenance is identity crisis, deprivation of freedom and capability, educational failure (due to inadequate home language development and forced submersion in majority language schools), marginalization and poverty' (Mohanty, 2006: 266). Most of the marginalized linguistic groups accept the low status and exclusion of their languages as *fait accompli*. While their language is perceived as important for identity and integrative functions, instrumental functions are dissociated from the native languages in favor of the dominant ones (Mohanty, 2004); low vitality of their languages is perceived as legitimate by the victims of the processes of exclusion.

The tribal and minority language speakers are disadvantaged to begin with; they are usually poorer, mostly belonging to rural, backward and economically underdeveloped areas. Prolonged deprivation, exclusion from education and from domains of official and economic power further weaken these languages which are not allowed to develop, and the weakness of the languages are used to justify further neglect and exclusion in a vicious cycle of disadvantage. Thus, the so-called poverty of languages, disabilities and disadvantages often associated with minor languages, are not inherent; they are socially constructed by the institutionalized discriminations in educational, political, economic and other social spheres conspiring to strengthen the association between tribal languages and insufficiency. Sadly, the weaknesses and insufficiency of tribal languages are often cited as grounds for their exclusion from education.

Languages in Indian Education

An analysis of the use of languages – as media of instruction (MI) and as school subjects – in Indian education (Mohanty, 2006) shows that a large number of minority languages are weakened and endangered by their exclusion and non-accommodation in school education and literacy programs despite a clear constitutional provision that the state and the local authorities shall endeavor to 'provide adequate facilities for instruction in the mother tongue at primary stage of education to children belonging to minority groups' (Article 350A, *Constitution of India*). Altogether only 41 languages are used in schools either as MI or as school subjects and this figure actually declined from 81 in 1970 to 67, 58, 44 and 41, respectively, in 1976, 1978, 1990 and 1998. The number of languages used as the language of teaching in schools (MI) has also declined. Between the years 1990 and 1998, the number of languages used as MI declined from 43 to 33 in primary grades (I to V), 31 to 25 in upper primary grades (VI & VII), 22 to 21 in secondary grades (VIII to X), and 20 to 18 in higher secondary grades (XI & XII). Thus, only the speakers of a limited set of languages are provided opportunities for education in their mother tongues. In adult literacy programs, 104 languages are used for literacy instruction. Limited success of adult literacy programs and frequent relapse of the new literates into illiteracy have been attributed to non-use of mother tongues (Karlekar, 2004; Mohanty, 2005). The mismatch between home and school languages and neglect of mother tongues, particularly for literacy and schooling, force the tribal (as well as other minority) children into a subtractive language learning experience, and their poor educational achievement limits their future opportunities. Studies in India have severally pointed to the negative consequences of such mismatches (e.g. Jhingran, 2005; Mohanty, 1994a, 1994b, 2000, 2005). Submersion programs, in which minority and indigenous children are forced to learn in the medium of a dominant language, result in subtractive language learning, have negative consequences, and violate right to quality education: "In subtractive language learning, a new (dominant/majority) language is learnt at the cost of the mother tongue which is displaced, leading to diglossic situation and later often replacement by the dominant language. Subtractive teaching subtracts from the child's linguistic repertoire, instead of adding to it. In this enforced language regime, the children undergo subtractive education . . . . This also contributes to the disappearance of the world's linguistic diversity. . . (UNPFII, 2005: 3)

The use of a dominant official language as the language of instruction in primary schools has been held to be a main feature of 'collapsed models of schooling', which reinforce inequality (Tomasevski, 2004). In India, the exclusion of mother tongues from formal education follows from the perception of powerlessness and low vitality ascribed to minor, minority and tribal languages compared to the dominant majority languages, such as English. In fact, English happens to be the most preferred MI and has a significant presence in school curricula all over the country. The role of English in triggering a power game and a hierarchical pecking order of languages has been discussed elsewhere (see Mohanty, 2004, 2006). Preference for English-medium education has relegated Hindi and other major regional and constitutional languages to lesser positions in education (Kurien, 2004), considerably weakening them in all spheres of the Indian society. These major regional languages, in turn, tend to push the tribal, minor and minority languages out of favor and are imposed on their speakers particularly in domains of education and official use. The prominent role of English in education has been viewed as a key factor in such outcomes in respect of the minor and dominated languages.

In the educational sphere, projected as a global language of science, technology and commerce, English has been seen in a primary role despite statutory attempts to enforce regional state languages in schools. In Hindi majority states as well as in non-Hindi states, alarmingly increasing proportion of the parents and students aspire for English medium education as a road to power and success. This is weakening the already weak system of state-sponsored regional majority language schools which are imposed on tribal language communities, other linguistic minorities, and the poor and disadvantaged groups who cannot afford high-cost English medium schools. (Mohanty, 2006: 269)

The power hierarchy of languages is socially constructed and legitimated. A process of early socialization for multilingualism as well as prevalent social norms and a host of complex social psychological processes associated with construal of linguistic identities result in the perception of legitimacy of the assigned roles of the languages lower down the hierarchy. Our studies of multilingual socialization in India (Mohanty *et al.*, 1999) show that children in India develop an early awareness of the higher social status of English vis-à-vis their own mother tongues, and that schools do contribute to development of such an awareness.

Besides the first category of children whose language is excluded entirely from schools, there are also children of other disadvantaged groups, such as the economically underdeveloped lower castes ('*Scheduled Castes*', SC), whose mother tongue variety is not the so-called standard language of the classrooms. Major Indian languages are characterized by high and low stylistic varieties, often associated with high and low caste speakers, particularly in rural areas. The distinction between high and low or standard and nonstandard varieties is often arbitrary and based on the degree of *Anglicization* and *Sanskritization* of languages. In India's hierarchical and class-differentiated society, the low, nonstandard and dialectical varieties of a language are separated from the standard language of the power groups by hypothetical standards of acceptability, perpetuating an elitist bias and nonaccommodation in schools and other formal social institutions. The speakers of the so-called lower or nonstandard varieties are put at a disadvantage because their language, even if it is one of the many varieties of a major language, is stigmatized, considered profane, inferior, erroneous and unacceptable for use in academic and formal domains. This creates a sharp discontinuity between home language and school language, particularly for the lower castes (SC) and other disadvantaged groups, whose mother tongues, despite being classified under the major language categories, are still discriminated against. This systematic discrimination makes educational success difficult to realize for members of these minority groups. Thus, the children from these groups suffer from linguistic discrimination in classrooms, causing large-scale nonattainment.

Language, Education and Poverty: A Closer Look at the Tribal Population in India

This section provides a broad profile of the tribes in India and some of the available data on tribal languages and their exclusion from education as it is related to poverty. A comparative analysis of educational attainment of students belonging to the STs and other groups (such as the SC) in India is presented to show how exclusion of the languages of the STs from their school education is related to their 'voicelessness' and capability deprivation. This point is further substantiated by citing a positive instance based on our study (Saikia & Mohanty, 2004) showing the positive role of mother tongue-medium schooling for the tribal Bodo children in Assam, India.

Tribal Communities and Tribal Languages in India

The Census of India (2001) shows that the STs, with a population of 84.3 million, constitute 8.2% of the total population (1028.6 million) of India. The lower caste groups, officially notified or recognized as SC, constitute 16.23% of the population. The Anthropological Survey of India (ASI), in its People of India project (POI) (Singh, 2002), listed 623 tribal communities out of which about 573 are notified or scheduled. The POI shows that the tribal groups speak 218 languages out of which 159 are exclusive to them; 54 languages are used by the tribals for intergroup communication. Most of the tribal languages do not have a script[4] and are written in the script of either the dominant regional language or another major language, but some tribal languages, such as Santali,[5] have developed their own writing system. Most of the tribal groups are bilingual or multilingual at the community levels. According to the POI, out of 623 tribal communities, 500 are bilingual ones. It must be noted that community level bilingualism reflects bilingual communicative skills of the adults, whereas the children usually grow up with the native tribal language which is the home language and language of early communication.

Tribal Languages in Education

The *Sixth All India Educational Survey* of the National Council of Educational Research and Training (NCERT) shows that out of 41 languages used in schools (as MI and subjects) only 13 are tribal languages (see Statement 11.2 in Gupta, 1999). Except Nicobaree, all these tribal languages are from North Eastern (NE) States, which have a much higher concentration of tribal population compared to the rest of India. The literacy figures for the ST groups are also much higher in the NE States. Incidentally, these states also record a better rate of economic development. Further, out of the 13 tribal languages in schools, only three to four are used regularly as MI (Jhingran, 2005); the rest are languages taught as school subjects or used as MI in some special programs, but not on a regular basis. Thus, less than 1% of the tribal children get an opportunity for education in the medium of their mother tongues. This is quite striking as a very large number of classrooms throughout the country have a sizable proportion of tribal children. In 20 states for which the District Information System for Education (DISE) – a database of the Ministry of Human Resource Development, Government of India – is available, there are 103,609 primary schools (Grades I–V) with more than 50%, 76,458 schools with more than 75% and 58,343 schools with more than 90% ST children (Jhingran, 2005) who are taught in a submersion program of majority language education. The DISE does not even have any information on the first language of the ST or other children whose home language is different from the school language.

Education of Tribal Children and the Problem of Exclusion of Tribal Languages

Jhingran (2005), in his study of the language disadvantage faced by children with a mismatch between their home language and their school language, shows the problem of noncomprehension for tribal children in the following description of a primary school classroom in a remote tribal area in Chhindwara district in Madhya Pradesh (India):

> The children seemed totally disinterested in the teacher's monologue. They stared vacantly at the teacher and sometimes at the blackboard where some alphabets had been written. Clearly aware that the children could not understand what he was saying, the teacher proceeded to provide even more detailed explanation in a much louder voice. Later, tired of speaking and realizing that the young children were completely lost, he asked them to start copying the alphabets from the blackboard. "My children are very good at copying from the black board. By the time they reach grade 5, they can copy all the answers and memorize them. But only two of the grade 5 students can actually speak Hindi", said the teacher. (Jhingran, 2005: 1)

Similar observations are quite common in classrooms in many other tribal areas. From the beginning of schooling, tribal children take at least two to three years to learn the language of instruction which the teachers and the texts use (Mohanty, 2000). This effectively means that their learning of school content and concepts become quite slow from the beginning of schooling. Jhingran (2005) speaks of the 'double disadvantage' of children having new academic information and concepts 'thrown' at them in an unfamiliar language. Findings of Jhingran's (2005) fieldwork during 2004 in four states – Assam, Gujarat,

Orissa and Madhya Pradesh – show some striking problems of noncomprehension for the tribal and other children schooled in second language submersion programs. Children showed no comprehension of the teacher's language, even after having spent about six months in Grade I. They (Grade I children) showed no recognition of alphabets, except when the characters were arranged in sequence (showing rote memorization). Teaching emphasized passive participation, such as copying alphabets and numbers from blackboards or text books; there was very little conversation or oral work in children's L2, the MI. Interestingly, the study found the situation to be a little better when there was a tribal teacher who knew the mother tongue (L1) of the children and could 'unofficially' lapse into L1 in certain circumstances, particularly when the children had problems with L2. In respect of academic performance of the tribal children in Grade V whose first language was different from the MI, Jhingran (2005) shows the following:

> (They) read with a lot of effort, mostly word by word… Their oral skills in the second language are poor and they are definitely more comfortable speaking in their mother tongue. Such children cannot frame sentences correctly and have a very limited vocabulary. While they can partially comprehend text (of grade 2/3 level), were unable to formulate answer to simple questions in the standard language. In most schools, the tribal language speaking children could not score a single mark in the reading comprehension test. (Jhingran, 2005: 50)

Clearly, exclusion of mother tongues from early education has serious consequences for tribal children in India. This is reflected in the low literacy rate, high drop out rate and poor educational performance of the tribal groups, and, consequently, in their capability deprivation and poverty. We will examine some selected indicators of poor educational development of the STs in India before looking at their economic development. In most cases, a comparison is made with other social groups, particularly the SC, which constitute another disadvantaged group with poor economic development. As I have mentioned earlier, the SCs, particularly the rural majority, speak the 'nonstandard' (often, also labeled as 'low' variety) form of the regional majority language, and their children have passive (and somewhat partial) understanding of the majority language ('standard' or 'high' variety) classroom MI. It should also be pointed out that the SC are marked by a negative comparison in the traditional Hindu caste hierarchy, whereas the STs, generally, are out of the caste-based hierarchy and, hence, less stigmatized on this ground in social comparison.

Literacy, drop out and school attendance of the STs

The crude literacy rate, i.e. the percentage of literates in the total population, as determined in 2001, is 38.41% for the STs. The corresponding figures for the total population and the SCs are 54.51% and 45.20%, respectively. Effective literacy rate (percentage of literates among the population aged 7 years and above) is 47.10% for the STs and 54.69% for the SCs, whereas for the rest of the population it is 68.81%. Thus, the STs show a literacy gap of 21.71% compared to 14.12% for the SCs. Literacy rate for the STs is much lower if one takes out the figures for North Eastern states like Nagaland, Mizoram, Meghalaya and Manipur, where the rates are much higher. The gross enrolment ratio (GER, i.e. percentage of children in the age group enrolled in schools) and drop out rate between Grade I and later grades are shown in Table 7.1 As shown, more than 50% of the tribal children enrolled in class I drop out or, rather, are pushed out, before completing primary education, and over 80% drop out before completing high school. The enrolment ratio is relatively high in the early grades due to special government programs for the STs in recent years, which seek to universalize education up to 14 years of age. In higher grades, the GER for the STs remains lower than the corresponding figure for the SCs, as well as the national average.

Classroom achievement of tribal students

Beside the study by Jhingran (2005) discussed earlier, there are few other studies that have examined the classroom achievement of the STs. A recent assessment of learning achievement of students at the end of Class V, conducted by the NCERT in 2004 with a national sample of 88,271 children (Singh *et al.*, 2004), shows that the ST students scored

Table 7.1 Enrolment and drop-out rates (2002–2003)

Group	Gross Enrolment Ratio			Drop-Out Rate		
	Class I–V (6–11 years)	Class VI–VIII (11–14 years)	Class I–VIII (6–14 years)	Class I–V	Class I–VIII	Class I–X
Scheduled Tribe	98.67	48.19	80.50	51.57	68.67	80.29
Scheduled Caste	95.61	56.28	81.06	41.47	59.91	71.92
Total Population	95.39	60.99	82.51	34.90	52.80	62.60

Source: Ministry of Human Resource Development (2004)

Table 7.2 Mean achievement scores of Class V students

Subject area	SC (n =18,146)	ST (n =11,424)	Others (n =58,701)
Environmental studies	48.53	49.52	50.99
Mathematics	44.97	44.12	47.45
Language	57.01	58.19	59.54
Grammar and usage	60.78	61.37	63.00
Reading comprehension	50.99	52.89	53.78

Source: Singh et al. (2004)

significantly lower than the 'other' students (i.e. excluding the SCs and STs) in tests of learning achievement in mathematics, environmental studies, language, reading comprehension and grammar and usage (see Table 7.2 for details). The tribal students performed somewhat better than their SC counterparts (except in mathematics), but their performance was significantly below the performance of other students.

The performance level of the tribal students in high school examinations (i.e. after 10 years of schooling) has also been found to be much below than that of the SCs and other groups. Table 7.3 shows the percentage of failure and success with different levels of achievement[6] or divisions in the state level high school examinations for the years 2003, 2004 and 2005 in the state of Orissa, the population of which includes a large minority (over 22%) of tribal members. These examinations are common examinations for all the students of government (and other recognized majority language (Oriya) medium) schools in Orissa, in which over 250,000 students are educated. Table 7.3 shows that the ST students have a higher failure rate compared to the SC and other students. Their level of achievement is also quite low. Low achievement of the tribal students effectively reduces their chances of joining institutions of higher education, in which the representation of tribal students is strikingly low, as shown in the following section.

Representation in higher education

The STs are grossly under-represented in higher education, and the proportion of their enrolment declines with the higher levels of education. Figures available for the year 2002–2003 show that out of 122.4 million children enrolled in primary classes (I–V), 9.67% (11.8

Table 7.3 Percentage of SC, ST and other students in different achievement levels in high school examinations in Orissa (India)

Year	2003			2004			2005		
Group	SC	ST	Others	SC	ST	Others	SC	ST	Others
No. of students	30,290	26,214	183,055	33,924	30,604	199,169	37,415	34,378	210,231
First division (60+)	4.94%	3.34%	12.91%	5.16%	3.41%	13.19%	5.39%	3.65%	13.85%
Second division (45–60)	13.82%	12.53%	19.88%	14.54%	13.79%	20.62%	16.28%	15.83%	22.18%
Third division (30–45)	19.70%	20.43%	21.05%	21.89%	23.02%	20.41%	23.17%	24.38%	23.42%
Fail (<30)	61.54%	63.69%	46.15%	58.40%	59.77%	43.77%	55.15%	56.13%	40.54%

Source: Board of Secondary Education, Orissa

million) were STs and 17.70% (21.7 million) were SCs, proportionate to the size of their respective populations. However, the corresponding enrolment in classes IX–XII drops to 5.37% for the STs (1.78 million) and 13.25% (4.40 million) for the SCs out of the national total of 33.20 million. In higher and technical education, the representation of the STs is dismally low, despite programs that reserve places for students belonging to the STs or SCs. Table 7.4 gives the figures for enrolment in higher and technical education in the years 2000–2001 and 2001–2002. The proportions of STs in higher and technical education over the two-year period have varied from 2.97 to 4.64%, far below their 8.2% share of the population.

The previous discussion shows large-scale educational failure and nonattainment, as well as lower literacy rates, among the tribals in India. These conditions are evidently related to the neglect of the tribal mother tongues in the areas of education and literacy instruction. The exclusion of tribal mother tongues from education limits the chances of tribal children to succeed in academics and, consequently, limits their freedom and restricts their ability to influence the direction of their lives. Saikia and Mohanty (2004) compared the language and mathematics achievement of Class IV Bodo tribal children enrolled in Bodo mother tongue-medium schools (BB), Bodo tribal children enrolled in Assamese-medium schools (BA) and Assamese children enrolled in Assamese-medium schools (AA). The three groups were matched for socioeconomic status, quality of schools and the ecological conditions of their villages. Group BB (Bodo children in Bodo-medium schools) performed significantly better than BA group (Bodo children in Assamese-medium schools) on all the measures. There was no difference between BB and AA children in the language measures, but the latter group performed better on two of the three mathematics measures. This study shows the educational benefits of the use of mother tongue tribal languages in an official classroom setting.

Educational failure and the consequent lack of access to higher education limit the upward socioeconomic mobility of tribal groups in India. As the *Handbook of Poverty in India* (Radhakrishna & Ray, 2005) observes, 'Due to low educational and skill levels, majority of tribal workers are involved in low quality of employment such as agricultural and non-agricultural casual wage laborer' (23) and 'proportion of regular workers is abysmally low at merely 4 per cent among the STs' (24). According to a recent report of the Planning Commission Task Group on Development of SCs and STs (Government of India, 2004), the percentage of marginal workers who find work only for less than six months a year is

Table 7.4 Enrolment in higher and technical education

Year	Higher education				Technical education			
	All categories	SC	ST		All categories	SC	ST	
2000–2001	9.937 million	769,000 (9.69%)	236,000 (2.97%)		1.665 million	184,000 (11.05%)	68,000 (4.08%)	
2001–2002	7.139 million	940,000 (13.16%)	306,000 (4.28%)		1.894 million	191,000 (10.08%)	88,000 (4.64%)	

Source: Planning Commission (2004)

31.1% for the STs, compared to 27.0% for the SCs and 19.8% for others, and most STs are engaged in work which does not require formal education or training base skills. The failure of educational programs, at least partly due to the systematic exclusion of mother tongues, is clearly reflected in the capability deprivation, economic underdevelopment and general poverty of the tribals in India, which evidently is a complex multi-dimensional phenomenon and process. For the tribals, as well as for other groups, '(P)overty indicates multiple deprivation, caused by a host of economic, social, political, and institutional factors. It mainly connotes low income, inadequate consumption, low human capability in terms of skill, education, health and nutrition, and insecurity' (Radhakrishna & Ray, 2005: 26). Thus, incapability and 'unfreedom' due to educational failure and illiteracy constitute integral aspects of the complex and multidimensional processes of capability deprivation and poverty. I have tried to show how the nonaccommodation and exclusion of language(s) in education contributes to these processes by limiting access to resources and denying equality of opportunity. Language(s) that people speak or do not speak can and do contribute directly to poverty in many other contexts of discrimination and the perpetuation of inequality by the deprivations of linguistic human rights, democratic participation, identity, self-efficacy and pride. In the case of the tribals in India, linguistic discrimination forms a core of their capability deprivation through educational neglect and in many other complex ways, all of which contribute to their poverty in a vicious circle. Their languages are weakened by marginalization and exclusion from education, official use and other instrumentally significant domains, and then castigated as inadequate forms of language to justify further exclusion. The next section shows the extent of poverty among the tribals in India by citing some broad indicators.

Poverty among the Tribals in India

An estimation of the Head Count Ratio of poverty (Planning Commission, 2001) shows that 26% of the population of India is below the poverty line. The proportion of population below the poverty line is highest for the STs (44%) compared to the SCs (36%) and others (16%). The decline in the percentage of poor (below the poverty line) between 1993 and 1994 and 1999–2000 was 7% among the STs as against 12% among the SCs and 9% among other categories (Radhakrishna & Ray, 2005). In terms of monthly per capita consumption figures, approximately 50% of the ST households in rural areas belong to the consumption class of less than 340 Indian Rupees (approximately $7.80). The corresponding figures for the SCs, other backward castes (OBC) and others are 40%, 30% and 17%, respectively (Radhakrishna & Ray, 2005). It may be noted that the national estimates of poverty among the STs include those in the North Eastern states, which have a high concentration of ST groups and where the incidence of poverty is low (less than 20%). Thus, the picture of economic development is even more dismal for the STs outside the North Eastern States in India.

The tribal communities suffer from poor economic development and deprivation and, in terms of various indicators of poverty, they are at the bottom in comparison even to other disadvantaged groups. 'The deprivation and exclusion that the tribal communities face are multidimensional and the factors that perpetuate deprivation are intrinsically interlinked and reinforce exclusion' (Radhakrishna & Ray, 2005: 21). Health, nutrition and other indices of human development reflect the same picture of deprivation for the tribals. The trends of poverty and deprivation among STs in India are summed up in the following words:

> Macro-level data substantiates the fact that tribals in the country constitute the poorest category not merely in economic terms but in all aspects of human development. They are deprived of access to quality education and health care; they are resource poor and their traditional sources of livelihood are dwindling; labor market discrimination and lower skills only afford them occupations with low productivity and limited scope for diversification. Therefore, the slow pace of development among the tribals in India, needs to be contextualized in the vicious cycle of deprivation and poverty. This not only impedes their engagement with mainstream development, it also keeps their entitlements and capabilities low. (Radhakrisna & Ray, 2005: 29)

The Voiceless Minority and the Silent Elites: The *English* Lollipop in Indian Education

Any discussion of how inequality is perpetuated through discrimination against the languages of the disadvantaged in India is incomplete without consideration of the role played by the English language and English-medium schooling in Indian education. The powerful presence of English as an international 'killer language' (Skutnabb-Kangas, 2000) has obliterated the traditional complementary relationship between languages and the strong maintenance norms. It has triggered a hierarchical competitive relationship in which tribal and minority languages are pushed to be marginalized, rendering the minorities and the disadvantaged voiceless. In postcolonial India, 'English is the language of power, used as an indication of greater control over outcomes of social activities' (Mohanty, in press) and, despite evidences to the contrary, the myth of English-medium superiority makes it the most sought-after medium of schooling, giving rise to a new basis of socioeconomic stratification of the society (see Mohanty, in press). Education in English is considered to be preferable to the poor quality public education given in the major regional languages. Thus, the demand for English-medium schools has increased at an alarming rate. In a foreword to the book based on the People of India project (Singh, 2002), noted sociologist the late Professor M.N. Srinivas mentions the growing demand for English-medium schools and the changing content of the regional identities. He refers to the demand for English-medium schools in rural Karnataka and mentions that 72 Members of the State Legislative Assembly (MLAs) signed a letter to the Chief Minister of Karnataka requesting permission to open English-medium schools in rural areas.[7] English-medium education has now emerged as the single most important predictor of socioeconomic mobility. While failure in English as a major language subject in school curricula throughout the country accounts for over 50% of the failures in high school examinations of the regional majority language medium schools, the privileged English-knowing elites are placed in a position of distinct advantage; their children, with a positive attitude towards learning English, linguistic support in the home environment and more expensive, better quality English-medium schooling, outperform the new aspirants – the first generation of English learners from the lower social strata. In face of the hegemonic status of English and the unequal power relationship between languages, while the minority, minor and tribal language speakers are rendered voiceless, the English educated elites have remained silent beneficiaries of the economic, social and political advantage that accrues to them from the pre-eminence of English in Indian multilingualism. Despite evidences to the contrary (Mohanty, 2003, 2004, in press), the myth of English-medium superiority has thrived, ironically widening the social gap in India. With the mounting pressure on English-medium schools, the quality of the regional language medium government schools has become indifferent. While the low cost government-supported regional language MI schools have catered to the educational needs of the poor and the disadvantaged (mostly the speakers of minority and nonstandard languages), the majority language speakers remain satisfied with poor quality, low cost private English-medium schools. The English-knowing elites of the privileged class, who have the capacity to be critical, quietly enjoy the pre-eminence of English in the society and the benefits that accrue to them and their children educated in high cost private English-medium schools.[8] While English-medium schools continue to attract the nation, there is little serious concern for the general public education. Policy rhetoric multiplies with little practical impact. Despite the assurances given in the Indian Constitution, research evidences, political statements and academic exercises such as the formulations in the National Curricular Framework (2005) commending mother tongue education, the other tongue English thrives in the complex dynamics of the postcolonial India which, like most other former British Colonies, finds in English an easy escape from balancing the demands for recognition from multiple native languages.

In this process of domination by English and marginalization of mother tongues, the marginalized do not speak because they cannot, and the privileged do not speak because they silently enjoy the benefits of the advantages they have acquired due to the pre-eminence of English. Several experiments seeking to bring mother tongues into children's early education, such as the bilingual transfer model of the CIIL (Mohanty, 1989) and the creation of tribal language textbooks[9] under the District Primary Education Programs (DPEP), have been attempted and abandoned due to apathy on the part of the elites and policy-makers who matter. The tribal language groups continue to face a language barrier that limits their access to and success in schools, as well as their social and economic opportunities.

Concluding Observations

When language becomes the basis of power, control and discrimination, socioeconomic inequality is perpetuated; the language(s) that people speak or do not speak determines their access to resources. Education is a critical factor in this relationship between language and power. The exclusion and nonaccommodation of languages in education denies equality of opportunity to learn, violates linguistic human rights, leads to the loss of linguistic diversity and triggers a vicious cycle of disadvantage perpetuating inequality, capacity deprivation and poverty. Education provided only in English and other dominant languages leads to a great inequality of educational opportunities between the advantaged speakers of the 'correct' and culturally promoted languages and the strongly handicapped speakers of the 'incorrect' and stigmatized languages. '(E)ducational flexibility and adaptability are vital to the educational welfare of most low income and minority students, although many educational regulations – and limited resources – makes this task daunting', says Professor John Baugh (2000). But this is much more than a matter of regulations and resources: it is the respect for diversity – and the will to translate that respect into action – that really matters.

Notes

1. The indigenous or the aboriginal communities in India are officially called 'tribes' (*ādivāsi*) and are listed as 'scheduled tribes', which are identified on the basis of 'distinct culture and language', 'geographical isolation', 'primitive traits', 'economic backwardness' and 'limited contact with the outgroups' and also, sometimes, on political considerations. Anthropological Survey of India, in its People of India project, has identified 635 tribal communities of which 573 are so far officially notified as scheduled tribes. In this article, the term 'tribe' (rather than 'indigenous peoples') is used in its formal/official sense.
2. The term 'push out' (Mohanty, 2000; Skutnabb-Kangas, 2000) is more appropriate as it captures the essence of the phenomenon.
3. This status was initially given to English for a period of 15 years in the Indian Constitution. But it has now been extended for an indefinite period.
4. There are 25 scripts used for writing Indian languages. Eleven major scripts are used to write the main scheduled languages and 13 minor scripts are used for writing some minor and tribal linguistic communities. Besides, the Roman script has been adopted by some languages in recent years.
5. The Santals have developed a script of their own – *Ol Chiki* – invented by the Guru Gomke (the 'Great Teacher') Pandit Raghunath Murmu. This script has become a rallying point for the identity of Santal tribals. There are other tribal communities where sporadic and unco-ordinated efforts are made to evolve language specific writing systems.
6. In the high school examinations, students scoring above 60% are graded as first division, 45–59% as second division, and 30–44% as third division. Those securing less than 30% are graded as failed.
7. There was a ban on opening English-medium schools in the state of Karnataka since the early 1980s.
8. English-medium schools are market driven and with the rising demand the cost of such schooling has spiraled. As a result, while some parents pay almost nothing for education in government run regional language medium schools, others pay up to Rs.15,000 ($330) per month for better quality schools for the privileged class. In some elitist residential English-medium schools, parents pay around $1000 (Rs.40,000 to Rs.50,000) per month.
9. I was involved in a project of the DPEP, Orissa for preparation of textbooks in six tribal languages. The books were prepared with great effort and enthusiasm by the teachers from the tribal communities, but were never taken to the classrooms because of bureaucratic apathy and lack of conviction among the policy-makers. Jhingran (2005) also mentions several sporadic and failed attempts for mother tongue education for the tribal and other minorities.

References

Dreze, J. and Sen, A. (2002) *India: Development and Participation*. New Delhi: Oxford University Press.

Gupta, M.K. (1999) Languages and media of instruction in schools. In *Sixth All India Educational Survey: Main Report*. New Delhi: NCERT.

Jhingran, D. (2005) *Language Disadvantage: The Learning Challenge in Primary Education*. New Delhi: APH Publishing.

Karlekar, M. (2004) *Paradigms of Learning: The Total Literacy Campaign in India*. New Delhi: Sage.

Kurien, J. (2004, 30 April) The English juggernaut: Regional medium schools in crisis. *The Times of India*, New Delhi.

Ministry of Human Resource Development (Department of Secondary and Higher Education) (2004) *Selected Educational Statistics, 2002–2003*. New Delhi: Government of India.

Mohanty, A.K. (1989) Psychological consequences of mother tongue maintenance and the language of literacy for linguistic minorities in India. *Psychology and Developing Societies* 2 (1), 31–51.

Mohanty, A.K. (1994a) *Bilingualism in a Multilingual Society: Psychosocial and Pedagogical Implications*. Mysore: Central Institute of Indian Languages.

Mohanty, A.K. (1994b) Bilingualism in a multilingual society: Implications for cultural integration and education. Keynote address in the area of Psychology and Language. Proceedings of the 23rd International Congress of Applied Psychology, Madrid, Spain, 17–22 July.

Mohanty, A.K. (2000) Perpetuating inequality: The disadvantage of language, minority mother tongues and related issues. In A.K. Mohanty and G. Misra (eds) *Psychology of Poverty and Disadvantage*. New Delhi: Concept.

Mohanty, A.K. (2003) Multilingualism and multiculturalism: The context of psycholinguistic research in India. In U. Vindhya (ed.) *Psychology in India: Intersecting Crossroads*. New Delhi: Concept.

Mohanty, A.K. (2004) Multilingualism of the unequals: The 'killer language' and anti-predatory strategies of minority mother tongues. Keynote address at the International Conference on Multilingualism, Southern African Applied Linguistics Association, University of the North, South Africa, 13–15 July.

Mohanty, A.K. (2005) Review of M. Karlekar (ed.) *Paradigms of Learning: The Total Literacy Campaign in India* (New Delhi, Sage, 2004). *Contemporary Education Dialogue* 2 (2), 249–252.

Mohanty, A.K., Panda, S. and Mishra, B. (1999) Language socialization in a multilingual society. In T.S. Saraswathi (ed.) *Culture, Socialization and Human Development*. New Delhi: Sage.

Mohanty, A.K. and Perregaux, C. (1997) Language acquisition and bilingualism. In J.W. Berry, P.R. Dasen and T.S. Saraswathi (eds) *Handbook of Cross-cultural Psychology: Vol. 2. Basic Processes and Human Development* (2nd edn, pp. 217–253). Needham Heights, MA: Allyn & Bacon.

NCERT (1990) *Fifth All India Educational Survey*. New Delhi: National Council of Educational Research and Training.

NCERT (1999) *Sixth All India Educational Survey*. New Delhi: National Council of Educational Research and Training.

NCERT (2005) *National Curricular Framework 2005*. New Delhi: NCERT.

Planning Commission (2004) *Report of the Task Group on Development of Scheduled Castes and Scheduled Tribes on Selected Agenda Items of the National Common Minimum Program.* New Delhi: Government of India.

Robeyns, I. (2006) How can the capability approach be used to serve marginal communities? Paper presented in the International Conference on Culture Matters: Understanding Development from the Perspectives of Marginal Communities, Deshkal Society, New Delhi, 13–15 October.

Saikia, J. and Mohanty, A.K. (2004) The role of mother tongue medium instruction in promoting educational achievement: A study of grade IV Bodo children in Assam (India). Unpublished paper, Zakir Husain Centre for Educational Studies, JNU, New Delhi.

Sen, A. (1982) *Poverty and Famines: An Essay on Entitlement and Deprivation.* Oxford: Clarendon Press.

Sen, A. (1985) *Commodities and Capabilities,* Amsterdam: North-Holland.

Singh, A., Jain, V.K., Gautam, S.K.S. and Kumar, S. (2004) *Learning Achievement of Students at the End of Class V.* New Delhi: NCERT.

Singh, K.S. (2002) *People of India.* New Delhi: Oxford University Press.

Skutnabb-Kangas, T. (1995) Review of *Bilingualism in a Multilingual Society: Psychosocial and Pedagogical Implications,* Ajit K. Mohanty. *TESOL Quarterly* 29 (4), 775–780.

Skutnabb-Kangas, T. (2000) *Linguistic Genocide in Education or Worldwide Diversity and Human Rights?* Mahwah, NJ: Lawrence Erlbaum.

Tomaševski, K. (2004) *Economic, Social and Cultural Rights: The Right to Education.* Report submitted by the Special Rapporteur Katarina Tomaševski. Economic and Social Council, Commission on Human Rights.

UNPFII (2005) *Indigenous Children's Education and Indigenous Languages.* Expert paper written for the United Nations Permanent Forum on Indigenous Issues.

Part 3

Language and Poverty:
A Cross-disciplinary Perspective

Chapter 8

Biodiversity, Linguistic Diversity and Poverty: Some Global Patterns and Missing Links

SUZANNE ROMAINE

Introduction

Many of the world's poorest people live in areas richest in both biodiversity and linguistic diversity. Nettle and Romaine (2000: ix), for instance, observe that the greatest linguistic diversity is found in some of the ecosystems richest in biodiversity inhabited by indigenous peoples, who represent around 4% of the world's population, but speak at least 60% of its 6000 or more languages. Meanwhile, research on biodiversity has established connections between some of the hottest 'hotspots' and poverty (Beck, 2003). Although there is considerable overlap between development needs and conservation priorities, and it is increasingly being recognized that indigenous peoples are critical partners in determining strategies for sustainable ecosystem management, the preservation of biodiversity and linguistic diversity are all too often cast as obstacles to development.

This results from the global predominance of Western scientific modes of knowledge and the discourses articulating those modes, which have framed the issues of linguistic diversity, biodiversity and poverty as unrelated to one another at the same time as they have dictated development strategies that are the source of hegemonic monocultures. As Vandana Shiva (1993: 7) observes, monocultures first inhabit the mind and are then transferred to the ground. They generate models of production that not only destroy diversity, but also at the same time legitimize the destruction as progress, growth, modernization and improvement.

The primary concern of this chapter will be to identify some global patterns of linguistic diversity, biodiversity and poverty. These are the missing links alluded to in my subtitle. I will argue that the measures most likely to preserve small languages are the very ones that will help increase their speakers' standard of living in a long-term, sustainable way. This entails rejecting prevailing models of development, such as those proposed by Jeffrey Sachs, an influential development economist, director of the United Nations Millennium Project, and author of *The End of Poverty* (2005a). Instead of Sachs's plan for ending poverty, I propose a new agenda based on the triple goals of promoting rural development, sustainability and cultural-linguistic pluralism.

Sachs's neglect of language is not only shortsighted; much of what he says about poverty, its origins and how it is best remedied is also misguided. Here we come to a critical role of language, namely its power to shape discursive practices in such a way as to highlight some dimensions of complex problems while downplaying or even hiding others. Language is never just a neutral instrument for conveying 'objective' thoughts or facts, but instead offers different points of view and ways of constructing social reality. Thus, the flip-side of the problem referred to as the 'feminization of poverty' is the masculinization of wealth (Goldin, 1990). Likewise, McLuhan (1964) said that affluence creates poverty: by this he meant that affluence is the ground that makes the figure of poverty noticeable. In a similar vein, G.K. Chesterton (1910: Chapter VII, l.3) noted nearly a century ago that the difficulty is not the problem of poverty, but the problem of wealth.

Whoever controls the language of poverty controls the agenda on poverty, how it is conceptualized and how it is to be remedied. Much of the debate on poverty has taken place within the field of development economics, a discipline that evolved largely in English-speaking universities. The critical actors and agencies are often international financial institutions such as the World Bank and the International Monetary Fund, transnational organizations such as the United Nations, and increasingly, multinational corporations. When poverty is problematized in economic terms, as low income of individuals or low gross national product (GNP) of countries, it seems 'natural' to look for both causes and solutions in economics. The perspective thus dictates the terms of the solution. The poor of the world are caught in a poverty trap: they lack the money to invest in infrastructure, education and health care. Lack of income then becomes the cause of poverty and so the solution to poverty is economic growth. Poor people need jobs in order to make money and create new products so that they have more income to buy more products. Note also that when the poor and poverty are problematized in terms of what they lack, we are operating within a deficit theory.

Poverty does not exist independently of the discourses that produce it. This does not mean there are no poor people, but simply that economic poverty is only one form of poverty. Such is the power exercised by a dominant discourse that it is hard to find anyone who disagrees with an agenda dedicated to economic growth and modernization. As Williams (1983: 145) notes, one of the key features of hegemony is 'a particular way of seeing the world and human nature and its relationships'. Moreover, the continuation of hegemony depends on its acceptance as 'normal reality' or 'commonsense'. The hegemony of a purely economic account of poverty has been little challenged.

A similar hegemony operates with respect to linguistic diversity. Diversity has been problematized while monolingualism or linguistic uniformity is normalized. Just as development and modernization have been taken to be synonymous with the introduction of Western science, technology and languages, it is still widely believed that indigenous languages are not suited for modern purposes. Widdowson (2005: 18n), for instance, claims that making Inuktitut the official language of the newly created territory of Nunavut 'creates tremendous problems because it is a pre-literate language not suited for use in complex legal and bureaucratic procedures'. The modernization and instrumentalization of a variety of languages, such as Indonesian, Welsh and Basque, for use in such official domains contradicts this claim.

Mapping Poverty, Biodiversity and Linguistic Diversity

Mapping has become an increasingly important tool for understanding a range of social, economic, linguistic and environmental problems. Sachs (2005a) relies heavily on data collected for individual countries or regions by economists at the World Bank, displayed in the form of maps with measures such as per capita income and GNP. Such maps yield a so-called 'geography of poverty'. Figure 8.1 reveals that sub-Saharan Africa, the Andean and Central American highlands, and landlocked nations of central Asia show high concentrations of poverty defined in economic terms, in these cases per capita income of lower than $2000. According to the World Bank, the source of these statistics, per capita production in Africa declined in the last three decades of the 20th century.

There are many ways in which people may be poor or rich. Geography reveals as much as it hides and income is only one measure. The situation of indigenous and tribal peoples is often not reflected in statistics or is hidden by national averages. Development theories often assume that people and places are poor because they lack resources. Yet, when we look at the geographic distribution of biodiversity, we see that some of the world's least developed countries are located in the areas with the

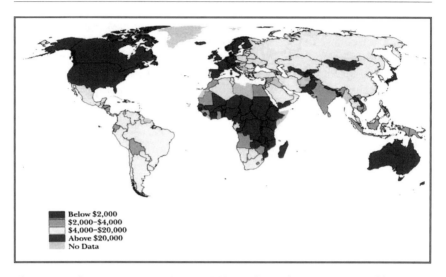

Figure 8.1 Income per capita in 2002, adjusted in current US$ 'Maps' copyright © 2005 by Jeffrey D. Sachs, *Source*: Data from World Bank (2004), from THE END OF POVERTY by Jeffrey D. Sachs. Used by permission of The Penguin Press, a Division of Penguin Group (USA) Inc.

most plant and animal species. The Andean highlands of Peru, for instance, are arguably the region with the richest gene pool for potatoes, including about 3000 varieties. In another hot spot, Papua New Guinea, there is wide genetic diversity in sweet potatoes, with possibly 5000 varieties. These natural resources comprise what the World Resources Institute (2005) calls 'the wealth of the poor'.

Figure 8.2 shows selected terrestrial hotspots plotted in relation to the United Nations' Human Development Index (HDI), a comparative measure of poverty (i.e. GNP per capita), literacy (i.e. adult literacy rate), education (i.e. combined primary, secondary and tertiary enrollment), life expectancy and other factors. In 2005, HDI showed improvement for countries around the world with two major exceptions: the post-Soviet states and sub-Saharan Africa, both of which declined. Thirty of the bottom 32 countries are in Africa,[1] and all of the bottom 10 countries are African (i.e. Mozambique, Burundi, Ethiopia, Central African Republic, Guinea Bissau, Chad, Mali, Burkina Faso, Sierra Leone, Niger).

Figure 8.3 shows that linguistic diversity (in terms of number of languages) is concentrated through the tropics and tails off towards the poles, just like biodiversity (Nettle & Romaine, 2000: 43).

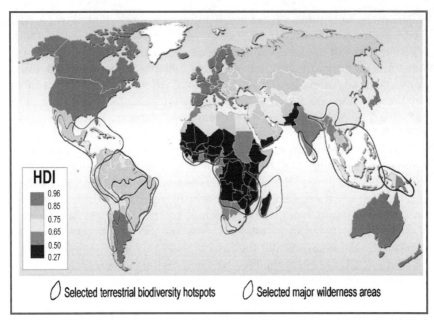

Figure 8.2 Global development and biodiversity. [*Source*: Hugo Ahlenius (2004)]

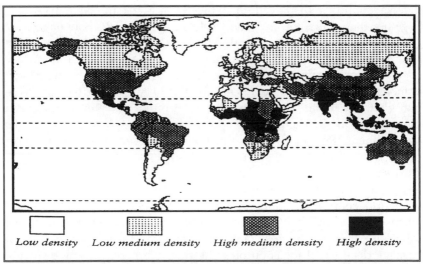

Figure 8.3 Geographic distribution of languages of the world (Nettle & Romaine, 2000: 33, Figure 2.1, page 33, adapted from Daniel Nettle, *Journal of Anthropological Archaeology* 17 (1998): 354–74. With permission from Elsevier)

The maps in Figures 8.1, 8.2 and 8.3 illustrate a substantial overlap in the distribution of languages, species and the rural poor. Satisfactory understanding of the links can only be as good as the available data, and there are many difficulties in obtaining reliable statistics in all three domains. In addition, there is the problem of what to measure. By almost any measure, however, the African continent (and sub-Saharan Africa in particular) is high in linguistic diversity and economic underdevelopment, so I will examine this area in more detail. Looking first at the issue of linguistic diversity in terms of number of languages, Africa has 2092 languages or about 30.3% of the world's languages (Gordon, 2005). Another way to look at the geographic distribution is to use Greenberg's index based on the probability that any two people within a country selected at random would have different mother tongues. The highest possible value, 1, indicates total diversity (i.e. no two people have the same mother tongue), while the lowest possible value, 0, indicates no diversity at all (i.e. everyone has the same mother tongue).[2]

If we consider the 10 countries with the highest index, six are African: Tanzania, Central African Republic, Chad, Democratic Republic of Congo, Cameroon and Mozambique.[3] If we extend our consideration to the top 20 countries with the highest diversity, the only other non-African country in the list is East Timor. Thus, 15 of the 20 most linguistically diverse countries displayed in Table 8.1 are in sub-Saharan Africa. Together they contain 47% of the world's estimated 6912 languages.

Many conclusions might be drawn from such statistics. Although it has been widely believed that linguistic uniformity is a necessary condition for economic development, this has not been convincingly demonstrated.[4] What matters is not the fact of linguistic diversity itself, but whether it is taken into account. Most often, it is simply not taken into account at all. There can be no true development without linguistic development (Romaine, 1990). Yet, linguistic diversity receives almost no mention and no consideration in what is arguably the largest, most comprehensive and ambitious development initiative launched at the United Nations Millennium Summit in 2000. There, 147 nations of the world committed themselves to a global effort to reduce poverty when they adopted eight broad Millennium Development Goals (MDGs). Although the goals are inter-related and need to be seen as a package deal, I will focus on only the first two here: namely, reducing poverty and achieving universal primary education (UNDP, 2005b). I examine in particular Sachs's plans for reducing poverty, which were the centerpiece of the program.

Table 8.1 Twenty most linguistically diverse countries

Country	Greenberg's index	No. of languages
Papua New Guinea	0.990	820
Vanuatu	0.972	115
Solomon Islands	0.965	70
Tanzania	0.965	127
Central African Republic	0.960	79
Chad	0.950	133
Democratic Republic of Congo	0.948	216
Cameroon	0.942	280
India	0.930	415
Mozambique	0.929	43
Uganda	0.928	46
Gabon	0.919	41
Côte d'Ivoire	0.917	92
Liberia	0.912	31
Benin	0.901	55
Kenya	0.901	64
East Timor	0.897	19
Togo	0.897	42
Mali	0.876	54
Nigeria	0.870	516
Total $n = 20$	Average = 0.928	Total $n = 3258$

Note: Statistics for Greenberg's index and number of languages are from Table 6 of *The Ethnologue* (Gordon, 2005). Non-African countries are in italics. Countries in bottom 30 according to HDI are capitalized (from UNDP, 2005a)

MDGs and Sachs' Plan for Reducing Poverty

Sachs proposes to halve the rate of extreme poverty by 2015 by means of large external transfers of capital from developed nations to the rural poor in order to create and/or stimulate the growth of Western-style free-market economies. More specifically, the plan involves doubling the contribution of affluent nations to about 0.5% of the GNP of the world's rich countries ($160 billion a year), eventually reaching a target of 0.7% by 2015. According to Sachs's calculations, one out of six people still get by on $1 a day or less; around 70% are women. If aid targets are met, this number would be halved.

I am sympathetic to Sachs' call for more aid from donor countries. Total US international aid, for example, is currently around 0.21% of GNP, among the lowest ratios of all donor nations. Likewise, I welcome the recent decision on 25 September 2005 by the World Bank and International Monetary Fund to grant 100% debt relief to as many as 38 countries, most of them in sub-Saharan Africa. It will be an important step toward meeting the targets of the eighth MDG. Nevertheless, there is no such thing as a free lunch. In return for aid and debt relief, the agenda will focus on getting agreement on trade.

To evaluate Sachs's plan, one must again ask what the flip-side of giving is. It is taking, and this is conspicuous by its absence. Here I return to my earlier remarks about the need to consider poverty as a social construct of the discourse that creates it and the interests of those whose voices and interests define it. As Shiva (1993: 90) points out, you cannot protect your house against theft by begging the thief to give back a small share of the loot. You need to prevent the thief from taking the loot in the first place.

Sachs does not address the fact that the consumption of four fifths of the world's resources by one fifth of its population and the production methods of the powerful continue to undermine the livelihoods of the poor, who have no access to assets or means of production other than the resources of local ecosystems. Instead, Sachs dismisses the idea that globalization is making the rich richer and the poor poorer by citing high levels of economic growth in India and China. The poorest of the poor in sub-Saharan Africa are not held back by globalization, according to Sachs (2005b: 60); they are largely 'bypassed' by it. Likewise, he sidesteps the question of whether poverty is the result rather than the cause of exploitation of the poor by the rich by saying that 'exploitation is the result of poverty' (which leaves impoverished countries vulnerable to abuse). Instead, Sachs claims that poverty is generally the result of 'low productivity per worker'. In response to the question of whether higher incomes in poor countries will mean lower incomes in rich countries, Sachs again presents a rosy scenario in which economic development is viewed as a 'positive-sum process'. He maintains that the world as a whole has achieved a massive increase in economic output rather than a shift in economic output to one region at the expense of another.

Sachs (2005b: 60) also claims that in Asia the 'Green Revolution of the 1960s and 1970s introduced high-yield grains, irrigation, and fertilizers, which ended the cycle of famine, disease and despair. It also freed a significant proportion of the labor force to seek manufacturing jobs in the cities'. Urbanization is good for economic growth because as people become more urbanized, they tend to have fewer children. In a nutshell, then, abandoning traditional farming practices in favor of new biotechnology provides higher yields. Farmers get more income and fewer farmers are needed to grow more food, freeing surplus farmers to move to cities, where they have fewer children. A decrease in population means less pressure on food supplies. Moreover, Sachs insists that overall global economic growth is compatible with sustainable management of ecosystems.

If something sounds too good to be true, it probably is. The terms of the debate and the structure of the argument warrant careful scrutiny. These claims rest on a dubious inversion of cause and effect relations between poverty and economic development on the one hand, and between poverty and environmental destruction on the other. The thrust of this model is to blame the poor for their lack of productivity and to imply that developing countries need to boost their productivity to catch up with the living standards of developed countries. The reality is quite different for at least two reasons.

Firstly, it is misleading to characterize as 'unproductive' the many rural communities of the world that are largely self-sufficient in terms of food production. They may be poor in economic terms, but they do not lack the means to support themselves. A people's resource base consists of the physical geography where they live, its ecology, its plant and animal species and other environmental factors. Sachs claims that poverty is what causes environmental destruction. Map-makers working with the Center for the Support of Native Lands, in Arlington, VA, and the National Geographic Society, in Washington, DC, superimposed a map of indigenous territories on another showing forest cover and marine ecosystems in Nicaragua. The resultant map reveals a strong correlation between indigenous presence and the survival of natural ecosystems. This led Nietschmann (1992: 3) to propose what has been called the 'Rule of Indigenous Environments': where there are indigenous peoples with a homeland, there are still biologically rich environments. Where people have lost their traditional authority over their land or have been forced from it, large-scale transformations of the environment have occurred, accompanied by cultural and linguistic decimation. Flight to the cities, a movement Sachs favors, fuels language shift.

Secondly, economic development of the type that propelled Western countries to their present high standards of living is not an attainable goal for poor countries. There are ecological limits to growth that technofixes (i.e. technology-driven solutions) cannot transcend. Collapse seems to be an almost inevitable stage in the evolution of human societies, as Diamond (2005) has shown in his comparative study of past civilizations that undermined their ecosystems through unsustainable practices causing environmental damage.

The raw materials and energy are simply not available for the majority of people in China, India and elsewhere to achieve Western standards of living and consumption. According to the World Bank, India would have to boost energy production by a factor of 35 and Africa by a factor of 38 to match US levels. It is implausible that the entire world can consume energy at the rate of the industrial nations, who have largely stripped the world of readily available cheap energy sources. Cheap oil is the chief energy resource fueling globalization. Even if the earth were full of oil, all of which was recoverable, the supply would last only 342 years at the rate of 7.04% per annum consumption (Ehrenfeld, 2003: 108). Wackernagel and Rees (1996) estimate that seven to nine hectares of productive land are required to sustain the consumer lifestyle of the average North American. At this rate, five earth-like planets would be required to support the entire human population at North American material standards.

Moreover, Sachs totally ignores the damage done by the large ecological footprint of the so-called Green Revolution, which was designed not to raise the income of the rural poor, but to increase the food supply. Thus, it should not be surprising that hunger and poverty have not been eradicated. Although India has been self-sufficient in food for at least 15 years and its granaries are full, up to one fifth of the population is malnourished because they cannot afford to buy the food they need (Polak, 2005: 86). Increasing agricultural productivity with modern methods involves relying on new so-called high yield varieties (HYV) of a few key crops that require large external inputs of water, fertilizer, herbicides and pesticides. The Green Revolution in Asia and India enlarged the land area requiring irrigation from around 100 million hectares in 1950 to around 270 million today. Yet, the world as a whole faces acute water shortages. Most of the countries poorest in water are also in sub-Saharan Africa.

Meanwhile, increased use of chemical rather than organic fertilizers has led to deteriorated soil quality, greater erosion and contamination of the water supply and of farmers themselves (Yapa, 1993: 261, 263). Twenty years of the Green Revolution have destroyed the fertility of the Punjab, once India's breadbasket. According to Shiva (1993), soils that had been maintained over centuries could have retained their fertility indefinitely if international experts and their Indian supporters had not erroneously believed that chemicals could replace the organic fertility of the soil.

The discourse of the Green Revolution relies on key terms such as 'miracle' or 'improved seeds' or 'high yield' which, as Shiva (1993: 71) observes, are not neutral; they are value-laden and contextualized within the corporate viewpoint. The notion of yield as a measurable output of some system must be precisely defined in order to be calculated meaningfully. A monocultural cropping system may produce a higher yield of one crop than a mixed field, but that does not necessarily mean that it is producing more food (see also Cook, 2004: n5).[5] Mayan peasants of Chiapas are characterized as 'unproductive' because they produce only two tons of corn per acre, even though their overall food output is 20 tons per acre (Shiva, 2000: 110). The alleged high productivity of homogeneous and uniform systems relies on artificial measures artificially maintained through public subsidies and through discursive practices that emphasize narrow, reductionist notions of productivity, output and yield.

When considered in the local cultural context, traditional farming methods relying on cultivation of a variety of crops are not only highly productive but sustainable as well. Multicropping produces not just food but animal fodder and organic matter. In sub-Saharan Africa, women cultivate as many as 120 different plants alongside cash crops (Shiva, 2000: 111). Modern 'plant improvement' is based on enhancing the yield of one crop or part of it at the expense of other locally useful plants that are declared 'weeds' and eradicated by herbicide. Moreover, diseases caused by intensive monocropping of genetically uniform varieties have been intensified by increasing dependence on the use of chemical pesticides that destroy the pests' natural enemies and at the same time create pesticide-resistant forms.

Surpluses of HYV are not really surpluses when the value of what is lost is factored in (Shiva, 2000: 126). The nutritional value of the multicrop system is sacrificed for the sake of producing a higher yield of one crop, as are the livelihoods of rural Indian women who make their living by mat-making and basket-weaving, when herbicides kill the wild reeds and grasses typically grown alongside rice. From the business perspective, however, use of chemicals is more efficient and economical than weeding by hand, which requires more labor and thus reduces profits. But this is only true when labor is scarce and costly. When labor is abundant, as in India, the displacement of labor is unproductive because it leads to unemployment, dispossession and poverty (Shiva, 1993: 141). Thus, the poor are not so much 'freed', as Sachs puts it, but forced into seeking wage labor in urban areas. In addition, because these so-called improved seed varieties cannot be saved and used for future planting due to their erratic and poor yield, farmers have to purchase seed from seed companies every year. Poor farmers lose out in favor of farmers with access to large areas of irrigated land and with money to buy the package, and literate enough to follow a complicated set of new techniques (Yapa, 1993: 269). Thousands of poor farmers in India have been pushed not just into debt but also even to suicide because they do not have the money to buy fertilizer, herbicides and pesticides.

One of the most serious consequences of agricultural modernization of this type has been the loss of genetic species diversity (Yapa, 1993: 267). Shiva (1993, 2000) has written extensively about how the so-called Green Revolution in agriculture, the White Revolution in dairying and the Blue Revolution in fisheries are based on the deliberate replacement of biological diversity with monocultures. An area once rich becomes poor, as do the people dependent on it. A varied natural system is inherently more stable than a monoculture. Now that the supposed benefits of the Green Revolution are being seen, at least in some quarters, as an ecological disaster, a new revolution, this time in the form of genetic engineering, is being heralded as the latest miracle for agriculture. Proponents claim that it will launch a new era of chemical-free agriculture; however, the main focus of its research and development is not directed toward creating fertilizer-free and herbicide-free varieties, but on herbicide-resistant crops. The introduction of herbicide-resistant hybrids leads not to reduced, but to increased use of herbicide, and poses other ecological risks that are poorly understood. Through genetic engineering, biodiversity is transformed from a renewable into a nonrenewable resource. Both seed and herbicide have to be purchased from the manufacturer of the new herbicide-resistant varieties (Shiva, 2000: 31). Seeds once freely available in the local resource base become a nonreproducible commodity that is patented and controlled by outside interests who profit from their sale.

In 1998, Monsanto, the largest producer of genetically modified (GM) seed and of one of the world's most widely used herbicides, sent an appeal to all African heads of state entitled 'Let the harvest begin', calling upon them to endorse GM crops. Delegates from all 20 African countries (with the exception of South Africa) to the Food and Agriculture

Organization (FAO) of the UN negotiations on the International Undertaking for Plant Genetic Resources provided this response to Monsanto:

> We strongly object that the image of the poor and hungry from our countries is being used by giant multinational corporations to push a technology that is neither safe, environmentally friendly nor economically beneficial to us. On the contrary, we think it will destroy the diversity, the local knowledge and the sustainable agricultural systems that our farmers have developed for millennia and that it will thus undermine our capacity to feed ourselves. (Let nature's harvest continue, June 1998, cited in The Five Year Freeze, 2002)

The terms *begin* and *continue* are a good example of competing rhetorical strategies that cast different perspectives on traditional versus modern farming. Monsanto's use of the term *begin* suggests that traditional farming has been unproductive, a nonstarter. There is a great deal of pressure on all World Trade Organization (WTO) members to allow the patenting of plant and animal genetic resources. But what is free about so-called 'free trade', Shiva (2000) asks, when only one company (Monsanto) controls 94% of all GM seeds planted anywhere in the world? As part of 'free trade', the industrialized nations of the north want to retain free access to the developing world's storehouse of genetic diversity. They continue to press for legal and political frameworks to make the developing countries pay for what they originally gave. In this way, life itself has become capitalism's last frontier as the conditions on which it depends – food, water, health and knowledge – have become commodities controlled by a handful of corporations (Shiva, 2000: 28).

Development intervention based on increasing agricultural productivity leads to further impoverishment by depriving people of the agricultural biodiversity that has provided the basis of economic life for two thirds of the world's population living in rural communities (Shiva, 2000: 19). Sachs's plan offers the disease as a cure: growth will solve the problems of poverty and the environmental crisis it has given rise to in the first place.

Development with Diversity: Reconciling Development, Poverty, Biodiversity and Linguistic Diversity

It is now time to return to linguistic diversity and the poor. The closer development comes to the poorest, most marginalized peoples in the world, the more likely it is that they will speak a different language from their neighbors (Robinson, 1996: 10). Yet few have asked the rural poor what their conceptions and understanding of development are (see, however, Gegeo, 1998; Peel, 1978). For this, it would of course be essential to conduct on the ground surveys in local languages before planning intervention projects. This is seldom done, despite growing calls for development to come from within communities and to be based on local indigenous knowledge so that it is responsive to self-perceived needs, is culturally relevant and is sustainable (Lertzman & Vredenburg, 2005). Sachs's plan proceeds in the sort of top-down planning mode character-istic of the colonial period, whereby colonizers aimed to make their colonies self-sufficient, with profits flowing to and political control maintained by the metropole.

The idea that economic development causes poverty is not new (Yapa, 1993, 2002). Ironically (and sadly), the persistent failure of this single-sector type of development over the last 50 years is precisely what prompts Sachs' ambitious scheme in the first place. More of the same economic determinism will exacerbate a worsening situation. The idea that development comes from elsewhere and is synonymous with economic growth continues relations of external dependency and under-development. It confers more power on outsiders who, in their guise as experts, consultants and financial backers, are needed to solve yet more problems created by their products. Economic planning and decision-making in poor countries will remain firmly controlled by external powers. Under these conditions, we will have little hope of achieving most of the MDGs, no matter how much money the rich countries contribute to the poor (Easterly, 2006; Polak, 2005: 86).

Consider the case of Cameroon, one of the most linguistically diverse and economically undeveloped African countries. In Ombessa, where most development intervention has addressed cash-crop farming, many overlapping agencies dispense sometimes conflicting advice to farmers about increasing production, fighting pests and other farming-related issues. In the face of low prices for cocoa, government policy has aimed to maintain and increase production in order to make up in quantity what is lost through falling prices, so that farmers will be ready to gain if prices recover and start to rise (Robinson, 1996: 109, 152). Many farmers are confused by the conflicting advice they receive and they question continuing cocoa cultivation.

Robinson (1995: 167) observes that among the Nugunu people, the idea of development, like French, the language in which is it most often offered and delivered, is seen as belonging to official spheres of activity. Like French, development is remote and not theirs. Villagers with little status rarely have any interaction with development agencies and their agents;

only 4% (mostly men) had contact personally, and only in organized meetings. Development thus reaches local male elites more readily than it reaches the ordinary villager. These same local elites also have the highest level of schooling and greatest competence in French (Robinson, 1996: 212–213). The educational system relies exclusively on French. The development encounter exacerbates a self-perpetuating cycle involving language, development and education. Just as children cannot benefit from schooling in a language they do not understand, the rural poor cannot benefit from development assistance rendered in a language they do not understand. Robinson (1996: 219–223) shows how language use is intimately connected with the exercise and distribution of power and control in meetings held by development agents and other officials. Where French is used, the agenda and discussion remains outside the control of villagers. One official told Robinson that communication problems in the village would be solved when 'everybody had learnt enough French' (Robinson, 1996: 221). Here again the cause of the problem is offered as the solution.

Use of the local language is inseparable from participatory develop-ment. By relying on French, development activities and resources reach those who are relatively well-educated and whose access to resources is already higher; all the while, they serve to still further marginalize the less advantaged. Despite the widespread recognition of lower levels of literacy and access to schooling in women, development does not address the fact that speaking a minority language compounds the marginalization of women (Robinson, 1996: 216). The third MDG is to promote gender equality and empower women, but it says nothing about the role of language.

The continuation of educational policies favoring international lan-guages at the expense of local ones is part of the development fiasco (Gegeo & Watson-Gegeo, 2002; Romaine, 1990). Although common sense dictates that a child's basic right to education cannot function equitably unless the child understands the language of instruction, fewer than 10% of the world's languages are used in education (Skutnabb-Kangas, 2000). This means that in most parts of the world, schooling is still virtually synonymous with learning a second language. The problem is particu-larly acute in Africa, where few African languages are used in government or education.

Mackey (1989: 5) estimates that some 90% of people in Africa 'have no knowledge of the official language of their country even though it is presumed to be the vehicle of communication between the government and its citizens'. Brenzinger (1998: 95) believes that fewer than 10% of

African languages are included in bilingual education programs, with the result that more than 1000 African languages receive no consideration in education. In this respect, Africa is not unlike the majority of countries in the world, which operate either *de facto* or *de jure* as monolingual states in recognizing only one (or sometimes two) language(s) for use. Bamgbose (2004) concludes that although there has been a great deal of improvement and a number of experimental programs and projects are underway, the use of African languages as the medium of instruction is generally limited to the lower classes of primary education. Only in a few countries (Tanzania, Somalia, Ethiopia, Eritrea, Madagascar and Nigeria) and in certain pilot projects is an African language used for the full duration of primary education (see also Mazrui & Mazrui [1998] for a critique of the World Bank's educational policy in Africa).

Learning through a language other than one's own presents a double burden. Not only must new knowledge be mastered, but another language must be mastered as well. It is for this reason that UNESCO's (2003) position paper on education in multilingual contexts reaffirmed the value of mother tongues as essential for initial instruction and literacy. The use of mother tongues should be extended to as late a stage in education as possible. At the same time, however, UNESCO stressed the importance of balancing the need for local languages in learning and access to global languages through education.

Conclusion

I have argued that dominant discourses are embedded within a network of systems of knowledge and power that influence how people think about development, poverty, biodiversity and linguistic diversity. We must not neglect the key word *human* in the discourse of development. In Sachs's approach, growth is defined only as growth of capital, which is seen as the solution to all problems. Human development is about more than increasing GDP and per capita income. GDP is not a measure of well-being (Daly, 2005). It is a narrow measure of overall economic activity that does not take into account the destruction of natural resources on which people's daily subsistence depends. Nor does it factor in inequalities in the distribution of wealth within and between countries due to power disparities in control of markets.

From the Solomon Islands, another part of the world with extremely high linguistic diversity, Gegeo (1998) comments that the kind of life that rural development based on modernization aims for is alienating and problematic for West Kwara'ae villagers on the island of Malaita. With its strong emphasis on Western values, knowledge, cash accumulation and consumption at the expense of social and cultural goals, villagers feel they have become more dependent on the global mode of production in the form of imported goods and foods rather than on their own skills and resources. As in Cameroon, there is no shortage of aid agencies and workers: Malaita's villages are littered with failed development projects of bygone years. Yet, despite the fact that villagers are self-sufficient and live primarily by subsistence agriculture, Malaita remains the least developed of the six major islands in the Solomons. For all its apparent attractions of modernity, villagers who migrate to town do not place high value on living a more European lifestyle. Dying in the capital, Honiara, or while in wage labor is seen as undignified.

It is time to ground development in a human rights-based approach as a matter of social justice. The United Nations Development Programme (2000: 17) stresses that the concept of human development is about 'the process of enlarging people's choices' and extends to elements such as 'participation, security, sustainability, guaranteed human rights – all needed for being creative and productive and for enjoying self respect, empowerment and sense of belonging to a community'. The UN Development Report (2005a: 4) states that the aim of multicultural policies is not to preserve tradition but to protect cultural liberty and expand people's choices in the way they live and identify themselves without penalizing them for their choices. At its Fourth Session in May 2005, the UN Permanent Forum on Indigenous Issues expressed concern that indigenous issues were often absent from the MDGs. They also endorsed a human rights-based approach, taking into account poverty indicators based on indigenous peoples' own perception. The members placed high priority on the right of indigenous peoples to sustainable development and called for relations between development agencies and indigenous peoples to be direct rather than mediated through institutions of the dominant society. They recommended promotion of multicultural policies, affirmative action and special measures for indigenous peoples, along with safeguards ensuring their participation in planning, implementation and monitoring of all projects and policies.

Addressing these concerns entails a new understanding of the critical role of language and linguistic diversity in human development and the maintenance of biological diversity. The biodiversity crisis is not just about the loss of thousands of species of plants and animals, but about the resources that sustain most of the world's indigenous peoples and that give their lives meaning.

Notes

1. The non-African countries are Haiti and Yemen.
2. The computation of the diversity index is based on the population of each language as a proportion of the total population.
3. The other four are Papua New Guinea, Vanuatu, Solomon Islands and India. The Solomons and Vanuatu are tied for third place.
4. A series of studies addressed the possibility of a causal connection between linguistic heterogeneity and economic development (Fishman, 1968, 1991; Fishman & Solano, 1989; Lieberson & Hansen, 1974; Pool 1972).
5. Cook (2004: 113) draws attention to another linguistic dimension in the debate about genetically modified food crops. Due to the metaphorical linkage between people and plants, apparently neutral terms such as *reaping, sowing, seeds* and *harvest* have evocative connotations that resonate beyond their literal use in the agricultural domain. Likewise, the term *monoculture* invites comparisons between the creation of agricultural and cultural uniformity.

References

Ahlenius, H. (2004) Global development and biodiversity. UNEP/GRID-Arendal On WWW at http://maps.grida.no/go/graphics/global_development_ and biodiversity. Accessed 27.7.06.

Beck, J.P. (2003) Poor people in rich lands: A first look at the socioeconomic state of biodiversity hotspots. Scholarly paper. Sustainable Development and Conservation Biology Program. University of Maryland.

Bamgbose, A. (2004) Language of instruction policy and practice in Africa. On WWW at http://www.unesco.org/education/languages_2004/languagein-struction_africa.pdf. Accessed 26.9.05.

Brenzinger, M. (1998) Various ways of dying and different kinds of death: Scholarly approaches to language endangerment on the African continent. In K. Matsumura (ed.) *Studies in Endangered Languages: Papers from the International Symposium on Endangered Languages, Tokyo, 18–29 November 1995* (pp. 85–100). Tokyo: Hituzi Syobo.

Chesterton, G.K. (1910) *What's Wrong with the World*. London: Cassell.

Cook, G. (2004) *Genetically Modified Language*. London: Routledge.

Daly, H.E. (2005) Economics in a full world. *Scientific American* 293 (3), 100–108.

Diamond, J. (2005) *Collapse: How Societies Choose to Fail or Succeed*. London: Viking Penguin.

Easterly, W. (2006) *The White Man's Burden: Why the West's efforts to Aid the Rest Have Done So Much Ill and So Little Good*. New York/London: The Penguin Press.

Ehrenfeld, D. (2003) Globalization: Effects on biodiversity, environment and society. *Conservation and Society* 1, 99–111.

Fishman, J.A. (1968) Some contrasts between linguistically homogenous and linguistically heterogeneous polities. In J.A. Fishman, C.A. Ferguson and J. Das Gupta (eds) *Language Problems of Developing Nations* (pp. 53–68). New York: Wiley.

Fishman, J.A. (1991) An interpolity perspective on the relationship between linguistic heterogeneity, civil strife and per capita gross national product. *International Journal of Applied Linguistics* 1, 5–18.

Fishman, J.A. and Solano, F.R. (1989) Cross-polity linguistic homogeneity/ heterogeneity and per-capita gross national product: An empirical exploration. *Language Problems and Language Planning* 13 (2), 103–118.

Gegeo, D.W. (1998) Indigenous knowledge and empowerment: Rural development examined from within. *The Contemporary Pacific* 10 (2), 289–316.

Gegeo, D.W. and Watson-Gegeo, K.A. (2002) The critical villager: Transforming language and education in the Solomon Islands. In J.W. Tollefson (ed.) *Language Policies in Education: Critical Issues* (pp. 309–327). Mahwah, NJ: Lawrence Erlbaum.

Goldin, C. (1990) *Understanding the Gender Gap: An Economic History of American Women.* New York: Oxford University Press.

Gordon, Jr., R.G. (ed.) (2005) *Ethnologue: Languages of the World* (15th edn). Dallas, TX: SIL International. On WWW at http://www.ethnologue.com/. Accessed 3.10.05.

Let nature's harvest continue (1998) In *The Five Year Freeze 2002. Feeding or fooling the world: Can GM really feed the hungry?* Genetic Engineering Alliance. On WWW at http://www.farmingsolutions.org/pdfdb/Feed_Fool_World.pdf. Accessed 3.10.05.

Lertzman, D. and Vredenburg, H. (2005) Indigenous peoples, resource extraction and sustainable development: An ethical approach. *Journal of Business Ethics* 56, 239–254.

Lieberson, S. and Hansen, L.K. (1974) National development, mother tongue diversity, and the comparative study of nations. *American Sociological Review* 39, 23–41.

Mackey, W.F. (1989) Status of languages in multilingual societies. In U. Ammon (ed.) *Status and Function of Languages and Language Varieties* (pp. 3–20). Berlin: Walter de Gruyter.

Mazrui, A.A. and Mazrui, A.A. (1998) *The Power of Babel: Language and Governance in the African Experience.* Chicago, IL: University of Chicago Press.

McLuhan, M. (1964) *Understanding Media: The Extensions of Man.* New York: McGraw Hill.

Nettle, D. and Romaine, S. (2000) *Vanishing Voices: The Extinction of the World's Languages.* Oxford: Oxford University Press.

Nietschmann, B.Q. (1992) The interdependence of biological and cultural diversity. Kenmore, WA: Center for World Indigenous Studies. Occasional Paper No. 21.

Peel, J.D.Y. (1978) *Olaju*: A Yoruba concept of development. *Journal of Development Studies* 14, 139–165.

Polak, P. (2005) The big potential of small farms. *Scientific American* 293 (3), 84–92.

Pool, J. (1972) National development and language diversity. In J.A. Fishman (ed.) *Advances in the Sociology of Language* (Vol. 2, pp. 213–230). The Hague: Mouton.

Robinson, C.D.W. (1996) *Language Use in Rural Development: An African Perspective.* Berlin: Mouton de Gruyter.

Romaine, S. (1990) *Language, Education and Development: Urban and Rural Tok Pisin in Papua New Guinea.* Oxford: Oxford University Press.

Sachs, J.D. (2005a) *The End of Poverty: Economic Possibilities for Our Time.* New York: The Penguin Press.

Sachs, J.D. (2005b) Can extreme poverty be eliminated? *Scientific American* 293 (3), 56–66.

Shiva, V. (1993) *The Violence of the Green Revolution*. London: Zed Books.

Shiva, V. (2000) *Tomorrow's Biodiversity*. London: Thames & Hudson.

Skutnabb-Kangas, T. (2000) *Linguistic Genocide in Education – or Worldwide Diversity and Human Rights?* Mahwah, NJ: Lawrence Erlbaum.

UNESCO (2003) *Education in a Multilingual World*. Position paper on education. Paris: UNESCO.

United Nations Development Programme (UNDP) (2000) *Human Development Report 2000*. Human rights and human development. On WWW at http://hdr.undp.org/reports/global/2001/en/pdf/completenew.pdf. Accessed 5.10.05.

United Nations Development Programme (2005a) *Human Development Report 2005*. International cooperation at a crossroads: Aid, trade and security in an unequal world. http://hdr.undp.org/reports/global/2005/pdf/HDR05_complete.pdf. Accessed 6.10.06.

United Nations Development Programme (2005b) *Investing in Development: A Practical Plan to Achieve the Millennium Development Goals*. On WWW at http://www.unmillenniumproject.org/documents/MainReportComplete-lowres.pdf. Accessed 19.9.05.

United Nations Permanent Forum on Indigenous Issues (2005) *Report on the Fourth Session 16–27 May*. On WWW at http://www.un.org/esa/socdev/unpfii/documents/doc_fourth_4session.htm. Accessed 20.9.05.

Wackernagel, M. and Rees, W. (1996) *Our Ecological Footprint: Reducing Human Impact on the Earth*. Philadelphia, PA: New Society.

Widdowson, F. (2005) The political economy of Nunavut: Internal colony or rentier territory? Paper prepared for the Annual Meeting of Canadian Political Science Association, University of Western Ontario, June.

Williams, R. (1983) *Keywords: A Vocabulary of Culture and Society* (2nd edn). London: Fontana.

World Resources Institute (2005) *The Wealth of the Poor: Managing Ecosystems to Fight Poverty*. Washington, DC: World Resources Institute.

Yapa, L. (1993) What are improved seeds? An epistemology of the Green Revolution. *Economic Geography* 69 (3), 254–273.

Yapa, L. (2002) How the discipline of geography exacerbates poverty in the Third World. *Futures: Journal of Forecasting and Planning* 34, 33–46.

Chapter 9
Language and Poverty: Measurement, Determinants and Policy Responses

FRANÇOIS VAILLANCOURT

Introduction

The purpose of this chapter is to examine the relationship between poverty and language using the tools of economics. This is done at the request of the editors of this volume and should contribute in providing a multidisciplinary approach to the analysis of this question. We address three questions. First, how does an economist measure poverty and the impacts of various determinants of poverty (multivariate versus bivariate analysis)? Second, how do economists operationalize the notion of language and measure the impact of language on labor income, and thus on total income and poverty? Third, what policies are appropriate to counter language-related poverty?

The Measurement of Poverty[1]

The measurement of poverty is a daunting problem insofar as it reflects on society's values and impacts on public policy directly or indirectly. Why? Because defining it requires the setting of a cutoff point between the poor and the non-poor, with said cutoff often used if not to set then at least to gauge the appropriateness of government and international agencies policies and, in particular, of income support policies against poverty.

There are two steps to measuring poverty:

(1) Defining the measurement tool to be used. One must first decide between monetary and non-monetary measures. Non-monetary measures include objective ones such as health poverty (incidence of illnesses), nutritional poverty (caloric intake) and educational poverty (literacy rate), and subjective ones – answers to questions such as 'Do you have enough?' Monetary measures can use either or

both consumption and income to establish poverty. In this chapter, we focus on monetary measures as economists have the most expertise in this area.

(2) Defining the standard (once given the measurement tool) used to define an individual or a group of individuals as poor. There are two broad approaches to defining poverty: the absolute one and the relative one.

The Absolute Approach

The absolute approach sets a poverty line (often a set of poverty lines) by size of target unit and/or by location of household. The larger the size of the target unit, the greater the monetary resources required to be above the poverty line; the larger the urban area the target unit lives in, the greater the monetary resources required to be above the poverty line. This requires defining:

• The target unit: this term covers the following:

  − households: a group of individuals sharing a housing unit;
  − spending units: a group of individuals sharing a housing unit and pooling together their income for major items (housing and food in particular);
  − economic families: a group of individuals linked by blood, marriage (legal or *de facto*) or adoption sharing a housing unit;
  − nuclear families: one or both parents and their children sharing a housing unit, or individuals.

  The proper unit will depend on the degree of sharing in a given society between more or less distant relatives.

• The appropriate amount for a single person unit to meet *basic needs*. One possibility is the food-energy intake method, often used in developing countries. Another is the cost of basic needs approach. This is done by first listing basic needs and then costing them. The list will of course include food and shelter, but may differ from country to country with respect to other items. For example, what is more basic: cable television or a daily newspaper? Is either to be used to remain a well-informed citizen or carry out job searches? Or should it be WIFI access? The answer depends in part on the availability and accessibility of publicly provided resources, such as newspapers in public libraries or free municipal WIFI. The estimation of food needs is traditionally done through detailed budget studies, assuming that nutritionally adequate meals will be prepared using lowest-cost ingredients. Of course, diversity may suffer and costing should take into account the fact that prices are often higher in areas where poor households reside.

• The appropriate amounts for various unit sizes. This is done using equivalence scales. Such scales assign decreasing weights and therefore decreasing amounts to additional members of the target unit. They are calculated by using budget survey information on spending by unit size. They start by giving a weight of 1 to the first adult, then a fraction for the second adult and/or the first child and so on to reflect the fact that there are economies of scale in housing (for instance, one kitchen can serve for more than one individual), in producing meals, in providing phone service and so on.

• The appropriate amount for a given unit size by place of residence. In general, the cost of living is seen as rising with the size of the urban unit one lives in as nominal rents are higher, reflecting the value of living in a larger labor market. This, however, may neglect the impact of high-energy costs on transportation expenditures in rural areas and small urban centers.

The Relative Approach

This defines poverty not with respect to a basic standard of living, but relative to a reference income. For example, a poor unit is defined as one whose income is 50% or less of the mean or median income of similar units. Therefore, when the mean or median income increases, the poverty line increases. The choice of mean or median is not without consequence, as the distribution of income usually follows Pareto's statistical law with the mean to the right of the median.

Having settled on what units to examine and what approach to use, one produces poverty lines that distinguish between the poor and nonpoor. In the space imparted to us, one cannot present all poverty lines used throughout the world. One notes:

• The World Bank's absolute poverty measure. This organization notes that 'When estimating poverty worldwide, the same reference poverty line has to be used, and expressed in a common unit across countries. Therefore, for the purpose of global aggregation and comparison, the World Bank uses reference lines set at $1 (US) and $2 per day (more precisely $1.08 and $2.15 in 1993 Purchasing Power Parity terms). It has been estimated that in 2001, 1.1 billion people had consumption levels below $1 a day and 2.7 billion lived on less than $2 a day'.[2]

• The American poverty lines. Two sets of poverty lines are reported in Table 9.1. They are fairly similar but not identical. One should note that:

   – the Census bureau calculates two different poverty lines for households made up of a single individual aged less than 65 ($9827) or more than 65 or ($9060) and for two person households ($12,714 and $11,430), respectively;
   – the Health and Social Services (HHS) poverty line reported in Table 9.1 is for the 48 contiguous continental states. The poverty line for a one-person household is $11,630 for Alaska and $10,700 for Hawaii.

Hence, we see that the first set adjusts for age but not for location, whereas the second adjusts for location and not for age. We can also infer that an additional adult is estimated to cost 30–35% ($3019/9645 or $3180/9310) of the cost of the first adult.

Having defined what units are poor, one can then turn to examining who is poor and why. This can be done by examining the following.

• The incidence of poverty; this gives the poverty rate, overall and for various groupings of interest such as rural and urban or old and young. It is calculated as the percentage of poor for the relevant target group.

Table 9.1 American poverty lines, 2004 Census Bureau and Health and Social Services (HSS)

Family size	Census bureau	HHS 48 states and DC
One	9,645	9,310
Two	12,334	12,490
Three	15,067	15,670
Four	19,307	18,850
Five	22,831	22,030
Six	25,788	25,210
Seven	29,236	28,390
Eight	32,641	31,570

Source: Column 1: US Census Bureau (http://www.census.gov/hhes/www/poverty/threshld/thresh04.html). Column 2: The 2004 HHS Poverty Guidelines (http://aspe.hhs.gov/poverty/04poverty.shtml)

- The depth of poverty; this is determined by calculating how far from the poverty line or cutoff a given group is or how much money needs to be transferred to it to pull it out of poverty (fill the poverty gap). For example, let us say that households with either an older or a female head have a 10% poverty rate, each facing, by coincidence, a $10,000 poverty line. But the older households have an average income of $9500 and thus a poverty gap of $500 and the female-headed households an average income of $8000 and thus a $2000 poverty gap. Then the female-headed households are poorer than the older ones.
- The severity of poverty, which is calculated as the square of the poverty gap (thus giving greater weight to poorer individuals).

Given this, one may wish to examine what factors, such as individual and family characteristics or locational characteristics, explain that a household is poor. To do this correctly, one must carry out multivariate analysis so as to identify the marginal contribution of each factor to the probability of being poor or, given that a household is poor, to its poverty gap.

The Determinants of Poverty: The Role of Language

As indicated previously, poverty can be measured using different approaches. Economists usually focus on measures using consumption or income. We will focus on the latter, total income, reflecting the existing body of work linking language and economic status. Total income is composed of labor income, capital income and transfer income. The most important source of income is usually labor income, the exceptions being rentier societies such as Monaco or oil-rich small nations. Thus, labor income should be the kind given the most attention, and it is the kind for which the impact of language skills has been the most studied. To carry out these studies, economists were first required to define language from an economic perspective.

One method followed by economists was to use the tools of international trade. Carr (1985),[3] Breton and Mieszkowski (1975, 1977) and Boucher (1985) all use the analogy of international trade between countries to stress the role of language as a means of exchange. Carr points out that a few currencies dominate international trade, and that the same could be expected in the case of languages; Breton and Mieszkowski compare language-related costs to transportation costs; and Boucher points out that language policy can be seen as a protectionist tariff. These analogies, while interesting, have not been used in empirical work.

More fruitful were approaches aimed at using multivariate techniques to link earnings and individual characteristics. The first approach treats language as an ethnic attribute or marker similar to race. This approach was inspired by Becker's (1957) theoretical model of racial discrimination, and by the empirical work undertaken in the USA in the 1965–1970 period to explain earnings differences between Black and White Americans. Raynauld *et al.* (1969) used this approach in their work for Québec, while Fogel (1966) applied it in the USA. Such a definition, however, overlooks the role of language as a communication tool. On the other hand, language was implicitly treated as human capital by Hocevar (1975) and explicitly described as such by Carliner (1976) and Breton (1978). This was an important development as it allowed the use of the Mincerian analytical framework to calculate the returns to language in the same way as the returns to education or experience. But defining language solely as a form of human capital overlooks the ethnic dimension of the first language learned, usually defined as the individual's mother tongue. Vaillancourt (1980) puts forward a model that distinguishes between the mother tongue, seen as an ethnic attribute and a form of human capital, and the other languages known by an individual, solely defined as elements of human capital.

The empirical relationship between the earnings of individuals and their language attributes, and in particular the net impact of such attributes (that is, once other factors such as education or experience have been taken into account), has been examined extensively for Québec, Canada and the USA and has been the object of some work in Australia, Germany and Switzerland. Empirical work on the issues is carried out using:

- the ordinary least squares multivariate analysis technique with or without a correction for the acquired language skills (sample selection issue);
- public use samples from censuses (Canada, USA, Australia) or survey data (Québec, USA, Germany, Switzerland);
- more or less narrow samples with sex (men) and age (25–64) often used as constraints;
- the logarithm of earnings, or only wages and salaries as the dependent variable;
- education, experience and its square and weeks worked (if the sample is not restricted to full year workers) as control factors

(independent variables), in accordance with the usual specification of Mincerian earnings equations. Other variables such as marital status, region, type of employment, etc., are also commonly used, depending on the availability of data.

In the case of Québec, Vaillancourt has carried out work using the 1971 (Lacroix & Vaillancourt, 1981; Vaillancourt, 1980), 1981 (Vaillancourt, 1988), 1986 (Vaillancourt, 1991), 1991 (Vaillancourt, 1996), 1996 (Vaillancourt & Touchette, 2003) and 2001 (Vaillancourt *et al.*, 2007) public use sample of the Canadian censuses. The variables used are as identical as possible, which facilitates intertemporal comparisons for the whole population and various subgroups. In addition, issues such as the returns to language for highly qualified workers (Lacroix & Vaillancourt, 1980) or to different levels of language skills (Vaillancourt & Pes, 1980) have also been examined.

In the case of Canada, there exists scattered evidence on the rates of return to language attributes, but no systematic intertemporal comparison had been made until recently. Bloom and Grenier (1992) do so for the 1971–1986 period, and review some of the existing studies. Vaillancourt *et al.* (2007) do so for the 1971–2001 period for Québec.

In the case of the USA, authors have used either census or survey of income and education data to examine first the impact of Hispanic ethnic origin (Carliner, 1980; Long, 1977; Reimers, 1983), and then the impact of the level of competence in English on earnings (Bloom & Grenier, 1993; Grenier, 1984a; McManus, 1985, 1990; Rivera-Batiz, 1991).

Research in Europe on the relationship between language and earnings has begun more recently, and includes work by Dustmann (1994) for guest workers in Germany and Grin (1995, 1996) for Switzerland.

We illustrate this work with recent results for Québec for 2000 in Table 9.2. The mean results show that differences in mean labor income between Anglophones and Francophones are smaller for women than for men, while labor income is higher for men than women.

These differences in mean labor income associated with a given set of language skills may not reflect the returns to language skills as such; they could be explained by differences in the education or experience of individuals with these language skills. This is why we calculate the net impact of language skills using multivariate analysis and report them also in Table 9.2.

The net impacts of language skills are as follows:

- The returns to English unilingualism for anglophone are negative. In the case of anglophone women, they are nonexistent (0).

Table 9.2 Average labor income and net returns by language skills, men and women, Québec, 2000

Indicator	Men: average labor income		Women: average labor income		Men: net returns	Women: net returns
Language attributes	$	RCR	$	RCR	%	%
Anglophones unilingual	34,097	1.15	23,002	1.11	− 18.06	0
Anglophones bilingual	38,745	1.31	26,247	1.26	0	7.40
Francophones unilingual	29,665	–	20,786	–	–	–
Francophones bilingual	38,851	1.31	26,644	1.28	12.20	17.04
Allophones anglophones	27,216	0.92	18,996	0.91	− 30.10	0
Allophones francophones	21,233	0.72	15,551	0.75	− 33.88	− 19.10
Allophones bilingual	33,097	1.12	24,034	1.16	− 11.78	5.32
Allophones other	20,146	0.68	15,379	0.74	− 25.82	0
Anglophones – francophones	27,192	0.92	23,002	1.11	− 11.66	0

Source: Vaillancourt *et al.* (2007).
Note: RCR: ratio of mean over category of reference, unilingual francophones

- The returns to bilingualism for anglophone men are zero when established with respect to unilingual francophones. The returns to bilingualism for anglophone women are positive.
- The returns to bilingualism for francophone men and women are positive.
- The returns to English and French language skills of allophones are negative.

Policy Responses

What are the possible policy responses to language-associated poverty? The answer depends on the nature of that poverty. One key issue is whether it is spatially determined. Let us at first assume this is the case.

Spatially determined poverty occurs when the physical characteristics of a region explain in part the income level of its residents. For example:

- residents of remote areas with limited access to markets in which to sell their goods and services will be poorer;
- residents of enclave areas (areas not far from potential markets but with difficult access to these areas due to topographical factors such as mountain chains, deserts, bodies of water and other obstacles) will be poorer;
- residents of areas with poor-quality soil will be unable to generate a surplus to invest in other sectors and will be poorer;
- residents of areas that have seen a substantial drop in the demand for the natural resources they harbor will be poorer.

How is this relevant to language-related poverty? Often, poorer language groups will be made up of the descendants of the losers in a struggle for territory. This group will have been forced to migrate to remote, less hospitable areas (e.g. Lands' End in Cornwall or Finistère in Bretagne or Acadia in New Brunswick). This will make them poorer. Alternatively, these language groups will always have occupied areas that were not invaded because they would have yielded few benefits to potential conquerors. Another scenario is that the residents of a given area were once rich (e.g. the Walloons in Belgium), but are now poor as a result of a change in industrial activity (in this case, the decline of steel and coal industries). In these various cases, one can either encourage outward mobility in the minority group or carry out regional development policies to reduce regional cum language-related poverty.

In the first case, one will probably see a decrease in first the use and then the knowledge of the minority language as its value for its native speakers goes down when they take up residence elsewhere. The average labor income of the remaining minority members in their region of origin may go up due to decreased competition for natural resources if a smaller number of workers have access to the same natural resources and thus can farm larger farms, gather more fish or cut more trees. But if there are economies of scale in the production of publicly provided goods and services or in the provision of imported private goods, then one may see an increase in the costs of such goods and services, which will erode away partially, totally or more than totally the increased labor earnings. The labor income of the mobile minority members will probably go up at least in the long term as they assimilate in the majority society.

Turning to regional development, one encounters two questions: 'Who will carry out these policies?' and 'Who should pay for the required investments in physical or human capital?' The answer to the first depends on both the demographic situation and the governance arrangements. They are summarized in Table 9.3.

Hence, a poor language group that is a majority in a region with some autonomy may be better able to carry out policies to improve its lot than one that is a minority in a relatively powerless region. Of course, the type of power available will matter greatly with autonomous governance arrangements that facilitate investments in human capital (responsibility for postsecondary education, labor force training) and investments in physical capital, financed through domestic savings or foreign investments (responsibility for savings incentives, financial markets, infrastructure of use to businesses), preferable in this case to more autonomy in road policing or care of the elderly.

Table 9.3 Demographic situations and the governance arrangements for national minority languages

Demography/governance	Unitary state	Decentralized state (federal)
National minority language group is regional minority	Alsatians in Alsace	Hispanics in several US states
National minority language group is regional majority	Hungarians in eastern Slovakia	Québec, Catalonia

On financing, the answer will depend on the degree of equalization, implicit or explicit, between regions. If there is no equalization, then the poor region must save and invest to pull itself out of poverty; if there is some equalization, then outside funds can be helpful. Singapore is an example of a poor region (formerly of Malaysia) that self-financed its growth, while Ireland is an example of a poor region benefiting from outside funds (in this case, transfers from the European Union).

Let us now assume that there are no differences in the income potential of the various regions, but that there are two language groups, a majority and a minority, in a given labor market. What are the possible combinations of poverty status and regional distribution? (Table 9.4)

Let us examine each case in turn.

- Case 1: the poor language group is the majority. Is it poor because its members are undereducated or because they are discriminated against due either to language or to another factor such as race or religion? The policy response will vary according to which factor is at play, recognizing that past discrimination may explain current undereducation.
- Case 2: the poor language group is a labor market minority but a majority in one part of it. The issues are the same as for the first case except that one must also take into account the issue of the knowledge by the minority of the majority language (extent and mastery).
- Case 3: the poor language group is a labor market minority and never a majority in a region. The issues are the same as in the second case, but the importance of mastery of the majority language is probably accentuated.

If the cause of poverty is undereducation, then public policy changes, such as offering more schooling in the relevant language to educate the poorer group, will allow it to break out of poverty. However, it will

Table 9.4 Possible combinations of poverty status and regional distribition

Poor group is regionally concentrated	Majority is poor	Minority is poor
Yes	Not possible	Possible
No	Possible	Possible

take probably 40 years for the educated workers to replace the undereducated ones.

If the cause of poverty is linguistic discrimination, then public policy changes such as quotas or mandated use of a language can be implemented. These policies will produce an effect faster than policies aimed at changing the level of education. The same holds for racial or religious discrimination.

Conclusion

Poverty can be measured using various indicators and more importantly making various choices as to what is the cutoff between the poor and the non-poor. The latter choice is a societal one that reflects preferences. Economics as such has nothing to say on this while economists must state clearly what cutoff they use and argue why it is the relevant one.[4] Once a poverty measure has been selected, one can examine what makes individuals and thus the group they belong to more or less likely to be poor. Language is one of various factors that influence poverty. Depending on the interaction of factors, such as minority or majority status and regional concentrations, various policy responses are appropriate. Two in particular stand out: regional development policies and language laws. The first will be appropriate if language and poverty are linked through the place of residence of a language group.[5] The second will be appropriate if language and poverty are linked through segregation and/or discrimination in the labor market.

Notes

1. For a non-technical discussion with applications to a wide range of countries, see World Bank Measuring Poverty on WWW at http://web.worldbank.org/ WBSITE/EXTERNAL/TOPICS/EXTPOVERTY/EXTPA/0,,contentMDK: 20238988 ~ menuPK:435055 ~ pagePK:148956 ~ piPK:216618 ~ theSitePK: 430367,00.html. Technical references are available for the interested reader.
2. From World Bank Understanding Poverty on WWW at http://web.world-bank.org/WBSITE/EXTERNAL/TOPICS/EXTPOVERTY/EXTPA/0,,content MDK:20153855 ~ menuPK:435040 ~ pagePK:148956 ~ piPK:216618 ~ theSite PK:430367,00.html.
3. First circulated in the early 1970s, but unpublished until 1985.
4. For example one can compare the positions put forward in Canada by the Fraser Insitute, a right-leaning think tank and the National Council of Welfare, a federal government sponsored left-leaning body. See http:// www.toronto.ca/legdocs/agendas/committees/cn/cn981203/it004.htm for a summary of the debate.
5. For a recent survey on this, see *Public Policy for Regional Development*, edited by Jorge Martinez-Vazquez and François Vaillancourt (Routledge, 2008).

References

Becker, G.S. (1957) *The Economics of Discrimination.* Chicago, IL: Chicago University Press.

Bloom, D.E. and Grenier, G. (1992) The earnings of linguistic minorities: French in Canada and Spanish in the United States. In B.R. Chiswick (ed.) *Immigration, Language and Ethnicity: Canada and the United States* (pp. 373–409). Washington, DC: American Enterprise Institute.

Bloom, D.E. and Grenier, G. (1993) Language, employment and earnings in the United States: Spanish-English differentials from 1970 to 1990. NBER Working Paper 4584.

Boucher, M. (1985) La Loi 101. Une approche économique. [Bill 101: An economic approach]. In F. Vaillancourt (ed.) *Économie et langue [Economics and Language]* (pp. 101–116). Québec: Conseil de la langue française.

Breton, A. (1978) *Le bilinguisme: Une approche économique [Bilingualism: An Economic Approach].* Montréal: C.D. Howe Institute. VII.

Breton, A. and Mieskowski, P. (1975) The returns to investment in language: The economics of bilingualism. University of Toronto, Institute for Policy Analysis, Working Paper No. 7512.

Breton, A. and Mieskowski, P. (1977) The economics of bilingualism. In W. Oates (ed.) *The Political Economy of Fiscal Federalism* (pp. 261–273). Toronto: Lexington Books.

Carliner, G. (1976) Returns to education for Blacks, Anglos and five Spanish groups. *The Journal of Human Resources* 11 (2), 172–184.

Carliner, G. (1980) Wages, earnings and fours of first, second and third generation American males. *Economic Inquiry* 18, 87–112.

Carr, J. (1985) Bilingualism in Canada: Is the use of the English language a natural monopoly? In F. Vaillancourt (ed.) *Économie et langue [Economics and Language]* (pp. 27–37). Québec: Conseil de la langue française.

Dustmann, C. (1994) Speaking fluency, writing fluency and earnings of migrants. *Journal of Population Economics* 7 (2), 133–156.

Fogel, W. (1966) The effects of low educational attainment on incomes: A comparative study of selected ethnic groups. *The Journal of Human Resources* 1 (2), 22–40.

Grenier, G. (1984) The effects of language characteristics on the wages of Hispanic-American males. *Journal of Human Resources* 19 (1), 35–52.

Grin, F. (1995) La valeur des compétences linguistiques: Vers une perspective économique [The value of language competence: Towards an economic perspective]. *Babylonia* 2 (95), 59–65.

Grin, F. (1996) Minority language and socio-economic status: The case of Italian in Switzerland. *Cahiers du Département d'économie politique*, University of Geneva. 96.10.

Hočevar, T. (1975) Equilibria in linguistic minority markets. *Kyklos* 28 (2), 337–357.

Lacroix, R. and Vaillancourt, F. (1980) *Attributs linguistiques et disparités de revenus au sein de la main d'oeuvre hautement qualifiée du Québec [Language Attributes and Income Differentials in the Highly Skilled Workforce in Québec].* Québec: Conseil de la langue française.

Lacroix, R. and Vaillancourt, F. (1981) *Les revenus et la langue au Québec, 1970–1978* [*Language and Incomes in Québec, 1970–1978*]. Québec: Conseil de la langue française.

Long, J.E. (1977) Productivity, employment discrimination and the relative economic status of Spanish origin males. *Social Science Quarterly* 58 (3), 357–373.

Martinez-Vazquez, J. and Vaillancourt, F. (eds) (2008) *Public Policy for Regional Development*. London: Routledge.

McManus, W.S. (1985) Labor market costs of language disparities: An interpretation of Hispanic earnings differences *American Economic Review* 75, 818–827.

McManus, W.S. (1990) Labor market effects of language enclaves: Hispanic men in the United States. *The Journal of Human Resources* 25, 228–252.

Raynauld, A., Marion, G. and Béland, R. (1969) *La répartition des revenus selon les groupes ethniques au Canada* [*Income Distribution by Ethnic Group in Canada*]. Commission Laurendeau-Dunton, rapport de recherches, 4 vol.

Reimers, C.W. (1983) Labor market discrimination against Hispanic and Black men. *Review of Economics and Statistics* 65, 570–579.

Rivera-Batiz, F.L. (1991) The effects of literacy on the earnings of Hispanics in the United States. In E. Menendez, C. Rodriguez and J. Barry-Figueroa (eds) *Hispanics in the Labor Force*. New York: Plenum.

Vaillancourt, F. (1980) Difference in earnings by language groups in Québec 1970: An economic analysis (PhD thesis, 1978). Québec: Centre International de Recherche sur le Bilinguisme, B-90.

Vaillancourt, F. (ed.) (1985) *Economie et langue* [*Economics and Language*]. Québec: Conseil de la langue française.

Vaillancourt, F. (1988) *Langue et disparités de statut économique au Québec: 1970 et 1980* [*Language and Socio-economic Status Differentials: 1970 and 1980*]. Québec: Conseil de la langue française.

Vaillancourt, F. (1991) *Langue et statut économique au Québec, 1980–1985* [*Language and Economic Status in Québec, 1980–1985*]. Québec: Conseil de la langue française.

Vaillancourt, F. (1996) Le français dans un contexte économique. In J. Erfurt (ed.) *De la polyphonie à la symphonie* (pp. 119–136). Leipzig: Presses de l'Université.

Vaillancourt, F. and Pes, J. (1980) Revenus et niveaux de bilinguisme écrit et oral: Les hommes québécois en 1971 [Income and written and oral levels of bilingualism: Québecois males in 1971]. *L'actualité Economique* 56, 451–464.

Vaillancourt, F. and Touchette, C. (2001) *Le statut du français sur le marché du travail au Québec, de 1970 à 1995: Les revenus de travail*. Toronto: C.D. Howe Institute, Backgrounder.

Vaillancourt, F., Lemay, D. and Vaillancourt, L. (2007) Laggards no more: The changed socioeconomic status of Francophones in Quebec. On WWW at http://www.cdhowe.org/pdf/backgrounder_103_english.

Chapter 10
Losing the Names: Native Languages, Identity and the State

PETER WHITELEY

The language and culture of the Hopi Indians of Arizona are at a turning point: the next two generations will see the near-total loss of their language or its persistence, but under altered social and linguistic conditions. A recent census department estimate suggests that out of a total Hopi population of approximately 12,000, two thirds of whom live on the Hopi Reservation, 5000 remain fluent in Hopi. My own impression, however, from serial visits since 1980, is that the fluency rate is significantly lower than that, perhaps by 50%.[1] Generally speaking, people in their forties and above are fluent, while people in their thirties and below are not, with some exceptions. There remains a substantial community of native speakers, however, and in that lies the potential for the language's active maintenance, but unless more consistent proactive measures are taken, the rate of loss would more suggest its precipitous demise. The potential loss is particularly resonant in the global decline of linguistic diversity, in addition to its obvious intrinsic salience to the Hopi people, for two reasons: up to now the Hopi are still generally regarded as the most 'traditional' of all North American Indians, retaining proportionally more of their pre-European practices and ideas than most. Second, for linguistic scholarship, the Hopi language has been perhaps the paramount exemplar of the Sapir-Whorf hypothesis; Whorf's studies of Hopi in the 1930s significantly shaped this, arguably the most powerful theory about the relationship between language and the world. Focusing primarily on Hopi, I want to address the consequences of a world and world-view under threat from linguistic decline amid sustained political-economic pressure.

Economy and 'Poverty'

Identifying the causal nexus tying language to economic conditions depends especially on the paradigm employed. 'Poverty' has typically been measured by the calculus of formalist economics that inherits the submerged prejudices held by market-industrialism against subsistence production (e.g. Brody, 1981; Sahlins, 1972). Formalist approaches are notoriously myopic with regard to the rationality of prestate systems of production. Old myths of the ceaseless toil and eternal want of a foraging lifestyle were shown to be baseless, especially after intensive studies of forager production in the 1960s and 1970s. But mainstream economics still seems uncomfortable with the rationality of productive practices not easily reduced to capital and labor flows. Even when surrounded by the forces of global production, many indigenous societies in North America retain extensive aspects of aboriginal subsistence practices – gathering, hunting, fishing and nonintensive horticulture – where products circulate within local reciprocity networks structured by norms of generalized exchange.

Indeed, such socioeconomic patterns are often the substrate for and integral to other forms of cultural persistence: traditional ritual activities and associated feasts, such as a Hopi Katsina dance, a Haida potlatch or Hodenosaunee Longhouse ceremonies, depend specifically on the preparation and exchange of nonmarket-based products (as well as commodities acquired with cash) that lie within a domestic mode of production and consumption entirely or largely outside state or global systems. Akwesasne deer-hunting for midwinter ceremonies, Hopi subsistence agriculture and the Katsina-dance cycle, or Haida collection of kelp and eulachon oil for a pole-raising feast, for example, reflect widespread persistence of precapitalist Native North American material praxis, even in cases where overt cultural distinctions from surrounding non-Native communities are unobvious. People may drive pick-ups, earn wages and buy commodities at supermarkets, but they still spend substantial time planting, hunting, collecting and exchanging.

Native peoples of North America have been losing their political and economic autonomy and along with it key cultural forms, including languages, since the 16th century. However, as with climate change and decline in biodiversity, the accelerated rate of linguistic and cultural loss at present is unparalleled. In the case of the Hopi, language loss only began to be a serious threat over the last three decades, ironically only after the decline of attempts at 'directed culture change' by the Federal Government to obliterate the language in Indian day schools and boarding schools that largely failed in their purpose. In the 1980s, many Hopis who had experienced the more brutal attempts to expunge their language remained completely fluent. Only with the advent of that prime agent of national hegemony and globalization, television, in the 1970s, has the language gone into such rapid decline. Focusing especially on Hopi names of places and persons, I want to address some of the consequences of this loss within the broader political-economic trajectory since the first extension of US dominion in the late 19th century (with the creation of the Hopi Reservation in 1882, the opening of a boarding school in 1887, and a militarily backed attempt to allot Hopi lands in 1892–1894).

A Cayuga Caution

Before stepping on this path, however, let me frame it with a cautionary tale. Cornell University stands at 'at the head of the lake', or Ne-o-däk'-he-ät in the Cayuga language (Morgan, 1851: 133). This area lies within Gwe-u'gweh-o-no'ga, aboriginal territory of the Cayuga, which, before the 1780s, ranged from Lake Ontario south to the Susquehanna Valley in Pennsylvania, covering an east-west strip from Owasco Lake to Seneca Lake and encompassing all of Cayuga Lake and its surrounding agricultural and foraging riches. Father Pierre Raffeix opined in 1672 that Cayuga land was 'the fairest country I have seen in America' (Thwaites, 1899: 56: 49–51), with abundant deer and other game, swans, bustards, salmon, other fish, eel, cornfields and soon, peach orchards – some 1700 square miles of plenty that supported several thousand Cayuga people. In the War of Independence, the Iroquois sought to retain neutrality. But pushed and cajoled by their old British allies, four of the Six Nations, including the Cayuga, eventually took up arms for King George (Graymont, 1972), led by Ojageghte ('he is carrying a fish with the forehead strap', or Fish Carrier). At the instigation of New York's land-hungry governor, George Clinton, one third of the Continental Army undertook a scorched-earth campaign into the Hodenosaunee heartland in 1779. All the Cayuga towns were destroyed (Cook, 1887). The Cayuga suffered a diaspora, with only a few (and for a brief period only into the late 1790s), under the leadership of Karistagia ('Steel Trap'), ever returning to their homeland.

Today, there are no speakers of the Cayuga languages who live in this area; indeed there are no Cayugas who live here either. Of some 10,000 people identified as Cayuga in the USA and Canada, only approximately 60 still speak the language, almost all of these at Six Nations Reserve in

Ontario (Raymond, 2005). Of two other successor communities – one in Western New York State living as landless tenants on the Seneca reservations and the other part of an amalgamated group in Oklahoma called the Seneca-Cayuga Tribe – only about 10 people speak Cayuga (Raymond, 2005). And so it is that, rather than Ne-o-däk'-he-ät within Gwe-u'gweh-o-no'ga, Cornell lies in Ithaca, near Syracuse, Rome, Scipio, Ovid, Manlius and Homer, thanks to the predilections of State Surveyor-General Simeon De Witt. He toponymically inscribed geographic dominion of the new nationstate over the Cayuga places, just as the settlers sought to remove the Ojageghtes and Karistagias from the possibility of sociopolitical comity.

Dislocation and associated impoverishment of the Cayuga are the direct cause of the decline in Cayuga sovereignty and ultimately of the Cayuga language. Lest we forget, languages – perhaps especially those of small-scale indigenous communities – are not neutral codes of communication, but rather are enmeshed in determining sociocultural and historical structures. To speak (and be) Chiricahua Apache in Arizona in the 1860s was *ipso facto* an expression of exclusion from and presumed enmity toward the expansionist American project, often with dire physical and material consequences. A critical component of the present survivability of indigenous languages concerns a group's social capacity to sustain and reproduce itself within an autonomous land-base and an at least partially autonomous economy, even as encompassed by global market capitalism. Moreover, an indigenous society's capacity to perpetuate and reproduce itself must not only be underwritten in national and international law; those laws also must be enforced by the appropriate powers of the nationstate within whose borders the indigenous people finds itself. The Cayuga case is not encouraging. While there may be some partial exceptions to this, such as the nonterritorial ethnoscapes of Arjun Appadurai's (e.g. 1996) devising, let me propose as a simple axiom that territorial and economic security are necessary conditions of indigenous linguistic survivability through time.

Persons and Places

Concepts of space and time, person and self are key constituents of worldview (e.g. Ortiz, 1972: 136–138). In the Hopi world, Whorf memorably argued for the intersection of these phenomenological and ontological axes. Instead of time and space, Hopi metaphysics:

> ...imposes upon the universe two grand cosmic forms, which as a first approximation in terminology we may call MANIFESTED and

MANIFESTING (or, UNMANIFEST) or, again, OBJECTIVE and SUBJECTIVE. The objective or manifested comprises all that is or has been accessible to the senses, the historical physical universe, in fact, with no attempt to distinguish between present and past, but excluding everything we call future. The subjective or manifesting comprises all that we call future, BUT NOT MERELY THIS; it includes equally and indistinguishably all that we call mental – everything that appears or exists in the mind, or, as the Hopi would prefer to say, in the HEART... (Whorf, 1956 [1936]: 58–59)

Whorf's views of Hopi linguistic concepts have been painstakingly challenged (Malotki, 1979, 1983). Yet, his characterization of Hopi phenomenology remains strikingly applicable to much Hopi discourse (for an eloquent defense of Whorf in general, see Lucy, 1992). For anyone with more-than-casual contact with Hopis fluent in the culture and language, there is a lingering sense that Whorf somehow got Hopi right, as evidenced in expressions, in Hopi and in Hopi English, that link intentionality to worldly conditions, that mistrust material fixity and that exhibit a somewhat fatalist sense of movement towards the here and now of as yet unrealized events and stages of existence. 'We're going to come to that yet', is a frequent expression, as are the successive phases/spaces (represented by color sequences in ritual displays), identified in Hopi mythic narratives, and the idea that life is presently in its fourth epoch, en route to a fifth and beyond. Outlines, shapes, color-effects, movements and de-emphasis on nominal quiddity (as opposed to verbal variety [cf. Whorf, 1956]) are all marked features of Hopi discourse, notably in personal names.

Names of places and persons do not *sui generis* instantiate metaphysical abstractions. However, place-names clearly adhere to concrete senses of spatial (perhaps 'manifested', in Whorf's terms) conceptualization, just as personal names enunciate aspects of social and personal ontology. Personal names objectivize social relationships in textual form, inter-relating selves and persons in a social system. Additionally, as Keith Basso (e.g. 1997) has demonstrated for the Western Apache, the named landscape, especially in oral cultures, resonates with historical, mythical and other social meaning: it is a textual archive (cf. Feld & Basso, 1997; Thornton, 2007). In short, if resolving questions of commensurability among metaphysics remains elusive, concrete identifications of place and person seen in names may allow a closer grasp of operational reality in the Hopi worldview.

Hopitutskwa and Hopi Place-names

Hopi settlements are grouped into three clusters, First, Second and Third Mesas, each of which designates a finger-like southern terminus of Black Mesa on the Colorado Plateau. The clusters are divided by long alluvial valleys. First Mesa villages are Wàlpi ('place of the gap'), Sitsom'ovi ('flower mound on top place') and Hanoki ('Hano village' of Tewa immigrants from 1700). Second Mesa comprises Songòopavi ('sand-grass spring place'), Musangnuvi (untranslated) and Supawlavi (perhaps 'place of the mosquitoes'). Third Mesa includes Orayvi ('place of the oray rock [a particular formation]'), Kiqötsmovi ('ruins mound on top place'), Hotvela ('juniper slope') and Paaqavi ('reed springs place'). Lower and Upper Mùnqapi ('[water] continuously flowing place') are two other villages that began as farming colonies of Orayvi. The Hopi Reservation represents a small fraction of Hopitutskwa, Hopi aboriginal land. Hopitutskwa remains the focus of subsistence and religious usages into the present, with the result that conflicts ensue – for example, over gathering of eagles on the Navajo Reservation or over pilgrimages to Nuvatukya'ovi ('snow butte on top place'), the San Francisco Peaks – when other users, more recent arrivals, do not acknowledge the Hopis' right to use the land. Several Hopi petitions over the last century reiterate these rights. For example (in 1951):

> The Hopi Tusqua (land) is our Love and will always be, and it is the land upon which our leader fixes and tells the dates of our religious life. Our land, our religion, and our life are one, and our leader, with humbleness, understanding and determination, performs his duty to us by keeping them as one and thus insuring prosperity and security for the people....
>
> It is upon this land that we have hunted and were assured of right to game such as deer, elk, antelope, buffalo, rabbit, turkey. It is here that we captured the eagle, the hawk, and such birds whose feathers belong to our ceremonies.
>
> It is upon this land that we made trails to our salt supply....
>
> It is here on this land that we are bringing up our younger generation and through preserving the ceremonies are teaching them proper human behavior and strength of character to make them true citizens among all people... (quoted in James, 1974)

In addition to farming, gathering, hunting and grazing sites, there are named ruins that belong to particular matriclans, multiple spring shrines, clan and religious-society shrines, clan eagle-gathering areas and many other specific forms of use throughout Hopitutskwa. Major sites are guarded at the perimeter by clan ancestor spirits who look toward the Hopi villages at the center, and to whom Hopis periodically make *homviikya* pilgrimages (a course of shrine visitations). Beginning with Tokòonavi (possibly archaic for 'dark mountain', Navajo Mountain in English), the course follows Pisisvayu (possibly 'river of echoing sounds [between canyon walls]', the Colorado River) to its junction with Sakwavayu, ('blue river', the lower Little Colorado), to the site of Sipàapuni,[2] the emergence place, thence to Kòoninhahàwpi ('Havasupai descent trail' – the shrine Potavetaqa, 'the one with the basketry-mark petroglyph' or migration-spiral symbol, is nearby), thence up Cataract Creek to Tusaqtsomo ('grass hill' or Bill Williams Mountain), south to Hoonàwpa ('bear springs'), southeast to the Mogollon Rim at Yot.se'ha-hàwpi ('Apache descent trail', the head of Chevelon Creek), northeast to Tsimòntukwi ('jimson-weed butte', Woodruff Butte), northeast up the Puerco River to Naamituyqa ('two points facing each other', near Lupton), northwest to Nayavuwaltsa ('adobe gaps', Lolomai Point), north to Kawestima (a Keresan-derived name for northern mountain, referring in Hopi to Tsegi Canyon area), and north back to Tokòonavi. Like village names, these illustrate a variety of denotative and connotative associations, some pertaining to appearance, others to diagnostic resources and still others to social or historical significance.

Hopitutskwa is not simply a temporal space; it is this level (the earth's surface) of a sacred cosmography. Prominent mountains, such as Nuvatukya'ovi ('snow butte on top place', the San Francisco Peaks), Aalosaqa ('the Two-Horn deity', Humphrey's Peak in the San Francisco Peaks) and other high or moist places, such as Kìisiw ('shady springs' near Pinon), are especially sacred and serve as powerful points of communication between this world and the world of the spirits. It is from these areas that both priests and laymen in ceremonies seek principally to draw moisture and to cycle it into natural processes leading to human, plant and animal growth. The Hopi are the stewards of Hopitutskwa, a responsibility they undertook in a sacred covenant with Maasaw, the deity of this earth, when they first emerged onto its surface (an event marked by the Sípàapuni shrine in Little Colorado Canyon). Hopitutskwa is markedly a sacred landscape, sung of and to in Hopi ceremonial songs, traversed frequently in religious pilgrimages, farmed, foraged, grazed and recharged in every season of the calendrical cycle of Hopi ceremonies.

The Hopi still have some limited territorial and subsistence-economic autonomy, having never yet been driven from the heart of their homeland. These are not the only reasons for the persistence of Hopi language and culture, but they are a critical substrate, and the very anchor of linguistic meaning. We can see that by looking at Hopi personal names, which are grounded in the landscape and a social order that is organized in terms of the meanings drawn from and attributed to that landscape. As Lévi-Strauss (1966) has argued, natural species and categories are *bonnes à penser* ('good to think'), providing a classificatory template of natural metaphors for social differentiation and relationality. The scheme of natural classification and the very particular ecosystem in which it operates are primary sources of social meanings for Hopi, governing clan identities, seasonal temporalities, the ritual order and quotidian subsistence-economic engagements.

Personal Names

Hopi personal names (cf. Whiteley, 1992) are imagistic poems, each thoughtfully composed by a name-giver and ceremoniously conferred upon a recipient. Naming occurs especially at birth and initiation into ritual sodalities. The child's 'aunts' (his or her father's clanswomen) arrive at the house 20 days after birth, each conferring a name of her own devising. One will *huurta* or 'stick' at least until the child is initiated, when she/he will receive a more formal name. In this matrilineal society, names are never conferred by one's own clan, but always by members of the father's clan or by members of the clan of an initiating godparent; in this way, names objectivize relationships in kin networks that exceed formal associations with co-members of one's clan. They are thus a primary index of community sociality, of *belonging* to an identifying social network.

Practically all names comprise between two and five syllables; they often embody dense meanings in poetic form, like haiku (Whiteley, 1992). Many names contain three morphemes: (1) an initial subject indicator (this might be a noun, but more often an adjectival or adverbial form, with the intended subject implied but not stated), (2) a verbal indication of motion or state of the subject, and (3) an ending suffix indexing gender that may or may not represent a verbal particle.[3] 'Lomakwaptiwa', a male name, and 'Qömahoynöm', a woman's name, are representative examples: *loma-* ('beautiful', male speaking), *kwap-* (get put on top [pl.]), *-tiwa* (male ending, possibly a causative passive); *qöma-* (dark, no stated subject), *hoy-* (fledge, become complete), *-nöm* (female ending, possibly contracted from *nööma*, wife). Yet without knowing what 'beautiful' things or processes, or which 'dark' forms are specifically intended, we cannot provide competent translations. Numerous beginning morphemes are color or other terms indexing apperceptive (implicitly or explicitly aesthetic) qualities: e.g. *kuwan-* (colorful), *puhu-* (new, fresh), *sakw-/sakwa-* (blue/green), *sikya-* (yellow) or *tangaq-* (iridescent). Where initial morphemes are nouns, they usually refer to natural species or elements: e.g. (rendered in combinatory form), *hon-* (bear), *honan-* (badger), *humi-* (shell corn), *kyar-* (scarlet macaw), *masa-* (wing), *si-* (flower), *talas-* (pollen), *tsu'-* (rattlesnake), *tuwa-* (sand). Following state/motion morphemes include: *-hay-* (hang), *-hong-* (stand [pl.]), *-lets-* (lie across), *-möy-* (spread out), *-ngay-* (sway), *-ve'y-* (be marked, drawn), *-way-* (move, walk), *-yes-* (sit [pl.], alight). Male name-endings include *-tiwa*, *-niwa*, *-ma* and *-va*; female endings are *-nöm*, *-si*, *-qa*, *-wuuti* and *-mana*. Names composed of fewer than three morphemes are also markedly apperceptive: *loololma*, the plural of the adjectival form *loma*, 'beautiful' (male speaking), refers, in the case of this specific appellation (the name of an Orayvi village chief), to a beautiful design of scarlet-macaw feathers.

Although specific meanings cannot be parsed without knowing the name-giver's clan and authorial intentions, general import is often suggested by the morphemic combinations and is often surpassingly beautiful. Their poetic basis builds on a foregrounded aesthetic sensibility, detailed ecological classifications, and often intricate and variegated cultural knowledge. Name images derive from a panoply of associations with the clan of the name-giver. Some names are generic references to the name-giver's clan totems: e.g. Tahòoya, little whipsnake (Snake clan), Honani, badger (Badger clan) or Kwayowuuti, hawk woman (Eagle clan). But most are tiny poems individually composed from the repertoire of a clan's proprietary interests (one cannot compose a name referencing bears, spiders or bluebirds unless one is of the Bear and its associated clans, for example). Unlike some naming systems that have come to be paradigmatic for some anthropological thinking on Native American subjectivity and personhood (cf. Mauss, 1985), where there is a limited stock of clan names passed down the generations, implicating social reincarnation, or where clan names are purported to suggest synecdochic subjects inseparable from a collective self (e.g. Bear claw, bear paw, bear arm, bear head etc. for members of the Bear clan), at Hopi there is no limited stock of orally archived names, but rather a

potentially limitless series of associations, and thus a strongly individ-
uating sense of subjecthood such names comport. The name-giver is
culturally required to think creatively to come up with a fresh image.
Among a cluster of, say, 8 or 10 names given at the naming ceremony, the
one that *huurta* is basically that which appeals most to the tastes of the
child's parents.

Let me give some examples. First, Sakwngaysi, a woman's name,
literally 'verdant green swaying [woman]', is a name given by a member
of the Piikyas or Young Corn clan, referring to the glorious appearance of
corn plants in full flower whose leaves sway in the breeze. Second,
Lomayayva, literally 'beautifully ascended', was conferred by a Badger
clan member onto a member of the Lizard clan. 'Beautifully ascended'
refers to a special group of many Katsinas (in this instance, that term
refers to masked representations of ancestral spirits) at the Patsavu
ceremony in February, as they ascend into the village of Orayvi from the
direction of the Badger clan's old home in the valley below at
Tuuwanasavi ('sandy middle place'). Incidentally, as these two examples
show, the need to know the name-composer's intended reference as well
as the cultural context is crucial, as the subject – in these cases, corn
plants or Patsavu Katsinas, respectively – is often lexically absent from
the name itself, thus confounding poststructuralist theory that treats
authorial intention as immaterial. Or (for natural history and ethnos-
cientific associations), take Hooqa'ö, 'pinyon pine conelet' (the ending
qa'ö also referring to a dried corn ear and thus suggesting metaphorical
association of maize ears with pine cones). Or again, Hamana, literally
'bashful', a single-morpheme name that refers to a badger's habitual
behavior (thus given by a member of the Badger clan). For aesthetics,
take for example Paatala, 'water light', a Patki (Water clan) name that
points up the beauty of light reflecting off new pools formed by
rainwater, Kuwanyesnöm, 'colorfully alighting', a woman's name conferred by a member of the Butterfly clan, Kyarngöynöm, 'chasing a
macaw woman', Tangaqyawma, 'iridescence being carried along',
referring to a rainbow or other iridescent forms, and conferred by a
member of the Water clan, or Puhunömsi, 'freshly covered [woman]', a
Rabbit clan name that refers to the beauty of a young rabbit's new fur. For
perceptual sensibility (*inter alia*), take Qötswisiwma, literally 'whiteness
turning around in a line' (a Katsina clan name), referring to a moment in
a katsina dance when katsinas wearing white mantas (cloaks) turn
around successively in a line; the image points up Whorf's identification
of phenomenological Hopi emphasis on shapes, movement and processes rather than the entities, masses and states that are characteristic of

standard average European (SAE) languages. Personal names are a genuine literary genre, giving a window upon myriad features of Hopi cultural knowledge, practice and values, and also serve as a mnemonic corpus of culturally meaningful texts.

Hopi Political Economy and the US Nation State

Persistence of Hopi language and culture through the 20th and into the 21st century is centrally framed against the background of US government policies. These began to affect the Hopi in the 1880s with the establishment of the Executive Order Hopi Reservation, a rectangle drawn around most of the existing villages – roughly an eighth of Hopitutskwa, the Hopi aboriginal land that covers the northeast corner of Arizona. At present, that reservation, reduced by successive actions of the Bureau of Indian Affairs, the Department of Agriculture and the US Congress, is about half its original size. Moreover, since the 1930s, there have been stringent limitations placed on Hopi economic usages within it, especially as regards livestock. Today, economic opportunities on the reservation are few and far between. Standard unemployment figures vary from more than 30% to 60%. The great majority of employment is provided by the Hopi Tribal organization and its various departments – Natural Resources, Education, Health and Tribal Court. There are some positions at the Hopi High School, Indian Health Service hospitals, the Indian Agency and the Police Department. Even though Hopi ceremonies have historically been a major attraction – as Hopi, especially via the Snake Dance, has been denominated an American Shangri-la since the late 19th century (cf. Dilworth, 1996) – the ethnic tourism industry has tended to benefit regional non-Hopi companies more than it has created Hopi employment opportunities. The Hopi Cultural Center, a tribally owned hotel and restaurant, does provide another source of on-Reservation employment, and there are a scattering of crafts shops and grocery stores. Crafts, especially silver jewelry, ceramics, basketry and Katsina dolls provide supplementary income for many people, but few are able to support themselves exclusively this way. Although the Indian art market is burgeoning in Santa Fe, Scottsdale and elsewhere, the enrichment of some Native artists is highly selective and has little effect on overall patterns in the community. In general, Hopis are poor and few have family incomes above the poverty line. The usual markers of rural poverty, a category in which Native Americans have consistently scored the highest of any ethnic group in the USA, are present in terms of such factors as life expectancy, suicide rates, diabetes and substance abuse, most recently among the youth, the scourge of methamphetamine.

Yet, unlike dislocated indigenous communities, Hopis still do have access to parts of their subsistence livelihood that tend to be effaced in standard measures of poverty. In terms of production for the market, the only resource Hopis grow is cattle, but grazing restrictions limit the number of cattle owners to about 5% of the population, and a 10-year drought since the mid-1990s has greatly curtailed cattle numbers. Massive government stock-reduction in the 1940s killed Hopi subsistence pastoralism's dependence on sheep, which had been significant to the economy since the 17th century. There is at present only one sheep herd comprising less than 200 head; mostly, Hopis buy or trade for mutton, a central element of ceremonial feasting, from nearby Navajos. As for agriculture, despite various well-meaning exogenous attempts to com-mercially market Hopi cultivars, such as blue corn, Hopis tenaciously cling to the idea that it is *qahopi*, un-Hopi or immoral, to exploit in this manner traditional subsistence crops such as maize, beans, squash, and even introduced crops like peaches, apricots, apples, chiles, onions, and gathered species such as pinon nuts, wild greens, deer, rabbits, etc., all of which circulate within domestic exchange networks.

The subsistence economy is bound up with the annual cycle of ritual works, which is explicitly concerned, in its songs, prayers and dances, with ensuring beneficial agricultural and foraging outcomes, and is thus inseparable from religious beliefs and practices in Hopi thought. When performing Katsina songs and dances, Hopis summon the spirits of the dead to return as clouds and pour life-giving rain onto the parched earth so that all life-forms – plant, animal and insect – may prosper. They do not imagine that this operates in a separate 'spiritual' or 'religious' sphere from hoeing weeds around corn plants or harvesting and distributing ripe produce: rather, the performative and practical aspects are mutually integral to productive processes. The meaning of produc-tion for more traditionally inclined Hopis is not simply a matter of putting food on the table for material sustenance, but is notably to demonstrate ongoing participation in a pattern of social life marked by reciprocal belonging and communality that is associated, especially in ritual discourse, with health and happiness. In general, Hopis tend to be skeptical of the reliability of the cash economy: although materially poor, they have often rejected actual and potential influxes of cash (e.g. government compensation for aboriginal lands). A woman with a steady job and a predictable source of cash may well be considered poor if she has no man (kin or affine) to regularly grow corn for her: corn, in addition to being a material staple, is the archetypal symbol of life, growth, health and social value. In addition to the recent drought, a general decline in youth participation in farming has produced a significant shortfall, especially for ceremonial occasions that require public redistribution of crops and domestic manufactures. Hopis will tell you with embarrassment and irony that nowadays at Niman (the Home Dance), a ceremony in which Katsina spirits bring the first fruits of the harvest into the village, much of the early corn and melons have not come from Hopi fields, but have in fact been acquired from Mormon farmers along the Little Colorado River to the south.

Until recently, the Hopi Tribe, the formal federally recognized entity presided over by an elected Tribal Council and encompassing an ongoing civil service, gained most of its operating revenue from coal and water leases to the Peabody Coal Company, which runs the largest open strip mine in the USA, north of the Hopi villages. The Company's pumping of groundwater, which amounted to more per annum than is used by the entire Hopi people, has had a severe impact on water available for domestic use. However, in spite of this and a significant grass-roots Hopi movement against the leases, the Tribal Council was long reluctant to abrogate the leases, in spite of a significant grass roots Hopi movement against them, because of the drastic impact this would have on revenues. Without those lease monies, the system of Tribal government, by far the largest employer on the Reservation, might collapse. After years of pressure, Hopi action groups recently celebrated the closing of the mine and the generating plant (in Laughlin, Nevada) that it fed. There have lately been renewed rumblings of a possible restart of the mine, although apparently without plans to resume transporting the coal via use of water in a slurry pipeline (*Navajo Times*, 2008). The economic challenge facing the Tribe is a classic dilemma facing underdeveloped economies on Indian Reservations and throughout the Third and Fourth World. Environmentally unsustainable and, in the long term, economically destructive extractive industries run by powerful multinationals, or massive civil engineering projects like government-sponsored hydro-electric dams or problematic industries based on social exploitation (like gambling), are frequently the irresistible 800 lb economic gorilla, whether it be nuclear waste storage on the Gosiute Reservation, clear-cutting old-growth forest on First Nations Reserves in British Columbia or damming the Columbia and Klamath rivers, producing massive reductions in indigenous subsistence fishing. The supposed instant panacea for Tribes of casino gambling has in fact brought benefits to proportionally few; at the same time much prior philanthropic support for Native causes has dried up in view of the unwarranted presumption of extensive gambling wealth. Despite pervasive unemployment and underemployment on the Hopi Reservation, continuing Hopi opposition to gaming (casinos have been rejected in two referenda since the 1990s) and distrust of the market economy, frequently voiced in conversation, suggest conscious commitment to ethical principles that lies behind the vaunted Hopi ability to retain more societal integrity and aboriginal culture and language than most.

Language Loss and Sociocultural Change

Though persistent against a century of political domination, Hopi linguistic and cultural practices and values of the sort encoded in place and personal names are losing ground in the labyrinth of federal policies, legislation and case-law, as Hopis lose cultural, economic and political sovereignty to the hegemonic ripples of market capitalism and popular culture. Name-givers are losing the practical experiential basis and the cultural contexts of the imagery of names, or losing sufficient control of the language to deploy it competently in this genre. Some namers have been turning to a written database of names recorded in the 1930s (Hill, n.d.), even though without the authorial intention, the direct translations of those are in many instances not transparent. But even where the meanings are easily discerned, the reference is now for many Hopi people memorate rather than lived: with apologies to T.S. Eliot, they 'have the meaning but missed the experience'. Namings were formerly occasions for the performative expression of social associations and for the regeneration of cultural value via poetic images that refer to a great variety of aspects of Hopi experience and practice; they now risk becoming recycled literary forms whose sphere of reference is greatly attenuated. Losing the names entails a weakening of the ties that bind and many of the ideas that animate Hopi thought, suggesting the imbrication of 'cultural loss' with linguistic loss. And disembedded from established cultural practice and social contexts, the language itself becomes semantically depleted.

Hopi place-names are getting lost too, both literally, as these cease to be known and transacted by younger generations, especially nonspeakers of the language, and also in the sense of appropriation, as places under non-Hopi authority. Examples include Tsimontukwi, Woodruff Butte, a sacred site for several Second Mesa Hopi clans, with multiple clan and ritual sodality shrines on it. This site, in private hands, has been turned into a quarry (selling its product to the Arizona Department of

Transportation for road surfacing) and had its top (including now all the shrines) blasted off. Sipàapuni, the geological formation in Little Colorado Canyon that marks the emergence of many Hopi clans from the world below, is currently under severe erosion threat because of altered flow patterns resulting from the damming of the Colorado River at Lake Powell for recreational purposes. Current plans to expand the ski resort on Nuvatukya'ovi, the San Francisco Peaks, will manufacture artificial snow from effluent (legal efforts against this by the Hopi tribe, Navajo Nation and others appear to have been defeated by an Appeals court decision in August 2008). The Peaks are a major spiritual home for the Katsinas, and their snow is a particular symbol of pure life-giving essence that is drawn through song and ritual toward the Hopi villages and fields to replenish life (effluent does not quite work in this regard). Losing 'control' of these places directly impacts aspects of Hopi cultural identity, as Hopi religion is tied into the specific landscape from which it draws its powers and to which Hopis remain ritually responsible. As in the case of the devastating pollution of Onondaga Lake in Central New York state, a sacred site for all the Hodenosaunee, or goldmining in the Black Hills for the Sioux nations, to mention only two more prominent examples, the imposition of the dominant society's extractive mode of production and accompanying attitudes toward the environment is having irreversible effects that not only clash with the religious and environmental values of indigenous societies, but also directly impact culture and language. If Tsimontukwi is no longer there to be visited, prayed toward, collect eagles from, or otherwise referenced in Hopi religious practices, the name is but an evanescent oral memorial to a vanished, formerly semiotically abundant landscape.

According to the neoliberal rationality that guides a sense of global democratic rights, the right to maintain linguistic diversity is basic; it is indeed a core value in the United Nations' pronouncements on culture and language (e.g. UNESCO, 2002). But where language has been used as a technique to preserve social privacy and what is left of indigenous sovereignty within a hegemonic nationstate, there is, as in many Native American societies, a desire to not textualize the language or allow others to learn and understand it. This has long been a primary sociolinguistic value in all the Southwestern Pueblos, from Taos in the east to Hopi in the West. Over the last decade, there have been a number of attempts by the Hopi Tribe, by private foundations, by local schools and even at the village level to address the problem of language loss among the youth. Some of these have concentrated on immersion with elders, but most come back to the idea that learning to read and write in Hopi is critical to perpetuating the language. Teaching Hopi literacy has been a focus for the last several years for teachers at the High School. But while missionaries have written Hopi for more than a century, and while there is as of 1998 an excellent Hopi Dictionary, many older Hopis consider writing to be for the Pahaana's ('whiteman's') language, not for Hopi. All Hopis nowadays are literate in English, but except for those studying Hopi in high school – very much as a second language – who tend to be the least fluent in Hopi cultural practices, few of the older generations, i.e. of those who are the language's most proficient speakers and users, are or wish to be literate in Hopi. To paraphrase a celebrated *koan*, those who write do not know; those who know do not write.

So, if name-loss is emblematic of culturally grounded linguistic loss, and if that culture and language is further enframed in an oral sensibility that undergirds societal and cultural persistence through deliberate rejection of literacy, can writing save Hopi, and if so, what are the consequences? The technologization of the word may be just another nail in the coffin of an autonomous oral indigenous culture; it is an instrument of modernity integral to the nationstate's hegemony, further incorporating indigenous societies and compromising their sovereignty (cf. Whiteley, 2003). In other words, saving Hopi language by the technical processes of linguistic recording, archiving and instruction requires that Hopis first completely accept 'Pahaana' views of culture and language. The Hopi-Pahaana opposition is much more than a racial or social division; it expresses a fundamental clash of values, of different ways of living in the world, just like the clash between subsistence production and the wage-economy. It is a division that continues to articulate Hopi perspectives on identity, ethical values and philosophical principles, and many Hopis, nostalgic for the loss of so much of their traditional culture, voice a fear of becoming 'just Pahaanas'. The assimilation in that 'just' is significant. It means the loss of distinctiveness in a mass social order, with the alternative often being incorporation at the lowest rungs of an ethnicized socioeconomic order; it also means the loss of specialness as members of a revered cultural form of which language is both the marker and the bearer. What does it mean for a young man not engaged in subsistence farming and monolingual in English to show up at the kiva wishing to perform (even 'rock out', as some refer to it) as a Katsina in the upcoming Home Dance? If he is from the right village and has been initiated, he will not be refused. But the elders deplore that, not speaking or understanding Hopi, he is enacting a religious role without singing the songs, following the dance-leaders' instructions or even being able to keep rhythm; how can he participate, liturgically or aesthetically, in 'turning around in line' at the right moment? How can he be or become a Katsina? The Katsinas' songs will call for ascendant kinfolk ('our fathers, our mothers') the clouds, the spirits of the Hopi dead, to come from Nuvatukya'ovi and elsewhere to pour their life-renewing essence onto the fields and springs so that all plants, people, animals and insects may flourish. And the believers – the practitioners watching the dance – will take the spruce branches from the costumes of the Katsinas at the appropriate time and go down to plant them in their cornfields so that they will serve as a magnetic conduit for the moisture-generating capacity they bring from the mountain peaks. Not speaking means not naming and not singing; that often accompanies not planting or harvesting and thus having no grounds for belief in some of the most fundamental of Hopi convictions. If, as a friend puts it, 'Hopi is first and foremost a farmer', and if the language is tied to the subsistence economy and its undergirding in religious beliefs and actions, linguistic perpetuation via a formally schooled ability to read and write textualized Hopi clearly entails a radically shifted sense of sociolinguistic value and cultural identity. Maintaining their language through literacy entails the surrender of sociopsychological autonomy: Hopi can no longer be a 'private language', so to speak, but must be reduced to the public space of democratic interchange that liberal rationality predicates for linguistic rights, and in that process lose the most cherished aspects of its capacity to socially, culturally, aesthetically and even perceptually distinguish.

In all probability, the Hopi language will only persist if it is regularly and habitually transferred to written forms. And this will run parallel with increasing incorporation into a global political-economic order in which the majority of Hopis will sell their labor in market capitalism at the lower end of the socioeconomic spectrum. At present, many are poor, but actively engaged in the reproduction of culture and the production of an autonomous subsistence economy that renders them socially and spiritually independent. But the transformation of both Hopi society and the Hopi language in this process – including the separation of meanings from their current embeddedness in particular patterns of sociality, ritual works, beliefs and domestic production, as well as a loss of the language's capacity to keep Hopi ideas private – represents a loss that is more than merely linguistic. Increasing influence of the values and practices of modernity, the nation and the market economy, including rationalist and logocentric notions of language itself, presents a paradox for all Hopis concerned about the language – not only philosophically, but also in terms of community decisions to deploy or not deploy specific language-enhancing policies.

Notes

1. Note the degree of contrast with recently published figures (Ichihashi-Nakayama *et al.*, 2007: 467), which indicate a 48% fluency rate for the Hopi population. My sense, albeit impressionistic and unquantified, is that Hopi language endangerment is much sharper than its rating (3 on a scale of 1–5, where 1 = most endangered) in linguistic accounts derived from government census records.
2. The etymology is obscure, but if originally Hopi – the same word, as Sipapu, Shipap, etc., is used by the Rio Grande Pueblos too – may refer, as earth navels for the Tewa, to an earthly crotch [*siip* in Hopi] or navel [*sipna*]).
3. See Whiteley (2008: 19) for a discussion of differing linguistic interpretations of name suffixes.

References

Appadurai, A. (1996) *Modernity at Large: Cultural Dimensions of Globalization*. Minneapolis, MN: University of Minnesota Press.
Basso, K.H. (1996) *Wisdom Sits in Places: Landscape and Language Among the Western Apache*. Albuquerque, NM: University of New Mexico Press.
Brody, H. (1982) *Maps and Dreams*. New York: Pantheon.
Cook, F. (ed.) (1887) *Journals of the Military Expedition of Major General John Sullivan against the Six Nations of Indians in 1779*. Auburn, NY: Knapp, Peck and Thomson.
Dilworth, L. (1996) *Imagining Indians in the Southwest: Persistent Visions of a Primitive Past*. Washington, DC: Smithsonian Institution Press.
Feld, S. and Basso, K.H (eds) (1996) *Senses of Place*. Santa Fe: School of American Research Press.
Gordon, Jr., R.G. (ed.) (2005) *Ethnologue: Languages of the World* (15th edn). Dallas, TX: SIL International. On WWW at http://www.ethnologue.com/.
Graymont, B. (1972) *The Iroquois in the American Revolution*. Syracuse, NY: Syracuse University Press.
Hill, K. (n.d.) Hopi kin database. Manuscript. Bureau of Applied Research, University of Arizona.
Ichihashi-Nakayama, K., Yumitani, Y. and Yamamoto, A.Y. (2007) Languages of the Southwest United States. In O. Miyaoka, O. Sakiyama and M.E. Krauss (eds) *The Vanishing Languages of the Pacific Rim* (pp. 460–474) Oxford: Oxford University Press.
James, H.C. (1974) *Pages from Hopi History*. Tucson, AZ: University of Arizona Press.
Lévi-Strauss, C. (1966) *The Savage Mind*. Chicago, IL: University of Chicago Press.
Lucy, J.A. (1992) *Language Diversity and Thought: A Reformulation of the Linguistic Relativity Hypothesis*. New York: Cambridge University Press.
Malotki, E. (1979) *Eine sprachwissenschaftliche Analyse der Raumvorstellungen in der Hopi-Sprache* [Hopi Space: A Linguistic Analysis of the Spatial Concepts in the Hopi Language]. Tübingen: Gunter Narr.

Malotki, E. (1983) *Hopi Time: A Linguistic Analysis of the Temporal Concepts in the Hopi Language*. Berlin: Mouton.

Mauss, M. (1985 [1938]) A category of the human mind: The notion of person, the notion of self. In M. Carrithers, S. Collins and S. Lukes (eds) *The Category of the Person* (pp. 1–25). Cambridge: Cambridge University Press.

Morgan, L.H. (1851) *League of the Ho-de'-no-sau-nee or Iroquois*. New York: Sage.

Navajo Times (2007, 27 December) Protectors of Mother Earth: With Environmental Victories, Green goes Mainstream on Dinétah, by Cindy Yurth. Windowrock, AZ: the Navajo Times.

Navajo Times (2008, 17 April) Black Mesa Studies to Resume; Slurry Appears Dead, by Marley Shebala. Windowrock, AZ: the Navajo Times.

Ortiz, A. (1972) Ritual drama and the pueblo world view. In A. Ortiz (ed.) *New Perspectives on the Pueblos* (pp. 136–161). Albuquerque, NM: University of New Mexico Press.

Sahlins, M.D. (1972) *Stone Age Economics*. Chicago, IL: Aldine.

Thornton, T.F. (2007) *Being and Place Among the Tlingit*. Seattle, WA: University of Washington Press.

Thwaites, R.G. (1896–1901) *The Jesuit Relations and Allied Documents: Travels and Explorations of the Jesuit Missionaries in New France, 1610–1791*. Cleveland, OH: Burrows.

UNESCO (2002) *Cultural Diversity: Common Heritage, Plural Identities*. Paris: UNESCO.

Whiteley, P.M. (1992) Hopitutungwni: 'Hopi Names' as literature. In B. Swann (ed.) *On the Translation of Native American Literatures* (pp. 208-227). Washington, DC: Smithsonian Institution Press.

Whiteley, P.M. (2003) Do 'language rights' serve indigenous interests? Some Hopi and other queries. *American Anthropologist* 105 (4), 712–722.

Whiteley, P.M. (2008) The Orayvi Split: A Hopi transformation. *Anthropological Papers of the American Museum of Natural History*, 87.

Whorf, B.L. (1956 [1936]) An American Indian model of the universe. In J.B. Carroll (ed.) *Language, Thought, and Reality: Selected Writings of Benjamin Lee Whorf* (pp. 57–64). Cambridge, MA: MIT Press.

Part 4

Language, Poverty and the Role of the Linguist

Chapter 11

The Role of the Linguist in Language Maintenance and Revitalization: Documentation, Training and Materials Development

LENORE A. GRENOBLE, KEREN D. RICE and NORVIN RICHARDS

Introduction

In recent years, an increased interest in language maintenance and revitalization comes not only from the linguistic scholarly community, but also from speaker communities as well as speakers of languages of wider communication. Funding agencies, such as the joint National Science Foundation (NSF), National Endowment for the Humanities (NEH) and Smithsonian venture for Documenting Endangered Languages (DEL) in the USA, the Hans Rausing Endangered Languages Documentation Programme (ELDP) at SOAS and the Volkswagen-Stiftung DoBeS (Dokumentation Bedrohter Sprachen/Documentation of Endangered Languages) Project, all have concerns and agendas, as do international organizations such as UNESCO. The multiplicity of concerned parties raises the question of the role of modern field linguists and how they can best be prepared to serve that role. In the present paper, we consider this question from a variety of angles, focusing on documentation, training and materials development in situations where language maintenance and revitalization is an issue, set against the background of poverty.

At the outset it is important to understand that there is no set pattern, no specific rules that apply to each and every situation for documentation, training and materials development. Settings vary greatly in terms of their needs and in terms of community desires. Poverty, broadly defined, lies at the heart of issues of language endangerment and the desire for revitalization, and is often a stumbling block to successful revitalization and/or language maintenance.

In considering language revitalization and maintenance, poverty must be considered from a number of different perspectives. From the human perspective, there are considerations of poverty of the community where the language in question is spoken and of the linguist working on a particular language. While economic poverty comes to mind first, intellectual poverty of both community and linguist can be issues as well. Poverty can also be considered in other ways: poverty of documentation available for a language and poverty of technology will have important effects on language revitalization/maintenance undertakings.

We begin with a brief overview of the role of the linguist in language documentation, language revitalization and language maintenance projects, and then discuss in greater depth the particulars of description and documentation and of training and materials development, stressing the responsibilities of the linguist, and taking poverty in its many forms as a background to all discussion.

On the Role of the Linguist

As background to understanding poverty and the role of the linguist, it is necessary to examine responsibilities of linguists engaged in fieldwork on endangered languages. In North America in recent years, fieldworkers are often trained to take on an important responsibility, often termed the Hale-Bach responsibility, to engage with the community on language maintenance and revitalization in endangered/impoverished language communities if this is desired by the community. Thus, the linguist becomes an activist. This position is taken by many linguists; see, for instance, Berardo and Yamamoto (2007), Bobaljik (1998), England (1998), Grenoble and Whaley (2006), Grinevald (2007), Hale (2001), Rice (2006) and others. While advocates of this view have been outspoken in recent years, nevertheless there exists debate about this stance. For instance, Dorian (1993: 578) takes the position that the linguist has a responsibility, emphatically stating that 'the linguist cannot enter the threatened-language equation without becoming a factor in it', but she continues to say that there is a great range as to exactly what kind of a factor the linguist may choose to be, ranging from minimizing his/her impact to maximizing it and taking an active stance. This is in reaction to Ladefoged (1992: 811), who argues, essentially, that linguists have no role in revitalization or language activism; 'the task of the linguist is to lay out the facts concerning a given linguistic situation'. Newman (2003) takes a similar position, noting that linguists who 'care too much' spend a significant amount of time in the field 'giving back to the community' in maintenance/revitalization, developing pedagogical materials and so on, detracting from the primary work of language documentation and description. Newman notes, however, that it is 'impossible to escape the practical and emotional pressures to behave like a caring human being in the field, nor would one want to' (2003: 6).

From our own personal experiences as fieldworkers in a variety of situations over the past few decades, an attitude of scientific detachment is difficult to maintain in the field. Conditions vary from place to place and time to time, but in every case the role of the researcher in the community requires careful thought. In many cases, it is not clear to us that the distinction between language activism and simply 'laying out the facts' can even be coherently drawn. The members of any community will have a variety of beliefs about the nature of their language; when the language is endangered, these beliefs often become a matter for debate, and this debate is one in which the linguist may usefully participate. A community may, for example, come to believe messages offered to them, explicitly or implicitly, by a dominant culture, to the effect that their language is primitive, or simple, or illogically constructed, or, almost paradoxically, too difficult or in some other way intrinsically unsuited to modern life. To the extent that these descriptions can be made precise, they are factual claims about the language, and the linguist may be in a position (and may have a duty) to lay out technical knowledge that contradicts them. Community members may hope that their children can 'get ahead' by learning the dominant language and may assume that this entails failing to learn the minority language of their families. Here, again, linguists may have access to a wider perspective on the benefits and costs of bilingualism and technical linguistic information that they ought to be able to share with the community.

For the linguist, engagement with the community can take a variety of forms. One is to be responsible to the needs of the community as perceived by the community, responding to wishes of the community and not just to their own agenda. Another way of engaging involves training – the linguist has a responsibility to train speakers of the language, when there is interest, in language documentation, as well as training students of linguistics. A third type of responsibility involves the development of materials, not only materials that document the language (e.g. the traditional triumvirate of dictionary, grammar and texts), but also pedagogical materials.

Just how the linguist and community work together to realize these different responsibilities will vary with place and time. The most important point, perhaps, is that the linguist is a presence in a community, having an effect on that community in one way or another, just as the community has an effect on the linguist. In as much as it is possible, the role that the linguist plays must be carefully considered, and the researcher and community must work together to determine the work to be done. Our personal experiences are not those discussed by Newman (2003), suggesting that taking on such responsibilities need not detract from the quality of research being done, but, in fact, may greatly enhance it.

Poverty and Language Maintenance/Revitalization

With an understanding of the various responsibilities of the linguist to the communities in which he or she works as background, we now turn to framing the role of the linguist in language revitalization with respect to poverty. It is important to note that we consider poverty to be *relational*. For instance, there may be poverty in a local community with respect to a dominant or national community (for instance Native American communities in the North American framework), but such communities may be relatively affluent on a more global scale. According to the 2000 US Census, the poverty rate among Native Americans was 26.9%, far above the national rate of 11.3%, making them the poorest group in the country. The World Bank defines the base of the international poverty line for households where the income or consumption is less than $1 per person per day, while at the same time noting that there is no indicator of poverty that is directly comparable across countries. This level of $1/day is more appropriate for lower-income countries, while in middle-income countries the poverty line would be more appropriately set at a higher rate (ranging from $2 to $11/day) (World Bank Glossary). Thus, there is no single set of criteria that one can employ to determine poverty.

With respect to poverty and language maintenance and revitalization, poverty can work at opposite extremes, working either against them or in their favor. Geographic isolation, for example, may result in a general lack of material wealth, along with limited health care and other resources, but that very isolation may help keep a local language strong and vital. For instance, in an informal survey of the status of Aboriginal languages in Ontario, a student of Keren Rice's found that the Aboriginal languages were far healthier in the more isolated Northern parts of the province than in the more densely populated Southern areas. Yet at the same time, people living in very impoverished communities, where there are scant resources for such basic human needs as food and shelter, rarely find themselves in a position to be concerned about language revitalization. For example, sub-Saharan African is home to over 1000 languages, but UNESCO (2006: 10) reports that one in three people living there is hungry. It is unrealistic to think of implementing active revitalization programs when speakers are starving. The fourth session of the UN Permanent Forum on Indigenous Issues (held in May 2005) reported alarming statistics for poverty on a global scale, with 370 million indigenous people living in extreme poverty; 'extreme poverty' is defined as living in conditions where one cannot meet basic needs, such as food, water, shelter and basic education (Sachs, 2005). The World Bank estimates approximately 1.1 billion people in the world live in extreme poverty; these statistics suggest that approximately one third of the people living in extreme poverty are indigenous. Thus, in some cases the isolation related to poverty can help keep a language robust, while in other cases poverty may make it impossible for communities to address language shift because of their struggle to meet basic human needs. This paradoxical nature of poverty can arise from its multifaceted nature.

Poverty can take a number of different forms. Consider, first, poverty from an economic perspective. Poverty and the desire for socioeconomic advancement are often cited as underlying causes for language shift (see, for instance, Mufwene [2004] among others). People want to improve their socioeconomic situation and may feel that their language is holding them back. This may lead to a rejection of the native language in favor of the dominant language. Such situations often involve another sense of poverty – the language itself may be regarded as being of low prestige and inadequate. These factors often lead to rejection of a language, with a desire for children to learn the dominant language in order to be able to get ahead. In some cases, this may be driven by pure economic necessity. To give just one of many examples, consider the case of a Teco-speaking community, Mazapa de Madera, in Chiapas, Mexico. Historically its economy was corn-based agrarian, but population growth led to a situation where the land could no longer support the community. As a result, many young people left to work in urban areas throughout Mexico; others became migrant workers, leaving seasonally to work in other areas. Working outside the community forced acquisition of Spanish and resulting language shift, with the community largely monolingual Spanish by the mid-1980s (Garzon, 1998).

That said, poverty considered from what we will call an intellectual perspective may facilitate language maintenance, language revitalization, language documentation, training and materials development. As we listen to elders, authors, poets and others from around the world, they often speak of the profound value of language (a good nonacademic example is Mark Abley's [2003] popular book *Spoken Here*; the 1996 Canadian Royal Commission Report on Aboriginal Peoples also contains a wealth of material). Peoples around the world are increasingly aware of language as a marker of identity; see, for instance, the 2005 Canadian report from the Task Force on Aboriginal Languages and Cultures. It is often noted that in communities where a language has been lost or is in a state of endangerment, there is also a loss of self-esteem and of cultural heritage. This is the intellectual impoverishment of language loss. As speakers of languages, and children of those speakers, become aware of the relationship between language, identity, culture, self-esteem and other similar factors, the recognition of that poverty can itself be a motivating factor in language revitalization. In a sense, language becomes the miner's canary for cultural vitality – in many cases, a threatened language is the first sign of cultural shift.

Conversely, successful language revitalization can help community members to take pride in their culture, reminding them that they have skills and traditions not available to the majority community. Indeed, in communities with severely threatened languages, skill in the language may become such a valuable resource that conflicts arise among community members over whose command of the language is most deserving of respect and prestige.

The Linguist and Poverty

The linguist entering a community where the ancestral language is endangered thus may find both economic and intellectual poverty. There are challenges that arise from both. In a community that faces economic poverty, the kinds of challenges might involve housing of a quality that the linguist is not used to, a different diet, perhaps inadequate food, potentially exposure to diseases. In a community in which intellectual poverty is found, people might not want to admit to being speakers of a language, and might be embarrassed about the language or feel that their language is inadequate.

We have so far focused on ways in which the community is faced with poverty. The linguist too may be faced with poverty (though typically on a very different scale from that of the community). While in some cases a linguist might have funding that is adequate, many field linguists enter a field situation without the kind of technology that has come to be expected today (a fact to which we return in the next section). A linguist may be taking time to do fieldwork, time away from a paying job.

The position of an endangered language is made more and more precarious by all these forms of poverty. An affluent community with a comparatively large number of speakers might be able to afford to bring in multiple specialists to address their linguistic needs; a poorer community must often rely on a single linguist (if anyone at all), who must often attempt types of work outside his or her area of expertise. As fewer individuals speak a language, the future of the language begins to hang on the welfare of individual speakers and on properties of their personalities; if some of these speakers are in ill health, for example, or are unwilling to cooperate with each other or with the linguist, then the prospects for the language as a whole grow correspondingly darker. All of these problems can be exacerbated by poverty.

Description and Documentation

The word 'description' has long been used in linguistics. This refers primarily to work that potentially leads to a grammar, lexicon and texts of a language. In recent years, a notion of 'documentation' has also become important in linguistics as well. Language documentation, as defined by Himmelmann (1998: 166), takes as its aim 'to provide a comprehensive record of the linguistic practices characteristic of a given speech community... This... differs fundamentally from... language description [which] aims at the records of a language... as a system of abstract elements, constructions, and rules'. Language documentation aims to create materials that would allow for the revitalization of the language even in the absence of speakers and other materials. On the ELDP website (www.hrelp.org), language documentation is described as involving the following: 'spoken language in a variety of styles and contexts, with transcriptions, translations, and annotations; written texts in a variety of styles with transcriptions, translations, and annotations; relevant sociological and cultural information; dictionary; thesaurus; pedagogical materials; grammar. Documentation thus is a major task, with attempting to record language in its fullest, with proper annotation, and appropriate archiving and availability in electronic format'. This definition of language documentation focuses on two aspects of the work – the materials to be gathered and advances in technology. Technology allows for high quality sound recordings as well as video recordings, and for archiving of materials in new ways, and facilitates the type of language documentation described earlier.

An important question to pose in each situation is why it is that documentation is being done. There could be a variety of reasons; some are given next in the form of questions:

• Is documentation for furthering linguistic theory?
• Is documentation for diachronic work?
• Is documentation for furthering our understanding of typology?
• Is documentation for the future needs of speakers?

Depending on many factors, including the goals of the linguist, the nature of the community and the relationship between the linguist and the community, the answer to why documentation is being undertaken might be different. This answer will in turn dictate the focus of documentation; documentation which aims to further linguistic theory, for example, will need to gather examples of phenomena that form part of the speaker's competence but may seldom or never appear in corpora (e.g. multiple wh-questions, parasitic gaps, judgments about ambiguity), while documentation intended to help future speakers with language revitalization might gather more data about conversational strategies, politeness, vocabulary for flora and fauna and so forth. If a linguist and community are working together, negotiating the goals of documentation is very important.

Poverty can have a major effect on the ability to document and archive a language, whatever the goals of the documentation are, as well as an effect on the quality of the documentation. With regard to the former, we have outlined some of this earlier. From the perspective of the linguist, there may be a lack of funding to support fieldwork. Perhaps more commonly, there may be a lack of proper equipment – tape recorders, digital recorders, video recorders, computers, and even batteries and tapes. While documentation in the technological sense may be a goal, it is not always a realistic one. Poverty within a community can also have an effect on the ability to document, and this may come about in many different ways. Levels of education may make it difficult to train people to do linguistic work – the time investment to give good training in literacy, for instance, can be very high, and people, while interested, might be unable to afford to spend the time on what might appear to be an unnecessary skill.

Poverty can also have an effect on the quality of documentation. If the linguist and members of the community come from very different types of educational systems, and are unable to spend the time to understand where the other is coming from, finding a meeting of the minds about what is important in language can sometimes be difficult. Training in linguistic thinking is a challenge at the best of times, and circumstances are not always ideal in a fieldwork situation, at least not ideal from the perspective of the linguist. In many communities around the world, the type of technological equipment that linguists routinely work with today may be quite foreign, and a challenge to learn. Providing training can raise other sets of problems in a community as well. When the linguist leaves the community, how is it possible for the now trained community members to continue doing linguistic work in the absence of funding? If the linguist hires individuals away from other work, what are the repercussions of this, both for the other work and, in the long-term sense, for the community member who has left a continuing job?

Training and Materials Development

In this section, we explore the role of the linguist with respect to training and materials development in a context of language endangerment and poverty. As discussed earlier, there is overall consensus among linguists working in these areas today that it is the obligation of the external linguist to work with a community as that community desires, to help train and to create language materials. In fact, many might even consider it unethical not to do so, if desired by the community. Critically, any of these programs must be centered around community interests and needs as community members, not external linguists, define them. That said, the linguist in such situations may be needed to introduce different possibilities, to discuss the merits and potential downfalls of these and to help community members make realistic assessments about their goals and interests in achieving them. This includes an honest evaluation of available resources, human and financial, and of the level of commitment of individuals as well as the community as a whole. Setting realistic, attainable goals is one of the biggest challenges at the outset of revitalization programs, and yet they are critical to their success.

Another challenge that many linguists in these situations face is that the needs and priorities of the endangered language community differ from the demands and expectations that the linguist's academic career imposes. An often unstated role of the linguist working in such communities is to build bridges between the indigenous communities and the academy; this is particularly true for those communities which are located near an academic institution and may have some kind of (formal) relationship with them. Just as poverty affects description and documentation, it affects training and materials development. Both economic and intellectual poverty can have negative effects on training and materials development: people may want to make efforts to maintain or revitalize the language, but their situation might not allow it; there might not be access to the types of things one needs to develop materials. We examine these issues in this section.

Training

There are a number of potential advantages to the both linguist and the community in training interested community members in linguistic work. Members of the community are much more likely than the linguist to be willing and able to spend long periods of time, possibly their entire lives, living within the community. They may be more powerfully motivated than the linguist to do certain kinds of linguistic work; as we said above, language revitalization is sometimes motivated partly by a desire to reclaim something of value to the community which is in danger of loss, and community members likely feel this loss more keenly than the linguist (a language maintenance or revitalization program is unlikely to be successful in any sense if the linguist feels the loss of the language more strongly than community members). Depending on the community, it may be easier for community members to gain the community trust and respect necessary for doing language revitalization work. In some communities, the reverse may be true, however; there are certainly communities in which a member who receives special training not available to other members may simply become an object of suspicion and dislike, accused of trying to make himself/herself more important than others (a phenomenon referred to in Australia as the 'tall poppy syndrome'). Certain types of language description may be easier for a member of the community, who can take advantage of the kind of privileged access that we have to our own mental grammars, discovering new linguistic data through simple introspection (see Hale [1965] for detailed discussion). The community member may also have privileged access to certain types of data generated by others, participating in types of conversations that the linguist never hears (here we can think of the many types of language that friends and family are more likely to share with each other than with strangers).

Training of a community member has the potential to make the community members equal partners in the development and implementation of a field project. They contribute to the project as linguists would, and act as educated consumers of the materials the linguist or team produces, able to interpret the linguist's terminology and catch his or her mistakes. In order to achieve these goals, there are several steps that need to be followed. First of all, it is important to find the right people to join the work, and then to agree on common goals. Critical to this is defining documentation and what the community hopes to achieve in this process, and what the role of individual community members will be, what the role of the community as a whole will be and what the role of the outside linguist will be. From the very start of a project it is necessary to determine who speaks the language and what their status in the community is. It is important to negotiate upfront such matters as payment, how an individual will manage to do the linguistic work while fitting it in with his or her other responsibilities, and some care should be given to the potential impact (on a personal and/or social level) which individuals may face in the community by virtue of having been singled out for this work. Finally, in most cases some sort of training is required as a precursor to engaging in the actual documentation. The level of training needed will depend on the goals of the project and the overall level of training among community members, and on the awareness of the linguist of the particular community and its goals and aspirations. Careful thought needs to be given to each of these various steps in setting up a documentation program that is truly collaborative. We will address each in turn.

Training in the field: The training of community members

Despite the existence of some outstanding programs at universities and an increasing number of programs designed to train speakers of endangered languages (at least in North America), the reality is that most linguists will be asked to do some kind of training while in the field. This stems in part from financial considerations – few community members can afford the money and the time needed to enroll in such programs – as well as practical considerations of the kind of background knowledge needed to participate in these programs. (For example, the university-based programs cited next all require knowledge of English, the language of instruction.)

What type of training is needed varies widely from community to community. A community with a large number of comparatively young speakers, for example, is in a very different position from one with a small number of elderly speakers; a community with a language that has been well-described in the linguistic literature will have different needs from one whose language is relatively undocumented. When all the speakers are too elderly to take an active role in regularly teaching children, some of the training will crucially involve teaching the language itself to younger community members who can pass the language on (see Hinton [2003] for some discussion). For some communities, the major training needs may center on the development of pedagogical materials; this may involve, for example, learning how to use whatever writing system has been developed for the language, along with how to teach it to others, and strategies for teaching the grammar and vocabulary of the language. For other communities, the linguist may need to offer training in linguistic documentation, including skills in recording, phonetic transcription and morphemic analysis. Depending on the individuals involved, this training may be tailored more or less specifically to the particular language under study; many community members will be interested mainly in the ability to analyze their own language, while some may want the wider perspective granted by a more general linguistic education, which would let them play a different kind of role in analysis. If a linguistic literature already exists, community members may want to learn the terminology of that literature, so that they can take advantage of existing work.

In this section, we have focused on the training of community members. It is very important to keep in mind that there is a different kind of training that is necessary, the training of the linguist to work in the community. The linguist may enter the community with knowledge of linguistics, but no knowledge of the community, the people, the culture, the epistemologies. For work to be truly collaborative and empowering, the training will often need to go in both directions.

Formal training: University programs

A number of universities offer training programs that are designed for community members who wish to learn enough linguistics to work on describing, documenting, revitalizing or maintaining their language. These include the University of Arizona, MIT and the University of Texas, Austin, for example. The University of Arizona launched its program in 1999 with the mission of providing a one-year Master's degree in Native American linguistics. The goal of this program is to train members of Native American communities 'to do descriptive research on their languages, and to prepare for academic careers in teaching these languages and related fields'. Students begin by attending the American Indian Language Development Institute (AILDI), which is in and of itself a program designed with many of the same goals. AILDI is an annual four-week summer program at the University of Arizona, founded in 1978 with the primary goal of ensuring linguistic and cultural diversity in large part through training members of Native language communities in the Americas. Similarly, the MIT Indigenous Language Initiative is a Master's program in linguistics designed specifically for speakers of threatened languages. The University of Texas, Austin, offers a concentration in documentary and descriptive linguistics; its work is closely affiliated with the Center for Indigenous Languages of Latin America (CILLA), which promotes linguistic collaboration with members of indigenous language communities in Latin America. Other universities have recently developed programs in language documentation aimed at both speakers/community members and linguistics students who wish to do documentation work; these include the University of Hawaii and the University of Alaska Fairbanks.

A few funding agencies (such as DoBeS of Volkswagen-Stiftung and the Hans Rausing Endangered Languages Programme) offer short term, intensive training sessions for grant recipients and others. AILDI represents a well-rounded (multipurpose) program that focuses on training community members to acquire the skills needed for their own purposes. These include not only teacher training and curriculum development, but also the kind of knowledge needed by tribal communities to enable them to craft tribal language policies and language planning documents. It is very specific to a Northern Native American context (the majority of the participants typically come from the American Southwest), but its structure can serve as a model for communities elsewhere. Several other universities located in the USA (e.g. University of Oregon) and a few Canadian universities (e.g. University of Alberta, University of Victoria) offer summer training programs for speakers of languages to develop skills for language teaching and language revitalization.

Poverty affects access to such training programs in critical and often fatal ways. Interested speakers maybe not be able to afford to attend, even if they receive a fellowship to go. People may be able to go for one year, but not be able to get the follow-through that is often required to receive the full benefits of such training. Those speakers in language teaching and language revitalization may not have the knowledge of educational institutions that is sometimes necessary to make such programs successful.

Materials Development

Communities interested in revitalizing or maintaining their language are often keen to develop materials to do so. Their primary interest is quite frequently in pedagogical materials, but often also reference materials, particularly dictionaries, aimed at language learners (as opposed to linguists). Few linguists are trained to create such materials; few, if any, graduate programs in linguistics offer courses in creating dictionaries or orthographies, let alone textbooks (although some such programs are being developed). There are few manuals available for creating materials or revitalization programs (Hinton *et al.* [2002] being an exception). Communities undertaking language revitalization and searching for ideas about how to do it may discover that other communities in the same position are among their richest sourcesfor ideas; there are already numerous conferences on language revitalization which are attended by members of such communities, ready to share their observations about the successes and failures of various techniques. Resources for learning about such conferences include Northern Arizona University's 'Teaching Indigenous Languages' website at http://jan.ucc.nau.edu/~jar/SIL9brochure.html, the Foundation for Endangered Languages website at http://www.ogmios.org/home.htm, and the Endangered Language Fund's website at http://www.endangeredlanguagefund.org.

It is our experience that writing pedagogical materials is a slow, labor-intensive process. Moreover, the value of these materials is seldom recognized by the academy, and so engaging in this kind of activity may actually hinder a linguist's professional advancement while at the same time being necessary if the linguist wants to work with a particular community. This conundrum points again to the need to train community members who can be the frontrunners on any such project, with the linguist contributing as needed and also to the need to educate the academy as to the intellectual value of such work. Linguistic work can be enormously facilitated through the creation of pedagogical materials, allowing linguists external to the community to learn things about the language that they never would have learned otherwise.

When the term 'materials' is used, by and large it is understood to be *written*, pedagogical materials. There is a basic assumption among many linguists and communities that literacy is a positive, and even necessary, step in revitalization/maintenance. This assumption is not without counterexamples; the Master-Apprentice model is one notable exception (see especially Hinton *et al.*, 2002). Nevertheless, literacy is controversial in many communities and for some linguists. In some communities, people believe that their language is not 'worthy' of writing; that it is not a 'real' language with 'real' grammar. In such cases the influence or prestige of the language of wider communication may have overwhelmed the local language. A community may also be leery of writing their language down for a variety of cultural reasons, including the worry that outsiders may be able to appropriate the language if it is written. In other cases, members of a community might believe that their language is too hard to learn and too hard to write. In still other cases, there may be an assumption that the very fact of writing a language will reinforce its maintenance, and development of an orthography and literacy may be valued for this reason (Wurm, 2003: 20–21).

One role of the linguist in the area of literacy is to clarify with a community those situations in which literacy would be most likely to assist in language maintenance/revitalization and be explicit about where domains need to be created, where social change needs to take place. It is often assumed that literacy can be added to an existing cultural framework, with a rather instantaneous boost in language vitality. But literacy, like every other aspect of language use, requires a context in which it can operate. For groups where there is no pre-existing literacy or where literacy exists only in a language of wider communication, it is necessary to create domains for the use of literacy in the endangered language. This may itself require a shift in cultural values about language: some oral cultures value orality more highly than literacy and may view a shift to writing as a downgrading of culture. (Alternatively, others feel that their language has little or no value because it lacks a written form. This attitude stems from the high prestige that is often attached to literacy in a language of wider communication.) Literacy can actually hinder the teaching of oral language and may provide no benefit at all if its existence is, in and of itself, seen as a solution to language shift. It is only a solution insofar as it creates new domains for language use, and new motivations for using the language.

In impoverished communities, it is important to keep in mind that creating domains for literacy, and the very use of literacy, requires both material and human resources: paper, printing facilities, teachers and so on. In North America, the internet is often cited as an easy solution to the problem of material resources, but its use requires access to the internet and computers, both of which are not available in many other parts of the world, and not in all Native American communities.

Finally, it is important to consider the overall timeline involved in this kind of work. Establishing a collaborative relationship with a community is extremely time consuming; actual clarification of goals and objectives adds time on top of this. It takes significant time to train people and to develop materials. This kind of linguistic research does not progress rapidly, and the timeline may be at odds with the expectations of an individual's home institution for career development. A community with an endangered language often does not have the time to wait for a 'perfect' description of the language before undertaking the creation of pedagogical materials; the linguist should therefore warn the community that the materials will unavoidably contain errors, which will later have to be corrected once the facts of the language are better understood.

Before beginning to develop any materials, we advocate what has been called 'prior clarification' of the goals and resources available to the community (see Dauenhauer & Dauenhauer, 1998). Given this myriad of difficulties, we see the role of the linguist as that of facilitator and as a resource to the community, as the linguist should be in the position to see the broader implications of the research, along with the wider range of possibilities and the challenges that are likely to arise.

The Navajo Language Academy (NLA; Fernald *et al.*, 2004) is one example of a program where many of these issues come together. The Navajo Language Academy, Inc., was officially created in 1998, although its roots trace to earlier Navajo linguistics workshops held in the 1970s and 1980s. It is a truly collaborative effort between trained linguists and community members, although at the outset it is important to make clear that Navajo is in the enviable position of having a number of Navajo community members who hold PhDs in linguistics, and that the collaboration of external and internal linguists has been a fundamental part of the NLA since its very inception. The summer workshops are aimed at training Navajo-language teachers as well as linguists; one specific goal is teaching people how to do research on Navajo, while another is the development of pedagogical materials to be used in language classrooms. It would seem that the NLA has successfully found a way to balance these demanding and at times conflicting goals. At the same time, the NLA is vulnerable because it does not have a steady, predictable source of funding. One result is that the NLA exists from year to year, and that its core members all hold full-time jobs elsewhere. This means that they have limited time to devote to the NLA outside of summer sessions, and achievement of all their goals suffers somewhat in the process. Thus, for example, although pedagogical materials are developed, the organizers feel that they could be better disseminated, and they are currently unable to provide support for teachers during the regular academic year, when the NLA is not in operation.

Through the Canadian Community-University Research Alliance (CURA) program of the Social Science and Humanities Research Council (SSHRC), a number of language programs have received five years of funding, renewable once. This program requires that participants work together to define their goals and define governance structures early in the process. Participants in these projects echo much of what has been said earlier – things take longer than expected; while there is interest, it is often difficult for people to find the time to devote to such projects, the goals of different communities and different linguists differ.

Materials development is a challenge at the best of times, requiring time and patience and a good team with members bringing different skills. Linguists should recognize that many communities will want and even expect external linguists to be engaged in developing pedagogical materials, yet they may find that their own training is insufficient in these areas. Tensions might arise because the expectations of an academic institution as to what counts as viable research may not include materials. Partnering with community members can help ensure that the creation of such materials does not fall solely on one person, and is more likely to result in materials that will be accepted and used by the community. Careful advance planning can help make the creation of such materials useful for the linguist's own knowledge of the language so that the time invested is beneficial to all. Conditions of poverty can introduce other kinds of challenges, and it is helpful if it can be anticipated that these will exist, even though the exact nature of such challenges might come as a surprise.

Conclusion

Ultimately the role of the linguist is dependent upon the goals of a documentation project and its overall purpose. Given limited resources, human and financial, the linguistic community as a whole has yet to reach consensus about how documentation should be approached, and there is likely not a single answer. Should we place a premium on documentation with the intention of future generations of linguists (or community members) going back to work on description (or revitalization/resuscitation) based on what was recorded? Alternatively, should we place a priority on language teaching and learning, especially where very few speakers remain, as a way of maintaining continuity of the language? Is there a way of accomplishing these seemingly very different goals at the same time? A model of the former type has developed in Alaska in recent years, where the outstanding dictionaries of Athabascan languages aimed to provide as deep and detailed descriptions as possible, and more recent work aims at making these dictionaries accessible to a more general public. Even a very basic documentation project requires a fair amount of time to record and transcribe material. Moreover, in many cases of endangerment there are few speakers and all are elderly, imposing an added urgency for rapid documentation. Time limitations are thus an important consideration in designing any documentation project.

As we have seen, many of the issues and concerns faced by communities with threatened languages are linked in some way to poverty. Poverty is often partly responsible for the threatened status of the language (though, as discussed earlier, extreme poverty may also, paradoxically, help to preserve a language by isolating the community that speaks it). The kinds of responses available to a community whose language is endangered are partly shaped and limited by poverty; poverty constrains everything from the ability of community members to seek linguistic training to the possibility of producing the pedagogical materials needed to revive the language. It is in the linguist's best interest to be aware of these effects of poverty, if language documentation and revitalization is to succeed.

References

Abley, M. (2003) *Spoken Here: Travels Among Threatened Languages*. New York: Houghton Mifflin.

Batibo, H.M. (2005) *Language Decline and Death in Africa. Causes, Consequences and Challenges*. Clevedon: Multilingual Matters.

Berardo, M. and Yamamoto, A. (2007) Indigenous voices and the linguistics of language revitalization. In O. Miyaoka, O. Sakiyama and M. Krauss (eds) *The Vanishing Languages of the Pacific Rim* (pp. 107–117). Oxford: Oxford University Press.

Bobaljik, J. (1998) Visions and realities: Researcher-activist-indigenous collaboration in indigenous language maintenance. In E. Kasten (ed.) *Bicultural Education in the North: Ways of Preserving and Enhancing Indigenous Languages and Traditional Knowledge* (pp. 13–28). Berlin: Waxman Verlag.

Dauenhauer, N.M. and Dauenhauer, R. (1998) Technical, emotional and ideological issues in reversing language shift: Examples from Southeast Alaska. In L.A. Grenoble and L.J. Whaley (eds) *Endangered Languages. Current Issues and Future Prospects* (pp. 57–98). Cambridge: Cambridge University Press.

Dorian, N. (1993) A response to Ladefoged's other view of endangered languages. *Language* 69 (3), 575–579.

England, N. (1998) Mayan efforts towards language preservation. In L. Grenoble and L.J. Whaley (eds) *Endangered Languages: Current Issues and Future Prospects* (pp. 99–116). Cambridge: Cambridge University Press.

Fernald, T., Perkins, E. and Platero, P. (2004) Navajo theoretical linguistics and language pedagogy: A report on the Navajo language academy. In G. Holton (ed.) *Athabaskan Languages Conference Papers.* Alaska Native Language Center Working Papers 4, 9–16.

Garzon, S. (1998) Indigenous groups and their language contact relations. In S. Garzon, R. McKenna Brown, J. Becker Richards and Wuqu'Ajpub' (eds) *The Life of Our Language* (pp. 9–43). Austin, TX: University of Texas Press.

Grenoble, L.A. and Whaley, L.J. (2006) *Saving Languages.* Cambridge: Cambridge University Press.

Grinevald, C. (2007) Linguistic fieldwork among speakers of endangered languages. In O. Miyaoka, O. Sakiyama and M. Krauss (eds) *The Vanishing Languages of the Pacific Rim* (pp. 35–76). Oxford: Oxford University Press.

Hale, K. (1965) On the use of informants in fieldwork. *Canadian Journal of Linguistics* 10, 108–119.

Himmelman, N. (1998) Documentary and descriptive linguistics. *Linguistics* 36, 161–195.

Hinton, L. (2003) How to teach when the teacher isn't fluent. In J. Reyhner, O. Trujillo, R.L. Carrasco and L. Lockard (eds) *Nurturing Native Languages* (pp. 79–92). Flagstaff, AZ: Northern Arizona University.

Hinton, L., Vera, M. and Steele, N. (2002) *How to Keep Your Language Alive. A Commonsense Approach to One-on-one Language Learning.* Berkeley, CA: Heyday Books.

Ladefoged, P. (1992) Another view of endangered languages. *Language* 68, 809–811.

Mufwene, S. (2004) Language birth and death. *Annual Review of Anthropology* 33, 201–222.

Newman, P. (2003) The endangered languages issue as a hopeless cause. In M. Janse and S. Tol (eds) *Language Death and Language Maintenance: Theoretical, Practical and Descriptive Approaches* (pp. 1–13). Amsterdam: John Benjamins.

Rice, K. (2006) Ethical issues in linguistic fieldwork: An overview. *Journal of Academic Ethics* 4, 123–155.

Sachs, J. (2005) *The End of Poverty: Economic Possibilities for Our Time.* New York: Penguin Press.

UNESCO (2006) The fight against extreme poverty. *SHS Views* (UNESCO Social and Human Sciences Sector magazine) No. 14, September to November, 8–11. On WWW at http://unesdoc.unesco.org/images/0014/001469/146990E. pdf#8. Accessed 15.5.08.

World Bank Glossary. On WWW at http://www.worldbank.org/depweb/ english/beyond/global/glossary.html#52. Accessed 15.5.08.

Wurm, S. (2003) The language situation and language endangerment in the Greater Pacific Area. In M. Janse and S. Tol (eds) *Language Death and Language Maintenance: Theoretical, Practical and Descriptive Approaches* (pp. 15–47). Amsterdam: John Benjamins.

Chapter 12

Preserving Digital Language Materials: Some Considerations for Community Initiatives[1]

HELEN ARISTAR DRY

Introduction

Many speaker communities with access to modern technology are taking an active role in the production of recordings and transcripts of their endangered native languages, often with the goal of creating teaching materials for language revitalization initiatives. Such material has great potential value for succeeding generations of heritage speakers, as well as for future researchers in the human and social sciences. Often the documentation produced by community members is not only more authentic, but also more extensive and varied than that which would be produced by an outside linguist, as community members have easier access both to speakers and to the range of natural settings in which the language is used. However, like all digital documentation of endangered languages, its long-term durability and accessibility is a matter of concern. Indeed, awareness of the threats to digital language resources is slowly spreading through indigenous speaker communities, as well as through the academic linguistics community. However, because so much excellent material is being created as part of ongoing heritage revitalization efforts in communities throughout the world, immediate steps must be taken to better educate community leaders – and the linguists who advise them – about issues and concerns regarding the effective preservation and stewardship of digital language data.

Just as the documentation produced by community members is potentially the most valuable, so too is it potentially the most at risk. For one thing, only the immediate community may know of the materials' existence. Rarely are they placed in an archive or furnished with metadata available to the public. Often, these community-generated materials are stored in a community center, local library or private home, where storage conditions are unlikely to be adequate for long-term preservation. Or – like much of the language documentation produced by previous generations of linguists – the original recordings and textual material may simply be discarded once they have served their original purpose. All too often a speaker tapes his/her grandmother for a language revitalization workshop or an educator interviews an elder in order to produce a vocabulary lesson; then the resulting audio or video is edited and compressed in order to produce a smaller file for download or display, and only this presentation file is retained on the school computers or in the community library.

Academic language documentation was often treated this way in the past, because documentation per se was considered only a means to an end. Documentation, as defined by Himmelmann (2002: 1) is 'a comprehensive record of the linguistic practices characteristic of a given speech community', and it is differentiated from descriptive activity, which employs the documentation as data in an analysis. As Himmelmann (2002: 2) notes, 'Conventionally, the documentary activity has been seen as ancillary to the descriptive activity (i.e. primary data are collected *in order to* make a descriptive statement of the language)'. And, partly as a result of this value hierarchy,[2] mid-20th century linguistic documentation was often abandoned after the linguist had completed the grammar, lexicon or dissertation for which the material was collected.

In the neglect of community documentation, a similar value hierarchy may be at work. In some communities, the goal of language revitalization simply overshadows the goal of resource preservation. And occasionally, an emphasis on the need to preserve language materials may be interpreted almost as an admission of failure, as part of the motivation for archiving derives from the fear that the language may die, which would render existing documentation irreplaceable. However, wherever a lack of adequate attention is given to preservation issues – both in speaker communities and in the academic community – the cause of the neglect is almost certainly a combination of the lack of awareness of the threat to digital documentation and the lack of knowledge of the practices recommended as countermeasures to these threats.

This paper attempts to provide a summary both of the dangers to language documentation and of the recommendations of best practice that have been designed to address them. Some technical information is included, as the recommendations would not be meaningful without it. However, technical information changes rapidly, and the reader is advised to consult the sources mentioned in the fifth section for more up-to-date information. Among these sources are the websites of a number of initiatives involved in digital archiving (e.g. OLAC,[3] DELA-MAN,[4] DOBES,[5] HRELP,[6] AILLA[7] and PARADISEC[8]). Representatives of these initiatives have been regular participants at the annual workshops organized by the E-MELD project,[9] a five-year NSF-funded project whose major objective was to promote consensus within the linguistics community about recommendations of best practice in digital language documentation. The recommendations set forth here derive primarily from the E-MELD workshops and are further explained in a reference website, The E-MELD School of Best Practices in Digital Language Documentation (http://emeld.org/school/), described in the fifth section.

Recommendations of Best Practice

'Best practices' are practices which are intended to make digital language documentation optimally durable, accessible and intelligible, now and in the future. They represent the informed response of language engineers and digital librarians to the threats to digital material posed by hardware and software obsolescence. However, 'recommendations of best practice' are just that: recommendations, not directives. And many are difficult for the ordinary linguist or native speaker to implement at this time, primarily because we do not yet have user-friendly tools facilitating implementation. Implementing best practices now requires some technical knowledge, which a busy teacher or linguist may not have the time or motivation to acquire. For that reason, a hierarchy of 'good, better, and best' practices has been proposed (Simons & Dry, 2006):

- good practice **ensures preservation;**
- better practice ensures preservation and long-term intelligibility;
- best practice promotes interoperability among resources, as well as ensuring preservation and intelligibility.

For those documenting a lesser-known or endangered language, *good practice* – or ensuring preservation – is clearly the most important consideration, as they are creating material which it may be impossible to replace in the future. *Better practice* – or ensuring long-term intelligibility – should also be a goal, because, as Whalen[10] puts it, 'We don't want to create another Rosetta stone'. Better practice is also becoming more easily attainable by the average language documenter, who can make a habit of providing contextual information and choosing software that uses unambiguous character encoding (see 'Encoding' section). By contrast, *best practice* – promoting interoperability – involves adhering to discipline-specific standards that make digital resources usable across platforms and readily available to web services, such as search engines. Although it will have a significant impact on future accessibility of resources, interoperability can be considered a less urgent concern for language documenters than preservation and intelligibility. Therefore, this paper will focus on recommendations related to *good practice* and *better practice*, specifically those that the language documenter can implement right now through good software choices and forethought in corpus management.

For corpus management, it is important to identify three forms in which the same documentary material can be represented:

- Archival form: the form in which information is stored for the future. An archival file is sometimes called a 'preservation master'.
- Working form: the form in which information is stored as it is analyzed and edited.
- Presentation form: the form in which information is presented to the public. A presentation form is usually associated with a smaller file size but a reduced amount of information.

Linguists often focus on working form ('I always put my data into Excel'). Native speaker communities often focus on presentation form ('I made all these lessons in PowerPoint and put them on the web'). But recommendations of good, better and best practice primarily concern the archival form of the resource. As explained in 'Preservation' section, the archival form should consist of the unedited and uncompressed original documentation. A 'production master' can be made from the original preservation master, and any number of copies in working or presentation format can be made from the production master. But it is the original preservation master that recommended practices are designed to preserve from multiple dangers: physical deterioration of digital storage media; obsolescence of computer hardware and operating systems, which makes the storage media inaccessible; and obsolescence of software, which makes file formats unreadable.

Threats to Digital Materials

As early as 1996, a special US Taskforce on Digital Archiving drew attention to the fact that changes in coding, formats, software programs and operating systems have made much valuable data inaccessible to modern computers, and therefore useless (Garrett & Waters, 1996). A case in point is the BBC Domesday Project, created in 1986, a cultural documentation project in which 'a vast archive of material was collected, which included some 200,000 photographs, 24,000 maps, 8,000 data sets, and 60 minutes of moving pictures' (Brown, 2003: 1). The material was collected and stored using the era's most modern technology (12-inch laser vision discs and innovative multimedia software). However, by 2000, the huge data store had become inaccessible: the videodisc players required to play the discs had come to the end of their working lives; and many parts of the complex hardware/software combination were incompatible with modern computers. Ironically, as noted by one commentator, 'after over nine centuries, the original Domesday Book can still be consulted... [but] the modern multimedia digital equivalent was unreadable after a mere decade and a half' (Brown, 2003: 2).[11] Such examples have led archivists to warn of an impending 'Digital Dark Age', proclaiming that 'due to the relentless obsolescence of digital formats and platforms... there has never been a time of such drastic and irretrievable information loss as right now' (Brand, 1999: 1).

Deterioration of the physical media

It is well known that paper, audiotapes and videotapes are prone to degradation and destruction. However, because digital files allow lossless copying, it is often assumed that material that has been digitized has been preserved forever. Many language documenters are not aware that optical storage media like CDs and DVDs also have a limited lifespan. When they first appeared, optical storage media were popularly thought to be invulnerable because, unlike phonograph records, they are not read by means of a physical object making contact with the surface. With CDs and DVDs, data is stored on the disc as a series of microscopic indentations, or 'pits'; and a laser is shone onto the reflective surface of the disc to read it. The pits distort the reflected laser light; and the pattern of changing intensity of the reflected beam is converted into binary data. However, writable CDs, such as those used to store language documen-tation, are constructed differently and do not have the same longevity. For CD-Rs, the reflection pattern is not composed of physical markers such as pits, but rather by an optical pattern created by controlled, heat-induced alterations in the opacity of a thin layer of translucent dye which coats the reflective surface of the disc. The pattern made by patches of heated and unheated dye produces changes in the reflected beam, which are converted into binary data. Unfortunately, some types of dye degrade quickly even under the best of circumstances, making CD-Rs more vulnerable to data loss than nonwritable CDs. Some CD-Rs, for example, last only a few years.[12] Most DVD-Rs, it is true, are projected to last over 100 years, given proper storage conditions. But facilities for proper storage, i.e. storage in a jewel case at 40°F, with controlled humidity and no exposure to direct sunlight, are often unavailable to community libraries.

Nevertheless, the greatest threat to information on digital storage media is not the physical deterioration of the media, but the rapid pace of hardware obsolescence. As the orphaned laser vision discs of the BBC Domesday Project illustrate, no matter how well-preserved digital media may be, it becomes useless when the hardware required to access it no longer exists.

Hardware obsolescence

As noted in Simons (2006), in the past 25 years alone, removable media on personal computers have evolved from 8" floppies, through 5.25" floppies, 3.5" floppies, Zip drives and CD-Rs, to DVD-Rs; and to these we can also add Blu-ray discs and USB flash drives. These changes have the advantage of producing media that are capable of containing ever greater amounts of information. But each advance threatens to make the earlier media obsolete and the information they contain inaccessible. Even if there exist 8" floppies that are themselves in pristine shape, computers that can read them are almost nonexistent. To find a machine able to read a 5.25" floppy would require contacting a professional or scouring resale shops in order to find an old machine. Indeed, although many of us still have racks of 3.5" diskettes on our desks, in all likelihood the desktop computer beside them has no slot for diskette insertion.

Software obsolescence

Software has evolved with similar rapidity, with vendors changing file formats and functionality with each version. In the last 20 years, for example, there has been a plethora of formats in which to display textual material, whether in print or on the Internet: WordStar, WordPerfect, MSWord 1.0–Word2003, LaTeX, PostScript, RTF, HyperCard, SGML, HTML 1.0–4.0, XHTML, XML, Hyper-G's HTF, Adobe's PDF and countless more. Though some of these are open standards – i.e. they are publicly described so that new tools can be created to read them – most are proprietary formats readable only by the specific software that created them. Just as almost no one can now read an 8" floppy, almost no one can read a document created with MSWord 1.0. Even current versions of Word cannot access such files – indeed they cannot access some types of material composed in Word 5.0.[13]

Toward a Solution

Preservation

To ensure that digital language documentation endures long into the future, linguists and community members are urged to create an archival copy in an enduring file format and to deposit the materials with an archive that will make a practice of periodically migrating them to new storage media as technology changes. Such an archive has sometimes been called a 'preservation archive', in order to distinguish it from a digital collection created by an individual or an organization without an institutional commitment to long-term preservation.[14] A preservation archive will have a migration program designed to shield the digital resource from hardware obsolescence.

Putting the material in an enduring file format will protect the material from software obsolescence. Although it is impossible to be absolutely certain what file formats will be readable by the software of the future, the software engineering community has now had 40 years of experience upon which to base some confident guesses. Recommendations of good practice are grounded in assessment of the file formats which are and have been most commonly utilized in software applications – i.e. not the formats which have the most users (e.g. MS Word), but rather the formats which can be interpreted by the greatest number of software applications, in part because they confront software developers with the fewest barriers to their adoption. Thus, Simons (2004), in a memorable acronym, posited that an enduring file format is one that offers LOTS. That is, an archival file format should be Lossless, Open, Transparent and Supported by multiple vendors. Each of these requirements will be discussed in turn next.

Lossless

Archival files containing documentation of endangered languages should be uncompressed and unedited. Documenters of endangered languages are creating material that will almost certainly increase in value as the years pass. And it is impossible to anticipate now all the needs and capabilities of the future. A segment of speech deleted to 'clean up' a file might include sounds that could answer a question for future phonologists or language learners. As Whalen (2004) and others have noted, much more sensitive tools for analysis and reproduction may someday be available, making it possible to analyze sound distinctions that are currently considered valueless because 'inaudible'.[15] Although it may be tempting to edit out what appears to be mere background noise, any editing of an archival file should be avoided. Numerous presentation and working copies can be made *from* the archival file, and these can be edited as needed; but the unedited file should be preserved as the archival master.

Similarly, compression of an archival file should be avoided if possible, as most processes that compress file size also reduce information in such a way that it is impossible to reconstruct it. Ideally, an archival file should be saved in an uncompressed file format, like WAV for audio, BITMAP for images or TXT for text. However, there are lossless compression algorithms that allow the original to be reconstructed during decoding without loss of information; for example, the.zip algorithm for text files is a lossless compression algorithm.[16] Table 12.1 lists some common formats and file extensions for compressed and uncompressed files.

For the reasons of transparency (see 'Transparent' section), uncompressed formats are to be preferred even over lossless compression; but with some file types this preference must be weighed against practicalities associated with file size and availability of compression utilities. For very large files, lossless compression may be a reasonable

Table 12.1 Common extensions of compressed and uncompressed file formats

Type	Uncompressed	Compressed (lossless)	Compressed (lossy)
Audio:	.wav,.aiff,.au (pcm)[a]	.ape, FLAC, TTA	.mp3, .aac,[b] .wma
Images:	.bmp	.tiff (or .tif) w/LZW, .png, .gif	.jpg
Video:	rtv	JPEG-2000	MPEG-2, DV, MPEG-4
Text:	.txt	.zip	NA

[a]Technically, .wav and .aiff are container formats, file structures that allow combining of audio/video data, tags, menus, subtitles and some other media elements. They could theoretically contain compressed audio formats, but in practice they usually contain PCM (pulse code modulation) data, which is an uncompressed format
[b]Apple audio codec (.aac) and Windows media audio (.wma) both have a lossless version. Confusingly, both the lossless and the lossy compression formats use the same file extension

choice. For large image files, for example, Portable Network Graphic format (file extension.png) or Graphic Interchange Format (.gif) may be more practical than BITMAP (.bmp) format. However, some caution should be used. Except for JPEG, most common image formats usually employ lossless, not lossy, compression; however, lossless compression is in fact optional in Tagged Image File Format (TIFF),[17] and GIF is lossless only if the image has a small number of colors. So to be safe.gif should be considered lossless only for black and white and/or grayscale images.

Video files are so large that, at the time of this writing, creating and archiving an uncompressed copy is usually impractical. Several lossless compression algorithms for video have recently been developed, and at least one (JPEG-2000) is supported adequately to be a reasonable choice for archives (Gilmour & Dávila, 2006); but lossless video compression is not yet widely implemented in software. For now, a language documenter is best advised to record audio and video separately, and to archive a compressed copy of the video and an uncompressed copy of the audio. Most video capture (i.e. transferring video from the camcorder to the computer) compresses the audio signal, so to secure an uncompressed archival copy, the audio must be recorded simultaneously on a different machine.

Open

Just as an archival format should ideally be lossless, it should also adhere to an open standard. Occasionally, 'open standard' is confused with 'open source', as the concepts referenced are often discussed as though they have a common opposite in proprietary commercial software. However, 'open source' and 'open standard' do not necessarily coincide; nor is 'open standard' necessarily incompatible with proprietary software.

The phrase 'open source' refers to software and describes an application whose source code is publicly available; any programmer can see how the program works and modify it at will. Open Office (technically OpenOffice.org) and Mozilla Thunderbird are good examples of open source software. 'Open standard', by contrast, refers to a format; and it means that the complete specification of the format is freely available. Some examples of open standards are HTML, XML and ODF (Open Document Format, which is used by OpenOffice.org).

Open standards and open source software frequently go together, as most open source software creates files in open formats; and, conversely, most proprietary software creates files in formats that only the proprietary program(s) can read. For many decades, for example, only

Table 12.2 Text file formats: open versus proprietary

Open standards	Open standard	Proprietary
Open development	.txt, .html, .xml, .odf, .csv	NA
Commercial development	.rtf, .pdf	.doc, .xls, .ppt

Microsoft applications could read the .doc format created by MSWord. However, some proprietary software companies do publish their file format specification, making the format open standard. Adobe's Portable Document Format (PDF) is an open standard, even though the Adobe Acrobat software that creates .pdf files remains a proprietary 'secret'. Similarly, RTF is an open standard, although it was developed by Microsoft. Table 12.2 lists the extensions of some common open and proprietary formats for text files.

When a format specification has been published, the threat of software obsolescence is ameliorated. Even if the program that created the file is no longer available, technicians can learn what constitutes a valid example of the format and, if necessary, write another piece of software to interpret it. For that reason, open standards are extremely important for archival copies; but it is much less important that such copies be created using open source software.

In fact, archival copies can be created even by programs whose native format is proprietary, as long as the program can create an export file that adheres to an open standard. Powerpoint and MSWord can both export into Rich Text Format (.rtf), for example. Moreover, an .rtf file is easily converted into plain text, the format of choice for archiving textual documentation. Similarly, most database programs export in plain text; some even export in Extensible Markup Language, or XML.[18] However, the danger associated with using proprietary software is that saving data in the native (proprietary) format becomes routine, and regular exports to the open format are never performed. Just as most people know that they should back up their data regularly but few actually do it, so many people realize that they should export their data regularly into an open archival format, but few actually click on 'Export'.

Transparent

Transparency of the file format constitutes a further argument for using uncompressed formats whenever possible. A transparent file format is one in which there is a one-to-one correspondence between the numerical encoding and the information it represents. In a plain text file, for example, there is a one-to-one correspondence between a character and the computer-readable binary number used to represent it. In a Pulse Code Modulation (PCM), audio file format (.wav, .aiff, .au), there is a one-to-one correspondence between the numbers and the amplitudes of the sound waves. In a transparent file format no special knowledge or algorithm is necessary in order to interpret the content. Consequently, .txt files can be read by any program that handles text and PCM files can be processed by any program that handles audio. By contrast, .zip and .mp3 files require implementation of a complex algorithm to restore the original correspondences.

Today, many programs provide automatic decoding of the common encoded formats, but we cannot be certain that such software will not become obsolete. Just as we have lost the ability to play the aluminum discs so popular in the 1940s, we may someday lose the .ape codec or even the .zip algorithm, or we may have no software capable of unpacking the file, or no operating system capable of running the software. Thus, for long-term accessibility, transparent, uncompressed formats are to be preferred even over formats with lossless compression.

Supported by multiple vendors

Just as lack of compression and transparency are paired in file formats, use of open standards and support by multiple vendors go together in software development. Open standards are more likely than proprietary standards to have wide vendor support, because development using open standards is typically less costly. If a file format is open, there is no inherent barrier to creating another program that handles it. It is not necessary to reverse engineer the format or purchase the specification from the developer. And the more software applications that handle a file format, the less likely that format is to fall victim to hardware and software obsolescence.

Long-term intelligibility

To make important documentation of endangered languages accessible to future generations, it is not enough to choose an enduring file format. We must also preserve the content in intelligible form, or – to use another acronym – the documenter must do MORE. That is, he or she must document the **M**arkup, **O**ccasion, **R**ubrics and **E**ncoding (Simons & Dry, 2006). In this formulation, 'markup' refers to descriptive annotation (which could indicate anything from speaker change to the grammatical function of a morpheme), 'occasion' refers to the recording situation and the speech situation which it documents, 'rubric' refers to any rule or set of rules adhered to in the documentation (e.g. the Leipzig glossing rules) and 'encoding' refers to the character encoding. Of these four, perhaps the most relevant to community documentation are 'occasion' and 'encoding'. And they are also the two aspects of the documentation that, if left unexplained, are most likely to obscure future intelligibility.

Occasion

Documenting the 'occasion' simply means noting when and where the recording was made, identifying the language(s) used and describing the speakers and the salient aspects of the situation. Such information about context is indispensable to long-term intelligibility of the content. As any archivist can attest, failure to provide it has produced numerous 'mystery' recordings in legacy collections – recordings without labels or any accompanying documentation, for which it is sometimes difficult even to identify the language(s) being spoken, much less guess at the meanings of the words. Anyone who has struggled to make sense of unlabeled documentation will recognize the importance of contextual information for interpreting a language resource.

Such information is called 'descriptive metadata', and it can be provided simply as free text added as a head note in a text file and/or as content of another text file which is stored with the documentation. However, to ensure that knowledge of the resource reaches a wider audience, the documenter can create machine-readable metadata according to a standard format and submit it to an Internet service or archive.

There are at least two metadata standards devised specifically for language resources, the OLAC standard[19] and the more complex IMDI standard.[20] These metadata standards were developed not only to tell documenters what resource information is necessary for interpretation, but also to ensure that information about the material can be found by search engines. Each standard specifies not only the set of descriptive elements to be listed (e.g. 'Title', 'Creator', 'Language', 'Date'), but also the proper format of a machine-readable file, that is, an XML schema for the metadata elements.

Both are also associated with software applications that facilitate the creation of a machine-readable file. A set of tools for creating and browsing IMDI metadata is available free of charge for download from the IMDI site (http://www.mpi.nl/IMDI/tools/). OLAC metadata participates in an open Internet service; any file that complies with the OLAC metadata standard can be registered with OLAC and made available to the OLAC harvester and Internet search engines. An online facility was developed to help the user create and register an OLAC-compliant metadata file. This is the OLAC Repository Editor, or ORE (http://linguistlist.org/ore/), which allows the user to fill out a simple 15-element online form, then click on 'Submit' to create an OLAC-compliant XML file and register it with OLAC. Providing descriptive metadata to such a public information service ensures that knowledge of the language documentation will not be lost.

Encoding

To understand character encoding, it is necessary to recognize that a character is an abstract entity, which is not the same thing as the rendering of the character in a specific font. To see this, imagine all the different ways that the Latin letter 'A' could be written, e.g. in cursive writing, in a schoolchild's printing, in the Times Roman font, in the Arial font. Though the letter shapes, or 'glyphs', are quite different, they all represent the same concept, the letter 'A'. The term 'character encoding' refers to a match between that character concept and a particular numerical value, or code point, which the computer interprets according to an encoding standard, or 'code page'. The character may then be rendered as one of many different glyphs, depending on the font chosen by the user. Table 12.3 summarizes this relationship.

Character intelligibility problems arise whenever more than one character is mapped to a single code point. The number of different code points available in any encoding standard is dependent on the number of bits, or binary digits, used to make up a unit of information.[21] Early encodings were seven-bit, and thus only 128 unique combinations of the binary digits 0 and 1 were possible. This in turn meant that only 128 (0–127) code points were available for assignment to characters. Later, an eight-bit standard was adopted, providing 256 code points. However, both were inadequate for unambiguous mapping of international character sets, so different fonts reused the same code points. Until recently, there were not enough code points available to support unambiguous mapping, so intelligibility problems still may occur when there is a mismatch between the encoding system used to enter and store a given set of data and the encoding system used to retrieve and view it.

Table 12.3 Character representation

Code point	Character (concept)	Glyph (symbol)
65	Latin 'A'	A, A, A, A, **A**, A

One familiar result of such ambiguity is a display problem, as for example when a message that is supposed to include a Chinese symbol is displayed with a completely irrelevant character from another alphabet. This occurs because of ambiguous mapping: the sender's font maps a Chinese character and associated glyph to a code point, while the recipient's font, which includes no Chinese characters, maps another character to the same code point. Installing the same Chinese font on both machines might solve the immediate problem (as long as both machines have the same default encoding standard). But if we extrapolate the problem far into the future, we see that ambiguous character mapping could make a resource uninterpretable.

Documenting the encoding. If a code point is mapped to different characters in different encoding standards and fonts, the linguist or speaker of the future may not know which character was intended. For this reason, the character encoding used in a file should be documented in the file itself, as well as in any separate metadata file that may exist. Documenting the encoding is better than simply listing the font used, as neither the particular font nor its description may be readily available at a later date, but another font using the same encoding may be. If the encoding is not known, however, providing the name of the font is certainly useful.

Also important is documenting any special characters used or any characters used with special meanings. Some linguists, for example, use a question mark or a seven to indicate a glottal stop. Correspondences of this kind should be noted within the file.

Using the Unicode encoding standard. Users can avoid providing so much documentation by using a recognized standard. The use of a common standard also increases the likelihood that necessary supporting software and/or migration paths will be available in the future. Unicode is the recommended standard because it offers unambiguous encoding. As a standard with up to 32 bits, Unicode has enough unique binary digit combinations to support one-to-one mapping of code points to almost all the characters in the world's writing systems.[22] Because Unicode fonts do not have to re-use the same code points for unrelated characters, ambiguities (such as the display ambiguity involving the Chinese character earlier) should not occur.

Currently, more and more software programs are adopting the Unicode encoding standard, so the user should simply check for Unicode support in software product descriptions and take that feature into account when making a purchasing decision. It may be worth upgrading to a newer version of existing software, as many programs that did not previously support Unicode have adopted the standard in their latest release. Alan Wood's pages provide a comprehensive listing of software that support Unicode (http://www.alanwood.net/unicode/ utilities.html), as well as a listing of Unicode fonts (e.g. Titus, Arial MS Unicode, Lucida Sans Unicode). As more and more programs support Unicode natively, however, it is becoming less necessary for an individual to find and install a Unicode font.

More Information

Character encoding, like most of the topics touched on in this paper, is a subject about which much more could be, and has been, written. For a more extensive (but still user-friendly) introduction to character encoding, the reader may wish to consult Constable (2003). Information about the other technology topics discussed, as well as about projects documenting endangered languages, may be found on a number of accessible websites.

Information on documentation projects

The E-MELD site, for example, includes a list of documentation projects involving collaboration with native speakers of endangered languages (http://linguistlist.org/emeld/school/case/projects/index. html). The 15-project list was compiled in 2005 by the Linguistic Society of America Committee on Endangered Languages and their Preservation; and it includes speaker-led projects in Pakistan-administered Kashmir, Mexico, Northern Tibet, Nigeria and Siberia, as well as the USA. Also in 2005, UNESCO launched an initiative to identify successful documentation projects via its Register of Good Practices in Language Preservation (http://portal.unesco.org/culture/en/ev.php-URL_ID= 23506&URL_DO=DO_PRINTPAGE&URL_SECTION=201.html). At the time of this writing, the registry is not yet available online, although there are websites listing projects in specific areas, e.g. projects on Siberian languages (http://lingsib.unesco.ru/en/projects/research/ index.shtml.htm), Caribbean Indigenous and Endangered Languages (http://www.mona.uwi.edu/dllp/jlu/ciel/pages/protecting.htm) and Endangered Languages of the Pacific Rim (http://www.elpr.bun.kyotou. ac.jp/essay/UNESCO_presentation_2003311.htm). More on UNESCO's support of documentation of endangered languages can be found in the UNESCO projects list (http://portal.unesco.org/culture/en/ev.php-URL_ID=8270&URL_DO=DO_TOPIC&URL_SECTION=-477.html) and on the website of the UK's Foundation for Endangered Languages (http://www.ogmios.org/215.htm), which also lists projects sponsored by the Volkswagen Stiftung as part of the DOBES project or by the Hans Rausing Foundation as part of the Rausing Endangered Languages Documentation project.

So far, most of the technologically sophisticated work in language documentation is linked to European or American projects or funding agencies. But a notable exception is the work in progress at Academia Sinica in Taipei. The Formosan Language Project, for example, aims to record and maintain the indigenous Formosan languages spoken in Taiwan through collecting and/or editing existing texts in digital forms with corresponding audio files. It is pursued in collaboration with native speakers who not only collect data (e.g. audio and video recording), but also transcribe and analyze their own languages. The Formosan Language Archive includes both Chinese and English browsing display on the Internet, and contains three main types of information databases: (1) the corpora of 11 Formosan languages with annotated texts (Amis, Atayal, Bunun, Kanakanavu, Paiwan, Pazeh, Puyuma, Rukai, Saisiyat, Siraya, Tsou), (2) a geographic information system and (3) four bibliographical databases (Zeitoun *et al.*, 2003; Zeitoun & Yu, 2005).

Similarly, an Academia Sinica project on the digital archiving of Yami language documentation (http://yamiproject.cs.pu.edu.tw/yami) includes a conceptual framework for integrating e-learning into language documentation and involves groups of native speakers in developing e-learning materials (Rau & Yang, 2007; Yang & Rau, 2005). Yang *et al.* (2007) have developed a web-based database to alleviate the short-comings of traditional software for language documentation in the hands of untrained users and enable community members to build their own dictionaries and digital archives over the web.

Information on technology

Additional information about the technologies discussed in this paper may be found on many of the project websites mentioned in the first section. For example, see the OLAC site for information on metadata, and refer to the DOBES and HRELP sites for advice on resource creation. Of particular value in this regard is the *Language Archives Newsletter* (http://www.mpi.nl/LAN/), which often evaluates new technologies designed for use in language documentation. Another technology-oriented site is the Resource Network for Linguistic Diversity hosted by the University of Melbourne (http://www.linguistics.unimelb. edu.au/thieberger/RNLD.html). And the Technology-Enhanced Language Revitalization project at the University of Arizona provides a particularly lucid manual for digital resource creators (http://projects. ltc.arizona.edu/gates/TELR_manual.html).

In addition, comprehensive information on most of the topics discussed here can be found in the E-MELD School of Best Practices (http://emeld.org/school/). The School is a reference website which contains information on audio, video, Unicode, XML and metadata, as well as case studies showing how documentation of 12 endangered languages was converted into best practice formats. The site is designed not just for linguists and language archivists, but also for members of speaker communities who may not have any particular technical training. To that end, each topic is introduced via a 'How to' page, summarizing the steps in a particular process. Developed under the auspices of the E-MELD grant, the School is maintained by the graduate student assistants who work on The LINGUIST List (http://linguistlist.org/), with the help of community input via Comments pages. The School site also hosts Ask-An-Expert (http://emeld.org/school/ask-expert/ index.html/), an interactive facility whereby any user can address a question to an expert in digital preservation, audio and video recording, character encoding, and/or annotation standards and receive an answer via e-mail.

Language technology changes so rapidly that regular consultation of up-to-date websites is recommended for linguists, language archivists and speaker communities who wish to remain current on the most recent recommendations of best practice. A well-known database of file and data formats (http://www.dlib.org/dlib/november04/stanescu/ 11stanescu.html#6) lists about 1000 digital formats and interim versions. Although many of these have not been used in more than a decade, the number does provide an indication of the speed at which file and data formats come and go. It is admittedly difficult to identify those most likely to survive the passage of time. But the practices recommended by language engineers and digital archivists provide the most reliable guide available to addressing the dual longevity issues for digital language resources: ensuring that the information is preserved in an enduring file format, and ensuring that it remains accessible and intelligible far into the future. The cultural and scientific importance of documentation of endangered languages can hardly be overestimated. Thus, both linguists and community members need to understand and implement practices designed to ensure that digital materials are as impervious as possible to the decay of the physical media, as well as to the premature obsolescence inevitably wrought by technological change.

Notes

1. This paper is an outgrowth of six workshops sponsored by the National Science Foundation as part of the E-MELD project (Electronic Metastructure for Endangered Languages Data. NSF Social Sciences Infrastructure Grant SES-1099652, 2001–2007). Very little of the material in this paper is original, although any errors are, of course, my own. The contributors from the E-MELD workshops are listed at http://emeld.org/workshop/2001/, /2002/, /2003/, /2004/, /2005/, /2006/, and those who reviewed the School of Best Practice are credited at http://emeld.org/school/credits/html#1003. They are too numerous to thank individually here. However, I would like to single out Gary Simons for special thanks. Simons's vision of an integrated web of digital resources and services has shaped all aspects of the E-MELD project, and most of the ideas in this paper were first discussed in his E-MELD presentations. For a more substantial exposition of the issues touched on here, see Simons (2006).

2. Other factors were, of course, involved, e.g. the fact that, before the era of Internet self-publishing, it was almost impossible to publish such material; only a few publishing houses were interested in grammars and lexicons of little-known languages, and almost none printed volumes of unanalyzed documentary materials.

3. OLAC. On WWW at http://www.language-archives.org.

4. Digital Endangered Languages and Musics Archive Network. On WWW at http://delaman.org.

5. DOBES. On WWW at http://www.mpi.nl/DOBES/.

6. Hans Rausing Endangered Languages Project. On WWW at http://hrelp.org/.

7. Archive of the Indigenous Languages of Latin America. On WWW at http://ailla.org/.

8. Pacific and Regional Archive for Digital Sources in Endangered Cultures. On WWW at http://paradisec.org.au.

9. Electronic Metastructure for Endangered Languages Data. National Science Foundation Social Sciences Infrastructure Grant SES-1099652, 2001?2006. On WWW at http://emeld.org/.

10. Personal communication, quoted in Simons and Dry (2006).

11. In order to rescue this valuable resource, a research group called Camileon (Creative Archiving at Michigan and Leeds: Emulating the Old on the New) not only had to develop a process and tools for data 'migration on demand' to a new hardware platform, but it also had to create an emulator, a program which mimics the functions and file-handling capabilities of the original playback software (Brown, 2003: 1).

12. These are early CDs (usually green or light blue in color), which were made with cyanine dyes; CD-Rs made with azo dyes (dark blue in color) may last

decades; and phthalocyanine dye CD-Rs (usually silver, gold or light green) are often given a rated lifetime of hundreds of years. (Wikipedia, quoted in Liberman, 2006). Many manufacturers have now found effective ways to stabilize cyanine dyes, but anyone with valuable information on early CD-Rs would be well-advised to copy it to an archival format.

13. 'Microsoft has historically made technical document files obsolete in a very short period of time. For example, mathematical equations created in Word 5 cannot be edited using later versions. Microsoft will not release the internal format of Word equations. This inhibits conversion from Word to anything else... Creating complex software to convert a file format that only has a 2–4 year life span is hard to justify' (K-Talk Communications, 2005).

14. The term was used, for example, in a recent resolution submitted to the Linguistic Society of America by DELAMAN. Although aware of the seeming redundancy of the terminology, DELAMAN members felt it was necessary to make a distinction between depositing material with a trusted repository and merely 'archiving it on the web'. Although collecting digital material and making it available via the Internet is often a valuable service, in most cases it does not ensure longevity of the resource.

15. Attention to 'future-proofing', to use a term current in audio engineering, has already produced salutary advice for linguists on more than one occasion. Plichta (2002), for example, was controversial at the time of presentation because it recommended a recording standard (96 KHz, 24-bit sampling rate) that was beyond the range of playback equipment readily available at the time (CD players supported only 44.1 KHz, 16-bit sampling). However, with the advent of DVD Audio, sampling rates of up to 192 KHz have now become possible, and 96/24 is the standard currently recommended by the Council on Library and Information Resources. See the CLIR report, 'Capturing Analog Sound for Digital Preservation' on WWW at www.clir.org/pubs/abstract/pub137abst.html.

16. See Ian Fieggen's graphics site for a clear and nontechnical explanation of compression types. On WWW at http://fieggen.com/ian/g_formats.htm.

17. The lossless version of TIFF is called TIFF LZW, after the original developers of the compression algorithm, but whether the encoding is lossless or not is not indicated in the file extension. Both lossy and lossless varieties can have the .tif or .tiff extension.

18. XML is the preferred format for text because it enhances interoperability and intelligibility. It is a content-oriented markup; that is, a title would appear between < title > tags, not just between tags indicating bold font or other formatting, as in HTML. XML is not discussed in this paper because it is difficult for individuals to produce at this time. However, if a database program has the ability to export in XML, this function should be utilized. To take advantage of the content-based markup, however, the user must provide meaningful field and table names. Merely using XML syntax does not promote the long-term intelligibility of the work unless the field names are meaningful.

19. On WWW at http://language-archives.org/ or for a less technical explanation of OLAC metadata see: http://linguistlist.org/olac/.

20. Isle Meta Data Initiative. On WWW at http://www.mpi.nl/IMDI/.
21. Information about what character to display is sent to the computer as a sequence of electrical impulses that can be represented as a binary number, with 0s and 1s. The sequence can also be represented as decimal, hexadecimal or octal number. The character 'A' in the Roman alphabet, for example, is represented by a sequence which is 65 in decimal numbers, 41 in hexadecimal and 101 in octal.
22. There are in fact some ancient alphabets and some little-used characters, e.g. in Chinese, which have no Unicode encoding. There are also, unfortunately, some duplications which were allowed into Unicode in order to ease the transition from legacy encodings and, it was hoped, promote earlier adoption of Unicode. A duplication occurs when the same canonical character is mapped to two code points. This occurred with the characters of the Latin alphabet when it was determined that legacy encodings required both a half-width and a full-width version of the characters.

References

Bird, S. and Simons, G. (2003) Seven dimensions of portability for language documentation and description. *Language* 79 (2), 557–582.

Brand, S. (1999) Escaping the digital dark age. *Library Journal* 124 (2), 46–49. On WWW at http://www.rense.com/general38/escap.htm.

Brown, D. (2003) Lost in Cyberspace: The BBC Domesday Project and the Challenge of Digital Preservation. *Cambridge Scientific Abstracts*. On WWW at http://www.csa.com/hottopics/cyber/oview.html.

Constable, P. (2003) *Guidelines for Writing Support: Technical Details: Encodings and Unicode: Part I*. On WWW at http://scripts.sil.org/WSI_Guidelines_Sec_6_1.

Garrett, J. and Waters, D. (1996) *Preserving Digital Information: Report of the Task Force on Archiving of Digital Information*. On WWW at http://www.rlg.org/ArchTF/tfadi.index.htm.

Gilmour, I. and Dávila, R.J. (2006) Lossless video compression for archives: Motion JPEG2k and other options. *Media Matters*. January. On WWW at http://www.media-matters.net/whitepapers.html.

Himmelmann, N. (2002) Documentary and descriptive linguistics (full version). In O. Sakiyama and F. Endo (eds) *Lectures on Endangered Languages: 5* (Endangered Languages of the Pacific Rim, Kyoto, 2002). This is an expanded version of the article published as Himmelman, N.P. (1998) Documentary and descriptive linguistics. *Linguistics* 36, 161–195. On WWW at http://www.hrelp.org/events/workshops/eldp2005/reading/himmelmann.pdf.

K-Talk Communications (2005) *Recommendations for Creating Technical Documents*. On WWW at http://www.ktalk.com/whylatex.html.

Kuny, T. (1998) The digital dark ages? Challenges in the preservation of electronic information. *International Preservation News* 17, 13.

Liberman, M. (2006) *Language Log*, 19 January. On WWW at http://itre.cis.upenn.edu/~myl/languagelog/archives/002770.html.

Plichta, B. (2002) Best practices in digital preservation of the spoken word. Presentation at the E-MELD Workshop on Digital Language Resources.

On WWW at http://www.emeld.org/workshop/2002/presentations/ bartek/bartek.ppt.

Rau, D.V. and Yang, M.C. (2007) E-learning in endangered language documentation and revitalization. In D.V. Rau and M. Florey (eds) *Documenting and Revitalizing Austronesian Languages*. Special volume for *Language Documentation and Conservation Journal* (University of Hawai'i Press), 111–133.

Simons, G. (2006) Ensuring that digital data last: The priority of archival form over working form and presentation form. *SIL Working Papers 2006003*, March 2006. Expanded version of a presentation at the EMELD Symposium on Endangered Data vs Enduring Practice: Creating Linguistic Resources that Last, LSA, Boston, MA, 8–11 January, 2004. On WWW at http://www.sil.org/silewp/2006/003/SILEWP2006-003.htm.

Simons, G.F. and Aristar Dry, H. (2006) Good, better, and best practice: The experience of the E-MELD project. A paper presented at the Workshop on Language Archives: Standards, Creation, and Access, Deutsche Gesellschaft für sprachwissenschaft, 22–24 February, Bielefeld.

Stanescu, A. (2004) Assessing the durability of formats in a digital preservation environment: The INFORM methodology. *D-Lib Magazine* 10 (11), November.

Whalen, D.H. (2004) From the field to the archive. Presentation at E-MELD Symposium on Endangered Data vs. Enduring Practice, LSA, Boston, MA. On WWW at http://www.emeld.org/school/readingroom/LSA-Symposium_whalen.ppt.

Yang, M.C., Chou, H.D., Guo, H.S. and Chen, C.P. (2007) On designing the Formosan multimedia word dictionaries by a participatory process. In D.V. Rau and M. Florey (eds) *Documenting and Revitalizing Austronesian Languages*. Special volume for *Language Documentation and Conservation Journal*. University of Hawai'i Press, 202–218.

Yang, M-C. and Victoria Rau, D. (2005) An integrated framework for archiving, processing and developing learning materials for an endangered aboriginal language in Taiwan. Paper presented at the ALR-2005, Jeju Island, Korea.

Zeitoun, E. and Yu, C-H. (2005) The Formosan language archive: Linguistic analysis and language processing. *Computational Linguistics and Chinese Language Processing* 10 (2), 167–200.

Zeitoun, E., Yu, C-H. and Weng, C-X. (2003) The Formosan language archive: Development of a multimedia tool to salvage the languages and oral traditions of the indigenous tribes of Taiwan. *Oceanic Linguistics* 42 (1), 218–232.

Conclusion

The chapters in this volume are reports by researchers working in a vast field of inquiry that spans a multitude of disciplinary boundaries, and each of them brings to bear a highly individual perspective, shaped by the particular subpart of the problem area on which they have chosen to focus, the particular linguistic contexts in which they have worked and the disciplinary framework by means of which they structure the problems. Distilling a single set of lessons from this diversity of views and perspectives without distorting them appears to us to be a precarious and premature task. Nonetheless, we will venture a few general observations by way of tying together some of the threads that run through these chapters.

Among the general lessons that can be extracted from the volume is first of all that the inter-relations between language and access to resources are a problem complex in which an extraordinarily large range of constituencies, both within academia and outside, have a significant stake. Besides speakers and their communities, these include (at least) linguists, ethnographers, sociologists, anthropologists, educators, language planners, economists, health workers, human rights advocates, politicians and national governments. A second lesson is that these constituencies naturally tend to approach the problems in different ways, which start from different premises, focus on different objectives, employ different methodologies, and therefore, not surprisingly, come at least sometimes to apparently opposing and irreconcilable conclusions. Members of a language community, for example, do not necessarily value or prioritize their language in the same way that a field researcher working in that community might. An economist will tend to assess the value of a language differently from an anthropologist. Indeed, the volume makes clear that there is no cross-disciplinary agreement on the best way to understand and measure concepts so fundamental to the discussion as 'wealth' and 'poverty'. The chapters in the volume also call into question, though, the prospect of reducing the problem area to a set of discrete problems, each of which can be approached in a wholly adequate way with the tools available to one of these individual constituencies. Language and wealth/poverty (whether defined in terms of capital, access to resources, freedom of choice, social empowerment or in still more abstract terms that take into account 'cultural value') are perhaps entangled to such an extent that they form a single complex puzzle that can only be solved by cross-disciplinary cooperation. Romaine suggests that the language/poverty problem complex is part of a still larger problem, into which biodiversity is also folded. Take as an example the problem of the twin goals of maintenance of endangered languages and advancing the economic well-being of their speakers. Is it the case that one must prioritize them relative to each other in determining how to allot resources? Is it the case that these goals are in conflict with each other, and that economic advancement necessarily entails movement from marginal language communities/switch to dominant languages? Or is it possible that the solutions to both problems converge? Is it possible to turn minority languages into economic assets, as suggested by Batibo, Brenzinger, Garcia and Mason, and Romaine? Is the maintenance of marginal languages indeed a worthwhile societal goal? What value is lost if languages are lost? How does one factor into the equations the loss of cultural value that accompanies language shift, as Whiteley asks? Given that poverty/wealth are, under one set of definitions, determined by empowerment and freedom of choice, how are the desires of the language community to be assessed and taken into account in determining courses of action? It is clear that no single discipline is situated to answer all of these questions. Consider another case. Alexander, Mohanty, Baugh, and Garcia and Mason all address in various ways the problem of costs and benefits of mother tongue versus other tongue education. In multilingual societies there are of course costs associated with offering all individuals education in their native tongues. There are also costs associated with failing to do so, and disadvantaging some part of the population by requiring them to receive education in a language not their own. How does one weigh these costs relative to each other? At one level it is a strictly economic question, measurable in monetary terms, and yet these authors make the case that a true understanding of the societal and individual costs of different choices requires a broader metric.

A final general lesson to be drawn from the preceding chapters is that this is an area of inquiry with respect to which traditional scholarly disengagement has become problematic. Languages, language communities, individuals, and the economies and ecologies of which they are a part confront crises, which seem to be unfolding with unprecedented swiftness and gravity. Scholars are becoming increasingly aware that they play a role in those economies and ecologies, and are giving increasing attention to the question of whether and to what extent that role imposes on them and on their disciplines an obligation to try to meliorate the peril, and how the scholarly and technical resources at their disposal might enable them to discharge those obligations. This lesson is developed most fully in the final section of the volume, but it informs much of the chapters which precede.

We have no more specific results to offer. We view this volume as the beginning, rather than the end, of an enterprise. Starting from the premise that language and poverty are connected in extensive, manifold and intricate ways that can be fully illuminated only by collaboration and dialogue across disciplines, this volume attempts to initiate such a dialogue. We thus offer it as the opening of a potentially fruitful conversation, which we hope will continue.